Cornelia James Cannon
and the Future American Race

CORNELIA JAMES CANNON

and the

Future American Race

Maria I. Diedrich

University of Massachusetts Press

Amherst and Boston

LC 2010037342
ISBN 978-1-55849-841-9 (paper); 840-2 (library cloth)

Designed by Steve Dyer
Set in Sabon by House of Equations, Inc.
Printed and bound by Thomson-Shore Inc.

Library of Congress Cataloging-in-Publication Data

Diedrich, Maria.
Cornelia James Cannon and the future American race / Maria I. Diedrich.
p. cm.
Includes bibliographical references and index.
ISBN 978-1-55849-841-9 (pbk. : alk. paper) — ISBN 978-1-55849-840-2
(lib. cloth : alk. paper)
1. Cannon, Cornelia James, b. 1876.   I. Title.
PS3505.A567Z57   2011
813'.54—dc22
[B]   2010037342

British Library Cataloguing in Publication data
are available.

All photographs are courtesy of Marian Cannon Schlesinger, private collection.

FOR

Marian Cannon Schlesinger

IN GRATITUDE

I shall disdain to cull my phrases or polish my style.

MARY WOLLSTONECRAFT,
"A Vindication of the Rights of Woman"

When the race cry is started in the neck of the
woods, friendship, religion, humanity, reason, all
shrivel up like dry leaves in a raging furnace.

CHARLES W. CHESNUTT,
The Marrow of Tradition

CONTENTS

ACKNOWLEDGMENTS

I have many people to thank for the assistance they provided during years of research, writing, and rewriting: librarians and curators of American libraries and historical societies; colleagues too numerous to mention by name for fear of forgetting one precious friend who "volunteered" to read the manuscript and offered abundantly of his or her expertise; patient family members; the fabulously supportive anonymous readers for University of Massachusetts Press. I thank Carol Betsch, Clark Dougan, and Amanda Heller, whose expertise was essential to transforming a manuscript into a biography. And then there is my reliable and devoted research team from Münster, Germany, without whose wonderful assistance I would have given up hope—Manuela Benus, Marie-Theres Brands-Schwabe, Katharina Pabst, and Jesper Reddig.

Walter B. Cannon's biographers—Clifford Barger, Saul A. Benison, and Elin L. Wolfe—graciously shared their expertise with me, and had Elin not taken me under her sisterly wing, I would have drowned in the deluge of material called "The Walter Bradford Cannon Papers" at the Francis A. Countway Library of Medicine in Boston. The Cornelia James Cannon Papers were still in Marian Cannon Schlesinger's residence in Cambridge when I was doing my research, and I am deeply grateful to the Radcliffe Institute for Advanced Study, and especially to Ellen Shea, for unbureaucratically granting me permission to quote extensively from these documents after the papers had been transferred to Radcliffe. In 1991/92 Radcliffe College also supported my initial research through a grant from the Mary Lizzie Saunders Clapp Fund. Cornelia James Cannon's descendants—her children, their spouses, and their grandchildren—generously shared their memories in numerous interviews and unforgettable roundtable discussions in Cambridge and Franklin, New Hampshire: Ellen and Bradford Cannon, Wilma and John Fairbank, Linda Cannon Burgess, Helen Cannon Bond, Arthur Schlesinger Jr., Cathy Kinderman, and Andrew Schlesinger.

My greatest inspiration, guidance, and encouragement, however, came from Marian Cannon Schlesinger, whose delightful Cambridge memoir, *Snatched from Oblivion*, aroused my interest in her mother's story. Marian invited me into her beautiful home; she hosted the family roundtables in Franklin; and she trusted me with the treasure her home contained—her mother's papers. Marian had expected me to write the life of the unconventional, progressive mother she adored. She was my most pertinent and severe critic during the long writing process; she and I disagree on many aspects of the narrative that emerged from my research. Still, the gratitude and respect that Marian's integrity and greatness inspired in me are beyond words.

ABBREVIATIONS

ABCL American Birth Control League

AM *Atlantic Monthly*

AMA "A Middle-Aged Adventure," CJCP

AmM "American Misgivings"

BCLM Birth Control League of Massachusetts

CB *The Clan Betrays,* CJCP

CJ Cornelia James

CJC Cornelia James Cannon

CJCP Cannon Family Papers, 1887–1980 (inclusive), 1917–1945 (bulk), series 2, Cornelia (James) and Walter Cannon, MC 553, Schlesinger Library, Radcliffe Institute for Advanced Study, Harvard University

CJCP/ MCS The Cornelia James Cannon Papers, Marian Cannon Schlesinger

COC "Can Our Civilization Maintain Itself?"

D *Denial,* CJCP

H *Heirs*

ERA Eugenic Record Association

FHJ Frances Haynes James

HMS Harvard Medical Library, Francis A. Countway Library of Medicine, Boston

HWH Harriet W. Haynes

HNJ Harriet Neil Jaynes

LAN *Life at Newport,* CJCP/MCS

MCS Marian Cannon Schlesinger

MHC   Mother's Health Council

NAR   *North American Review*

NAWS   National American Woman Suffrage Association

NL   "Newport Letters, 1887–1899," CJCP

PB   *The Pueblo Boy*

PPLM   Records of the Planned Parenthood League of Massachusetts, Sophia Smith Collection, Smith College, Northampton, Massachusetts

RQ   *Radcliffe Quarterly*

RR   *Red Rust*

SC   "Selecting Citizens"

SL   Schlesinger Library, Radcliffe Institute for Advanced Study, Harvard University

WBC   Walter B. Cannon

WBCP   Walter Bradford Cannon Papers, 1873–1945, 1972–1974 (inclusive), 1881–1945 (bulk), H MS c40, Harvard Medical Library, Francis A. Countway Library of Medicine, Boston

WC   *The Woman Citizen*

WI   "What Ideals Do We Wish to Preserve?"

Introduction

W HY COULDN'T HE JUST HURRY UP A BIT? CORNELIA JAMES Cannon could barely contain her joyous impatience as her husband, Walter B. Cannon, professor of physiology at Harvard, checked his bags once again to make sure that all the papers he needed for the conference were complete. So much to do, and he took his time admonishing the children to be good, and thanking his sisters for keeping Cornelia company! She gently pushed him into the driver's seat, playfully slapping the Model T's trunk as the car pulled away from the farmhouse.

Finally! Dr. Cannon must surely have developed second thoughts at the triumphant sparkle in his spouse's eyes as he took a parting glance in the rear-view mirror. So much to do! Walter would be absent for five days. This was Cornelia Cannon's chance to construct what had been her dream ever since they had purchased a dilapidated farm as their summer residence in Franklin, New Hampshire, in 1910, and, even more important, ever since she had decided to launch a writing career: a cottage that would be all hers. And she was well prepared, indeed. Tools were laid out, construction materials had been ordered, her sisters-in-law Bernice and Ida sworn in as construction assistants, the children as miniature carpenters. The moment Dr. Cannon disappeared from sight, the working crew sprang into action.

The Cannon farm already boasted one writer's retreat, "a tiny brown-shingled shack like something out of Hansel and Gretel,"[1] removed from the main house, under the huge twin pines from which the farm drew its name. This precious space had gone to Dr. Cannon; here he planned research projects, wrote lectures, articles, and books during the summer months. The family was always in sight, but the scientist was protected against intrusion by that powerful invisible wall which their respect for his work maintained. Cornelia had no room she could call her own. At home in Cambridge her desk was under the staircase; in Franklin she had created a tiny workplace for herself in the bedroom. But Cornelia Cannon had never faced a problem for which she could not design a solution: she would transform the farm's henhouse, a collapsing structure clinging almost desperately to the barn, into both a guest house and her writing space.

After all, she saw herself as a disciple of Jamesian pragmatism, equipped with a preference for action and results. Rather than entering into elaborate planning sessions with her husband, she would tackle the project all by herself. It was almost too good to be true — a gift to herself, entertainment for her youngsters, a service to visiting friends, a surprise for Walter. The henhouse was dismantled, and the material that was still usable, which for thrifty Cornelia meant every piece that did not crumble in her hands, was dragged uphill to the site she had chosen for the new structure. Situated on a hillside from where she could keep an eye on the main house and its surroundings, the cabin would offer a spectacular view of the valley and, on the horizon, Mount Kearsarge.

For days Cornelia Cannon and her "volunteers" sawed and hammered and painted away, adhering to construction plans whenever convenient, and improvising whenever the situation required just that. Cornelia and Bernice even shingled the roof, each "tied . . . to the chimney with a rope around her waist."[2] When Dr. Cannon returned, the proud team presented the result of their workmanship. Surprise, indeed. Surprise at an ingenuity that would reinvent a henhouse as "The Chalet," and surprise at just "how much work was left for him to do!"[3] Plus undisguised disgust at the negligence, if not outright sloppiness, with which the work had been performed.

And it was not just the meticulous husband who was torn between admiration for Cornelia Cannon's ingenuity, on the one hand, and despair at her improvisational leniency, on the other. The Harvard physicist and family friend George W. Pierce, after spending a week in "The Chalet," sent a thank you note that focused on the unique quality of the place and, probably unconsciously, brought together the craftswoman Cornelia James Cannon with the reformer and the writer. "Dear Madam," he wrote. "The Manuscript of your article 'The Leaky Chalet' has been received and read with pleasure. It is superb. We enjoyed especially the chapter 'Who Sleeps Bathes.'"[4] Included was a check so the roof could be reshingled.[5] And Cornelia laughed at herself and others — and enjoyed the space with a view which she had created for herself.

A strong woman's irreverent subversion of male norms of perfection and aesthetics? Vivacious inventiveness versus stale conventionality? A "typical American preference for action over reflection, for facts over theories, and above all for results"?[6] Feminist pragmatism rejecting "the a priori cookie-cutter model of knowledge and theory"?[7] All of that surfaces in this episode—and so much more. In that respect it becomes paradigmatic of Cornelia James Cannon's personality, and especially of the attitude she developed toward all her reform activities and the writing projects supporting them.

She was an ambitious, talented woman, with insatiable intellectual curiosity; Radcliffe had provided her with an education exceptional at the time even for women of her class and race; she possessed the gift of laughter and a jubilant joie de vivre. She had enthusiasm, vitality, and energy in abundance, and a powerful determination and courage to say and do what she thought proper and right. She was well read and full of ideas. Her Cambridge community knew her as a Deweyan participant citizen eager to tackle the most controversial issues of the day, as a progressive confident that any problem could be solved through the social and natural sciences and with committed, competent citizens working hand in hand. And she had always dreamed of becoming a novelist,[8] a novelist who, like her favorite nineteenth-century Victorian writers, would use her skills to support her reformist mission.

But life had kept her too busy for this dream to materialize. In the first decades after Radcliffe, the tasks of raising five children, of running a complicated household, and of supporting her husband's career, as well as a number of reform activities, had gobbled up her time. There was no space in her schedule for an all-absorbing project like a novel. Still, writing had been her daily companion even in those family years: her papers contain literally thousands of letters, sketches, poems, and plays for private use. Then World War I interrupted this happy routine and opened up new vistas. Like many American women she discovered a powerful sense of self and acknowledged a deep need within herself for space and mobility during the war. This revived her desire to share her experience with a larger reading public.

Now, in the 1920s, as she could afford a maid, all her children had entered school, and her husband had emerged as one of the scientific lions of the day, her urge to achieve visibility and fame increased by leaps and bounds. She decided to enter the literary marketplace as an essayist and a novelist. In the 1920s and 1930s she produced dozens of essays that were published in major American journals such as the *Atlantic Monthly* and the *North American Review*, four historical novels for children published by Boston's Houghton Mifflin, and finally four adult novels—*The Clan*

Betrays (1920s, unpublished), *Red Rust* (1928), *Heirs* (1930), and *Denial* (1934–35, unpublished). Her first published novel, *Red Rust,* made it onto the national best-seller charts; the success of *Heirs* was less dramatic as it hit the depression market. In addition, she left boxes of unpublished manuscripts.[9] There was visibility, lionization, extra income, the indescribable joy of having made it into print, the author's exultation at her achievement. Lasting fame, however, sidetracked her.

The texts she published—especially her provocative essays—attracted considerable attention because she broached topics that were hotly debated by the American reading public of the day: immigration law, welfare reform, intelligence testing, public education, women's rights, and eugenics. Her writing on social and political issues combined a wittily aggressive fierceness with exhilarating confidence. Yet she was well aware that the essay as a genre stirred the mind for a moment only; there was a brief spark, but it could not sustain itself beyond the moment.

Once we consider her essayistic production in its entirety, however, another problem surfaces that takes us beyond the generic: as time went on, the provocative tenor of her texts—rooted in her clear-cut social vision and commitment—was overshadowed by a reveling in controversy as an end in itself. Even more important, the pronounced distaste for perfection that had driven the construction of "The Chalet" now lent to her writing a precariousness that was counterproductive to her intentions. As in her "Chalet," the walls slanted, the roof tended to leak; hasty, makeshift craftsmanship surfaced; and as the demand for her contributions increased, there was too much recycling, too much willful eclecticism that corrupted the originality of intent. A "no-sooner-done-than-said"[10] quality crept into her compositions—a lifelong reluctance to polish skills beyond "just enough"; a determined, almost obstinate skepticism toward any kind of perfection; an undifferentiating admiration for "the amateur";[11] an intellectual curiosity that preferred the panoramic over depth; sheer enjoyment of a "slaphappy flow . . . intended mostly to amuse and provoke."[12] Her tongue-in-cheek motto was "There's almost nothing worth doing well. The important thing is to get it done,"[13] or "Whatever is worth doing is worth doing badly."[14] Provocative imperfection as program?

Cornelia James Cannon's response to my rather exasperated "verdict" would probably have been "So what?" After all, as her daughter Marian Cannon Schlesinger reminded me, she "never claimed to be Walter Lippmann,"[15] or, for that matter, Mary McCarthy—and she had no intention whatsoever of competing with the literary lionesses and lions of the day, with Edith Wharton, Theodore Dreiser, Willa Cather, Jack London, or her personal nemesis, Gertrude Stein. They all shared with Cannon a profound eugenic commitment,[16] but the naturalistic determinism of Wharton, Dreiser, Cather, and London conflicted with her optimistic progressivism, and Stein's experimental modernism simply appalled her, as we will see. Cannon's models were those British and American writers of the nineteenth century who took it upon themselves to arouse their readers' awareness of the most pressing issues of their day—the exploitation of the working classes, the suffering of the slave, the subjugation of women, and the scandal of child labor, to name only a few.

Within the American literary landscape the New England and midwestern regionalists attracted and inspired her; their loving yet realistic evocations of the nation's rural communities, their customs and mores, and the problems they encountered as the face of their region was transformed by industrialization, urbanization, and the westward movement.[17] She had grown up with novels out of this past, and in her writing for the American present and future she saw no need to revolt against these models.[18] Like Louisa May Alcott, Benjamin Disraeli, Charles Dickens, Elizabeth Gaskell, Harriet Beecher Stowe, and Sarah Orne Jewett, the progressive novelist Cornelia James Cannon was determined to confront her American readers with social and political problems clamoring for solution. Yet to cater to their interests, she, a woman dealing with twentieth-century issues, relied exclusively on representational strategies that had proven successful for the Victorian age. Enamored with books, she was familiar with the most innovative writers of the day. Her letters mention, among others, the naturalists, the social realists, and the modernists, even many of the then slowly emerging ethnic writers; they fascinated her without impacting her writing strategies. When it came to her own fiction, she opted for a didactic realism that was decidedly anti-experimental. Though intent on writing well, she suffered no headaches over questions of innovation, literary merit, and aesthetics. All she wanted was to get her political message across, and to establish herself as a guide with authority in the process of transforming public perception.

Cannon was involved in innumerable reform activities, so many in fact that her son-in-law Arthur Schlesinger Jr. called her an "all-purpose reformer,"[19] yet the various reform objectives to which she lent her writing skills came together in one unifying question: How could she, an educated white American woman, a progressive and pragmatist borne by the belief that the world was hers to shape, contribute to the improvement of

American life? What was to be her share in organizing American destiny and American progress? At a time when President Theodore Roosevelt, backed by eugenicists such as Charles Davenport, pleaded with upper- and middle-class Anglo-America to fend off dysgenic population trends, when nativists, supported by scientists such as the Cannons' friend Robert Yerkes, demanded that the nation preserve its (fictitious) racial purity and homogeneity by implementing a racially restrictive immigration policy, the mission Cornelia Cannon designed and defined for herself was what she and her husband used to call "the future of the race" or "the future race."[20]

The term "race" as used by the Cannons, and in the wider circles in which they moved, conflated race, ethnicity, and class; it negotiated both the fluidity of the concept as prevalent in the nineteenth century "to denote the human race, different ethnic Europeans, or wider ethnic differences between species"[21] and the essentializing classifications of contemporary biology. The term "future" evoked their commitment to eugenics, defined by Francis Galton in 1883 as "the science of improving stock,"[22] which was fundamental to this biologistic notion of race: the belief in the power and authority of science to improve their nation's racial quality by selective breeding as well as the belief in the obligation of the racially "desirable" American citizen to contribute to this noble scientific project through rational reproduction.

The "future race" was the definer of Cannon's commitment, and to this she subordinated all other reform interests as well as her writing. It motivated her fascination with immigration policies, her enthusiasm for eugenics, and her birth control activities; it inspired, intersected with, and more often than not clashed with her feminism, her outspokenness against machine politics and Klan violence. Cornelia James Cannon may have been "a novelist and an all-purpose reformer," but above all she was a novelist and a reformer with a clearly defined purpose: to serve her beloved America and, with that, "the race"; to see to it that America's destiny would remain white and vigorous in eugenic terms. It was essential that she be heard, that she be understood by as many readers as possible in the here and now, and that American citizens be moved to immediate action by what she had to say. Not only did her eagerness to enlighten the American reading public on her exclusive notions of national identity keep her trapped in nineteenth-century modes of perception and expression, but also she sacrificed those qualities to an exuberant didacticism that made her private writing sparkle: her wonderful sense of humor, her irreverent laughter, her love of self-ridicule, her embrace of hyperbole, her at times almost savage witticisms. All of that evaporated when she sat down to write for publication, to be replaced with a sense of mission that could tolerate neither laughter nor relief.

The public persona Cannon constructed in her correspondence was that of the spirited and outspoken woman reformer, inspired and invigorated by those who either applauded or assailed her for her enlightened fearlessness and rigorous consistency. Yet as this biography delves deeper into Cannon's private and public life, her reform activities, and the narratives they inspired, what emerges is a personal itinerary whose protagonist and her reformism are defined by fear—by an all-pervasive, bottomless dread of racial displacement.[23] "I wish we could have an Anglo-Saxon civilization," she sighed in a letter to her mother on 8 December 1920, recoiling against a Cambridge and Boston setting in which new (first- and second-generation) immigrants amounted to over 70 percent of the population.[24] Only three years later, alarmed by Lothrop Stoddard's study *The Rising Tide of Color against White World Supremacy* (1922), and at the height of the nation's struggle over the National Origins Act of 1924, she cried out, "But then, what if we *do* get blotted out?"[25]

The combined threat she saw emanating from white "race suicide" and the "excessive" fertility of those she loathed as racially and eugenically defective put her in a state of panic. The tide metaphor she employed illustrates that she perceived the demographic shift the United States was experiencing as an overwhelmingly dangerous force beyond her control. What surfaces at the heart of Cannon's public reformist agenda, at the heart of her conduct as a private woman, is an all-pervasive racially defined xenophobia and, as its companion, her determination to defend "the race" against the threatening eugenic apocalypse. Her public commitment was triggered by more than the progressive's devotion to social justice; it rested on the progressive eugenicist's view of the world, on her fear of the racial Other and of racial decline. Cannon's reformist patriotism and the discourse of race to which she subscribed were joined at the hip.

This narrative traces a eugenic career that takes its departure from a naïve faith in the promises of Darwinian evolutionary theories and that journeys, via trust in the potential of socio-biological engineering, toward an unconditional propagation of eugenic sterilization programs. Still, the argument made in this biography is not reductively developmental: xenophobia and eugenic fixation do not "grow" and "develop" as our protagonist matures and ages. The "moral" of this story is not that a life starting out as freedom-loving and oppositional discovers race and eugenics along the road and is tragically entrapped in a program of racial dominance and repression. Rather, race surfaces as the ultimate corruptor that is there from the very start—the powerful definer of American life.

This reading also has consequences for how Cornelia James Cannon's individual life experience is contextualized. What her kin and larger social circle explained with the privatizing and exasperated "That's just Mother" or "Oh, Cornelia" must be understood in its larger cultural significance. The life of Cornelia Cannon is of interest for us today not only for its uniqueness and exceptionality but also for its representative qualities. Cannon's reformist career and the ideologies that inspired her reformism mirror those of countless women who had an impact on American culture, society, and politics from the eighteenth through the twentieth centuries—that legendary league of women reformers who, almost as a rule, were born on American soil, white, Protestant, and middle class. It also mirrors the ideologies that fueled their reform efforts, and here again, race comes in as the ultimate definer and corruptor.

Cannon's story is significant neither as the life of a potentially heroic American freedom fighter tragically caught in the trap of a racism of her own making or as that of the eugenic scarecrow. It is culturally relevant because she comes to us, figuratively speaking, as the great-granddaughter of Abigail Adams, whose "Remember the Ladies" emanated from slave-holding Massachusetts; as the granddaughter of abolitionist women like Lydia Maria Child, Maria Weston Chapman, and Harriet Beecher Stowe, whose personal courage as well as racial biases have been brought before us by Hazel Carby, Jean Fagan Yellin,[26] and other revisionist cultural historians; the daughter of abolitionist suffragists like Elizabeth Stanton and Susan B. Anthony, vowing during the controversies over the Fourteenth and Fifteenth Amendments that they would "sooner cut off [their] right hand" than see "'Sambo' walk into the kingdom first";[27] as sister to Margaret Sanger, who effortlessly combined a feminist defense of birth control with eugenic legitimization strategies in *Woman and the New Race* of 1920;[28] as a sister also to the socialist feminist Emma Goldman and the eugenic discourse structuring *Why and How the Poor Should Not Have Many Children;*[29] and finally as mother of post–World War II white feminists and women's studies pioneers who, as black feminists and scholars such as Barbara Christian, Deborah McDowell, and bell hooks remind us, were blind to the experience of black American womanhood. These women, in turn, emerge as sisters, daughters, and granddaughters of revolutionary leaders who were slaveholders; abolitionist pioneers who demoted

Frederick Douglass for claiming his own voice; organized labor who stood for anti-immigration and black segregation policies;[30] a president who admonished white middle-class women "to breed freely," for "we have no business to permit the perpetuation of citizens of the wrong type."[31]

This genealogy of white reformers, women and men, who were motivated by both a longing for social justice and classist and racialized visions of Americanness, who initiated reform to preserve the nation's established social and racial stratification, is identified neither to denigrate the personal sacrifice, courage, and devotion that inspired these reform efforts, nor to demote national heroism or to normalize or even naturalize racism. Each and every one of these reformers would have rejected the label "racist"; they lived and performed, as whiteness studies has taught us, out of a "'whiteness' [that] may simply assume its own normativity."[32] Charles W. Mills coined the term "racial contract" for a racial discourse and praxis, a hierarchical agreement, explicit or implicit, formal or informal, "between those categorized as white *over* the nonwhites, who are thus the objects rather than the subjects of the agreement," a contract whose ultimate agenda is white hegemony—"a racial policy, a racial state, and a racial judicial system."[33] And yet if we want to understand the pervasiveness of the racism, xenophobia, and classism that impacted American political discourse of the nineteenth and twentieth centuries, including progressive reformers like Cornelia James Cannon, we also have to move beyond the analytical tools provided by the unifying agenda of the white contract. We must take into account that even whiteness was redefined, stratified, and hierarchized; it became exclusivist in the rhetoric especially of the eugenics movement and its conflation of race, ethnicity, and class.

This biography argues that race is a definer of the American experience; this biography contends that racism and xenophobia are mainstream American phenomena.[34] It also moves beyond the whiteness paradigm in contending that especially the racially programmed eugenic discourse—in its highly diversified expressions and objectives as well as its complex historical transformations—did not affect only white Americans from all strata of life and political orientations. In its heyday this powerful, all-pervasive eugenicism also permeated the political and social debates within the African American community even as African Americans were protesting the white supremacy assumptions it contained; writers and civil rights activists as diverse in their positions as Pauline Hopkins, W. E. B. Du Bois, Nella Larsen, Alice Dunbar-Nelson, Jean Toomer, and George S. Schuyler embraced a belief that "the selection process among modern humans could be improved."[35] With Daylanne English this biography contends that in the period under discussion, "eugenic thinking was so pervasive . . . that it attained the status of common sense in its most unnerving Gramscian sense."[36]

It must be the biographer's goal to portray with empathy individual experience as embedded in a complex social and cultural matrix, to understand the mechanisms both internal and external, the institutions, the power structures, the notions of gender, class, and race, the concepts of education as well as the ideas about culture that encouraged, inhibited, or even prevented the protagonist's development. The challenge in our pas de deux with Cornelia James Cannon is thus to place an individual woman's history *in* history,[37] to understand notions of gender, race, and class through individual life, or, to use Gayatri Chakravorty Spivak's words, "to situate feminist individualism in its historical determination."[38]

Cannon's grandson Andrew Schlesinger contends that she "is a type of American woman of her period—a conservative reformer—dedicated to 'improving' society (compelled to push and test boundaries), yet personally conflicted over gender issues and feeling constrained by society's boundaries." He remembers her as "a representative American woman wanting more out of life, but still bound up. Her novels provide the historian a unique insight into these contradictions and ambivalences, which shackled all American women, making their lives seem trivial and their efforts seem dilettantish."[39] Cornelia James Cannon was a woman moving within a network of women, native born, white, and middle class like herself. It was a community of powerful women in her own family that generated and formed her; she matured through the determination and pride of the women with whom she attended Radcliffe, the notorious "Nineteenth-Century Limited";[40] she had two sisters-in-law, successful professional women who, through sharing the responsibilities of motherhood, provided her with space to soar. Boston and Cambridge were communities vibrating with the activities of reformist women who, during the final decades of the nineteenth century and the first decades of the twentieth, founded literally hundreds of institutions and organizations, so many indeed that in 1900 the cartoonist Anna Bergengreen ridiculed Boston as "a mammoth woman's club."[41]

Cannon was always working with and among women equally devoted to the task of improving American society. A representative WASP woman reformer, stuck emotionally between selfhood and submission, and unable to resolve her inner conflicts, she was representative also of their limitations, their race and class biases, their unacknowledged fears, their contradictions; a woman who subverted accepted gender ideas of her time yet reconfirmed them when masking her reformism as a mother's duty; an ambitious writer who, accepting praise at face value, succumbed to the sexist low expectancy syndrome of the day; an advocate of the melting pot who, haunted by anxiety about "racial decay,"[42] clamored for restrictive racialized immigration legislation and ultimately sterilization; a liberal who saw no contradiction in demanding a redefinition of civil rights as privileges reserved for those racially and/or intellectually equipped to use those rights discriminately;[43] an essayist who perceived African Americans as a strain on "our racial blood,"[44] yet supported the NAACP and protested Klan violence as well as President A. Lawrence Lowell's refusal in 1923 to admit African American students to Harvard's freshman dormitories; a birth control pioneer who gloried in the role of mother of five and grandmother of twenty; a reformer who, "when it comes to the real test," was, as she herself admitted, "afraid of the new, the untried."[45] Courage, ruthlessness, and devotion, ambition and egocentrism, humor and zeal, racialized perception and humanitarian commitment intersect, fuse, and clash. At first sight there is no consistency, nor can there be a continuous narrative and a sense of closure; yet the continuity and consistency that surface among fragments of competing truths, once we perceive race as the definer, makes this story culturally relevant.

Cornelia James Cannon made herself up and over as she journeyed through life, and she was so certain she was special that, following family tradition, she documented her numerous activities in volumes of letters and memoirs she left for heirs and potential biographers. Hers was a long life to narrate: born in the year of the Hayes Compromise, she was a still vigorously combative woman when she died in a Franklin, New Hampshire, retirement home in 1969, at the height of the Vietnam War, at the age of ninety-three. This biography will not trace all facets of this busy life. It will focus exclusively on the roles she accepted as defining ones—mother, reformer, writer—all in the service of her racial agenda. It was an invention of self that was intimately linked to her pragmatist's dream that the world is ours to improve, and the belief that the sciences provide us with the expertise to do so; to her midwestern progressive conviction that we need to reform what we want to preserve; and, above all, to her creed as a white American that it was her duty as citizen and woman to contribute actively to the realization of her Anglo-American Dream and "the future race."

This biography delineates those factors that contributed to the mission Cannon designed for herself: her formative years in Minnesota and at Radcliffe, the family period and the transformational experience of World War I, her reformist activism and related writing of the twenties and thirties. As the novel was her preferred medium for negotiating her program of positive and negative eugenics, of race and national identity, we can gain insight into the intricacies of her agenda only if we move beyond cursory survey and biographical data toward in-depth analyses of these narratives; this is what chapters 6 through 9 provide. In the early 1940s she gave up writing for the American marketplace: Cornelia James Cannon, writer, reinvented herself as Cornelia James Cannon, grandmother. This biographer hesitates to accompany her into the (semi-)privacy of this role.

Part of the challenge in trying to reconstruct Cannon's life lies in the fact that this is—almost—what Isak Dinesen's biographer Judith Thurman called "a virgin subject."[46] Almost, for there is Marian Cannon Schlesinger's splendid family memoir *Snatched from Oblivion* (1979), which embraces Cornelia Cannon, "the dynamic, humorous, tender, irresistible force,"[47] as uncontested heroine. In addition we have the written testimony of family and community: husband, children, in-laws, and grandchildren; her Minnesota family; friends and acquaintances. We also have newspaper reports on Cannon's work as a birth control activist, her success as a writer, her public school campaigns, her travels, her ideas on immigration. These documents were carefully archived by Cannon, just as she filed every letter to the press, every review and comment on her published writing, every newspaper article on her many ventures, the collection a perfect illustration of her powerful sense of achievement and entitlement.

And there is the story told by my most stubborn competitor, Cornelia James Cannon herself, a woman convinced that her life, like Benjamin Franklin's, was "fit to be imitated." In the *Life* of Arthur M. Schlesinger Jr. we find the exasperated verdict that "she did her damnedest to form her daughters in her own image."[48] There is no denying that biography is always the business of "gossip writers and voyeurs calling themselves scholars,"[49] a "massive socially sanctioned invasion of the privacy of private life,"[50] but with Cornelia James Cannon it was an invasion she invited—and struggled to mastermind. It was her way of forever negotiating identity, of creating that myth of self. Shelves filled with thousands of letters and other writings suggest that more was on her mind than adherence to family tradition; she was prepared for the biographer, and determined to control the writing of her life, the images of self that would surface.

For more than seventy years there were weekly family letters—letters Marian Cannon Schlesinger characterized as "the unedited flights of her mind, funny, sometimes contradictory, satirical, often full of exaggeration, sometimes outrageous and often witty and self-parodying." Schlesinger also reminded me that "half of what she wrote her family recognized as hyperbole not to be taken seriously and said 'Oh, that's just Mother!'"[51] These letters were neatly divided into public self-representations expected to circulate, on the one hand, and more intimate notes to individual family members, on the other. The very fact that Cannon combined public and private proves her awareness that she was negotiating at least two competing inventions of self and life. It challenges us to decode her language of omission, to listen to her silences and decipher what Jean Strouse calls "the codes in all kinds of scattered evidence."[52]

In working with these competing narratives, one needs to remember Mary A. Favret's admonition that any epistolary discourse transgresses the boundaries between private and public spheres in its effort to construct and represent an authentic self through dialogue, in the carefully chosen posture and choreography the participants adopt; the self-generating and self-authenticating voice in letters is always also somebody else's.[53] Cannon kept carbon copies of every letter and filed them meticulously. But to make sure that a proper version of this semipublic correspondence would reach the public eye, she, following her mother's and sister's example, copied, and in the process often rewrote, passages from these letters that were then distributed among kin. She used her letters to compose memoirs of special periods of her life, such as "From a Hostess House" or "Birth Control in the United States, 1900–1965." With each rewriting the self that surfaced moved closer to that public persona Cornelia James Cannon longed to perform; as in all autobiography, interpretation hid behind the mask of representation, the freewheeling raconteur and the conscientious memoirist interact.[54] Memory was selected, molded, and even deleted until the invention of her life became indistinguishable from the images she had designed for public memory—a palimpsest approach to memory which Peter Gay has identified in many family archives, "material for a public shrine."[55] We have Cannon's voice as we attempt to reconstruct her life, a controlling voice; she was script writer and director in one.

As I stated in the introduction to my composite biography of Ottilie Assing and Frederick Douglass:

> It is the biographer's task to retrieve what we have lost from memory, to reclaim the past, and to build a bridge between this past and our present. We unearth bits and pieces of information—"evidence" we call it—and we rearrange and piece together those fragments, hoping that what we reassemble will bear a resemblance to the actual events and help us understand what actually happened—in spite of the inevitable gaps and fissures. In fact, these gaps and fissures are as important as the pieces we were able to recover. Any biographer struggles to narrow the range of that which can never be recovered with certainty, and in doing so we must draw a dividing line between what is possible and probable, between what is improbable and impossible, even as we realize that fact and fiction, memory and interpretation, are intimately intertwined. In the end we have to acknowledge that much of the person into whose life we delve must necessarily elude us, and, perhaps even more significant, that much of the life we re-imagine and reconstruct is about our own life, our own prejudices, dreams, agonies, and joys.[56]

These are the humbling aspects of biography; this is also its fascination.

CHAPTER I

"Personified Mischief"
CHILDHOOD AND YOUTH

N O MATTER WHOM I INTERVIEWED ABOUT CORNELIA JAMES
Cannon—her daughters, Wilma Cannon Fairbank, Linda Cannon
Burgess, Marian Cannon Schlesinger, and Helen Cannon Bond; her son,
Dr. Bradford Cannon, and his wife, Ellen; her sons-in-law John Fairbank
and Arthur Schlesinger Jr.; her numerous grandchildren and great-
grandchildren; former acquaintances and friends—the response was always a medley of admiration, exasperation, and awe, expressed in the
formulaic "quite a woman!" Arthur M. Schlesinger Jr. remembered her as
"vital, opinionated, incorrigible," as a woman whose curiosity was tireless,
"her activity endless"—as "short, plump, bustling, brusquely disdainful of
frocks and frills, despising all stigmata of worldliness, her hair and dress
in shapeless, no-nonsense Boston bluestocking style."[1] Boundless energy
seemed to be the defining feature of the woman when I first became interested in her life and work, an energy she had inherited from her maternal
grandmother, Harriet Williams Haynes, via her mother, Frances Haynes
James; an energy she passed on—almost undiluted—to her five children.

Composing her childhood memories for "My Beloved Descendants" in
1939, Cornelia James Cannon boasted good-humoredly that the family
was "of pretty royal blood, hardly an English king has been able to escape
being an ancestor,"[2] and she established an American genealogy that dated
all the way back to the *Mayflower*. The only complaint she made about
"My Ancestors" in an article published in the *Atlantic Monthly* in 1925
was "the ignominy of inheriting a germ plasm containing not even a single
gamete from a man radical enough to get jailed or deported or hung."[3]

These ironic and spirited narratives take on a more ambivalent tone, however, once we cease enjoying them in isolation and relocate them among the other texts Cannon published while she was composing these lighthearted personal memoirs. They intersect with essays in which she expressed her dread at the nation's "racial decay,"[4] including one in the *North American Review* in which she designed a racialized program for "Selecting Citizens"; they were part and parcel of a birth control campaign that had moved effortlessly from socio-biological engineering to sterilization; and they emanate from a pen that worked to reinstate "an Anglo-Saxon civilization" as a barrier against an ominous deluge of racial Others and undesirables that was haunting her white American Dream. The laughter of the family memoir and the cry of alarm against racial displacement by violators of her exclusive Americanness melt into one. She was dead serious about her claim to Anglo-Saxonness.

Royal kin, *Mayflower* glory, and a white Protestant New England ancestry: we begin our journey with Cornelia James Cannon with a family past encoded as challenge and pain, great ambitions and humiliating poverty; a history of disruption and dislocation, on the one hand, and of strength, endurance, mobility, and creativity, on the other—history that is both HER stories in the best sense of the word and the construction of WASP Americanness.

Only a few years after Harriet Williams, Cornelia Cannon's maternal grandmother, was born in Augusta, Maine, in 1826 to Seth Williams (1787–1838) and his wife, Hannah, née Waters (1791–1861), the family faced difficult times. Harriet's father, an engineer, built the first dam on the Androscoggin River; when it collapsed under the impact of a major flood, Williams died brokenhearted at the age of forty-five, leaving Hannah, four daughters, and a son destitute. The children were distributed among relatives. At first sight Harriet appears to have hit the jackpot, for she was taken under the wing of her uncle, U.S. senator Reuel Williams, and his wife, who lived in a luxurious mansion in Augusta. Once she moved in, however, Harriet quickly realized that her childhood was over. The girl, treated more like a servant than kin, offended her aunt's sense of propriety by displaying an independent mind rather than adopting the kind of humility expected of a poor relative—and a girl at that. "It takes two to achieve a snub," Harriet would later admonish her granddaughters. Like most middle-class girls of her day, she enjoyed little formal schooling; many public and private schools refused to accept girls, and higher education was still unavailable to young women.[5] Harriet's solution was escape into her uncle's library, where she trained herself to become a teacher. She never forgot, however, that she literally had to steal the knowledge she craved, and as a professional educator she made the improvement of public schools, coeducation, and women's access to higher education her lifelong mission. It was a commitment she passed on undiluted to Cornelia, her granddaughter.

At the age of twenty-six Harriet married Francis Greenleaf Haynes (1823–1858), a portrait painter, and they moved to Cambridge, Massachusetts. Haynes's profession forced him to adopt a nomadic life of wandering all over New England; his outgoing nature, combined with his skills as a storyteller and gossip, made him a cherished guest in many houses. Harriet's life, by contrast, was anything but easy. Their income was erratic, and the birth of two daughters—Frances Linda in 1853 and Helen Neil in 1855—and a son forced her to subject her family to strict economizing. Without the help of maids, she shouldered tasks that would have been the male provider's in a more conventional relationship.

Whatever precarious happiness the family enjoyed was of short duration. While painting a dead child in a family vault, Francis Haynes caught a cold that culminated in tuberculosis. In 1858, further weakened by the death of his own infant son, he died, barely thirty-five years old. Harriet was left with two sickly girls and no money, and for the first time in her life she allowed despair to overcome her—so much, indeed, that relatives feared for her life. They sent her off to St. Paul, Minnesota, which was then regarded as an ideal resort for consumptives. There she lived with her sister Emma, whose husband, Earl Goodrich, edited a local newspaper. Under their care Harriet overcame her inner paralysis. Anxious to reunite with her daughters, she searched for ways to make a living, and for once she was lucky: her intelligence and administrative skills obtained her a teaching position in one of St. Paul's new high schools. In those antebellum years teaching was just beginning to be professionalized, as individual states launched teacher training academies or "normal schools."[6] Especially in the Midwest, however, the need for teachers was greater than these schools could supply. This was Harriet's chance, and she grabbed it eagerly.

Nevertheless, she was able to enter into this career only because her husband's early death had liberated her from the married woman's worst enslaver: childbearing. Harriet opted for professional success rather than remarriage. It was a story that was obviously passed on among the Haynes women, for eighty years later it would resurface in Cornelia James Cannon's birth control novel *Denial,* in which a working-class woman, seeing her daughter caught in the spiral of incessant pregnancies, exclaims, "God was good to me and sent me only three children before your father died" (D, 68).

Securely established in this prospering frontier country, Harriet not only reclaimed her daughters but also talked her sister Margie into migrating to Minnesota. They rented a house and took in boarders to make ends meet, one of the few respectable avenues to modest independence open to white middle-class women of the day. Living in a household with no male provider, with a mother who ultimately became principal of her high school, and with an aunt who worked day and night to keep the boarders content, Harriet Haynes's elder daughter, Frances, grew up knowing that her world provided few viable alternatives for middle-class women to the conventional roles of wife and mother. She had to do without most comforts taken for granted by girls of her class, yet she defied anybody to describe her life as one of deprivation.

Her mother was one of the most respected women in this expanding city. As an educator she provided a service central to the reestablishment of those communal institutions and standards of living that were common in the East yet painfully absent from the West. And she executed the moral authority acquired through her profession by making her voice heard in her community when it came to discussing controversial issues such as slavery, public education, women's rights, or social reform. Theirs was a fatherless home, but there were two mothers who saw to it that the girls acquired a solid education in the local public schools that Harriet Haynes was determined to improve. "I believe in friction of mind with mind,"[7] she once wrote, and this was the attitude she passed on to her daughters. Carefully selected female boarders were transformed from paying guests into household friends; they formed a dynamic community of women, all contributing to the girls' intellectual growth, their pride in their womanhood.

Despite her intellectual preparedness, Frances's was a more gentrified biography than her mother's, but this very gentrification documents that this family of women had indeed arrived socially in the Midwest. In October 1874 Frances married Henry Clay James (1849–1930), a lawyer from Haverhill, Massachusetts, who, after graduating from Harvard, had moved to St. Paul to practice law. The couple lived on Seventh Street in St. Paul, where five of their seven children, all girls, were born within the next ten years—Margaret (1875), Cornelia (1876), Helen (1878), Ethel (1881), and Frances (1885). James speculated in land, almost a sport in the booming midwestern communities of the day. For years he made remarkable profits, and consequently the family could afford to move to a mansion in nearby Newport, Minnesota, in 1887. Here the couple's only son, Henry Clay Jr., was born in 1888, followed by a sixth daughter, Linda, in 1881. When Frances gave birth to Henry, Harriet Haynes received a telegram reading, "The family record broken at 6:30." To his uncle the proud father telegraphed, "The future President arrived at 6:30." Cornelia, then twelve, had a keen sense of what was happening. Under the pen name of Baby Henry she wrote a mock letter to her relatives, commenting on her father's numerous telegrams, "which, mind you, he did not do for my sisters!"

Frances James, grown up in a household defined by women, adopted the structure of that home as the model for her own domestic realm. Hers became a household of women, in which she and her mother ruled, surrounded by female relatives and friends.[8] Her husband appeared happy with this arrangement, for not only did his business make enormous demands on his time, but also his wife's happiness in her society of vivacious women provided him with personal freedom while offering him all the comforts of family. He gloried in the role of enlightened manhood, vigorously defending her ways against outside criticism. It seemed natural that so many girls were born into this circle, girls who again would grow up empowered by this proudly independent female environment.

Little Henry may have been the apple of his father's eye, but he was an outsider, and Frances never relaxed into raising a boy. Her granddaughter Marian Cannon Schlesinger remembered Frances James as "a gifted New England bluestocking and born executive with a will of iron."[9] Neither her status as a married woman nor motherhood could curb her passion for personal autonomy. She strove to form her children by respecting their individuality while constantly negotiating established norms of childhood and gender. The children grew up absolutely secure in her love. They were never a squad of presentable model children but rather a herd of strong-willed individuals, as one of Frances's close friends, a Miss Landerer, confirmed. "I am as much interested as ever in little Henry's exploits and periodical attacks of unhappiness due to relentless fate in the shape of his nurse and older sisters," she wrote in a letter of 1891; "in horsey Frances, in Cassandra Helen with her lofty scorn of buttons, hooks, stays and such like necessary feminine evils; in Cornelia, the personified Mischief; and in our Lady of Sorrows, Margharita, who after all, enjoys her woes so much more than any of the others do their pleasures."

Still, motherhood was a role Frances found difficult to fulfill, and in Harriet Haynes's letters we find numerous remarks that signify exhaustion and exasperation. "It is charming to see how Henry can govern any of his children," she admitted to her younger daughter, Helen N. Jaynes, on 25 October 1887. "Frances is driven to death." Frances James could never resign herself to the nineteenth-century woman's fate of continuous child-bearing. She suffered terribly from nausea, heart palpitations, and respiratory problems during her pregnancies. After Linda's birth she wrote to her sister on 1 December 1891, "Miss Landerer wrote a funny letter hoping that this was the last of the Mohicans," and she admitted, "This baby has been pretty hard on me." Her tired body rebelled against the physical challenge of pregnancy, and her independent mind against her bondage to the laws of biology, a fate and a disposition she shared with most American women of her day, for once across boundaries of race and class. It was no doubt reminiscences of her mother's tribulations that later strengthened Cornelia's determination to make the blessings of birth control available to American women.

Cornelia Cannon's commitment to birth control was not merely inspired by her mother's suffering; it would also bear the same marks of conflicting interest and systemic American determinants. Discourses of female self-liberation and self-empowerment intersected with discourses of racial obligation and awareness in Frances James as in her daughter, creating through race a highly constructed yet powerful alliance between incompatibles, and in that the two women were representative of middle-class white American womanhood of their time. Frances longed for physical autonomy, but she also was an early convert to evolutionary theories and their translations, by way of Herbert Spencer and Francis Galton, into social philosophy and eugenic praxis, as we will see.

They were living in a time when waves of immigrants from southern and eastern Europe, on the one hand, and millions of African Americans, emancipated from slaves to citizens, on the other, were changing the nation's ethnic—in contemporary terms "racial"—composition. This transformation triggered angry and anxious negotiations of national identity, and the Jameses, too, negotiated racial phobias, the fear of racial displacement. The family letters on which Cannon based her *Life in Newport* are colored by the sentimental images that nineteenth-century discourse imposed on white middle-class children. Aunts and grandmothers celebrated the angelic beauty of the "dear babes" and recorded every achievement of these chubby angels as paragons of a future white Americanness. Yet in the context of the racial defense paradigms of the day, these celebrations of the

James children are more than naïve expressions of personal enchantment or intoxication.

Each pregnancy, each baby born to an intellectually torn Frances was an investment in the nation's racial future, in not just white but Anglo-Saxon hegemony. What her deep-seated feminism rejected as woman's bondage resurfaced as racial commitment, duty, a woman's potential to initiate the progress of "the race" and empower its womanhood through biology. It was a renegotiation of woman as self and biology for which Angelique Richardson, in her investigation of British eugenics and the New Woman, coined the term "eugenic feminism." Sex and society, this position decreed, were biologically determined, but an enlightened woman "might work *with* rather than against nature, intervening in the process of biological evolution in order to alter biological destiny." [10]

Frances was determined to fulfill what she regarded as her woman's duties and racial responsibility, but she also realized that she would lose herself if she devoted herself entirely to the conventional roles of wife and mother. Consequently she was eager to develop a realm of activities adapted to her personal needs. As long as her children were small, she simply invited interesting people to her home. Thus she spent many an evening in the company of three individuals who shared her intellectual pursuits and her reformism: her mother, a lawyer named Fitzpatrick, and especially her friend, the teacher Mary J. Newson, or "Miss May." Together they read the great Victorian novelists—the Brontës, George Eliot, Elizabeth Gaskell, Charles Dickens, Charles Kingsley, William Thackeray—in combination with the social analysts who had influenced their writing, first and foremost Thomas Carlyle, Thomas Malthus, John Stuart Mill, and Karl Marx. They discussed the social issues these writers were raising: the industrial revolution, labor unrest, child labor, pollution, the working and living conditions of the working classes, reform efforts. From there, their quest took them almost inevitably to Charles Darwin, Herbert Spencer, and ultimately Francis Galton.

It was an itinerary that reveals how firmly these individual intellectual pursuits intersected with and were shaped by their larger social, political, and cultural contexts. Through comfortable parlor meetings, Frances and her circle invited the world in and reached out to that world in turn. Their reading of the Victorians thus was more than an escapist reveling in Old World problems; it was their way of approaching the dramatic transformations their own nation was facing in the decades after the Civil War, which catchphrases like "urbanization," "industrialization," "new immigration," and "westward migration" describe only imperfectly. These developments changed the face of the nation almost beyond recognition: they spelled ghettoization, catastrophic sanitary conditions, sweatshop exploitation, deficient medical services, an underprepared and overtaxed public educational system, as well as water, air, and food pollution. They spelled extreme forms of poverty for millions, and they invited social unrest, exploding crime rates, class and race violence.

In the second half of the nineteenth century, reform efforts proliferated all over the United States in response to these social challenges, usually organized and staffed by white middle-class reformers fully aware of the explosive potential of these transformations. These activists, especially the progressives of the late nineteenth and early twentieth centuries, were motivated by humanitarian concerns, by a sense of social responsibility that is best described by the secularized concept of stewardship of wealth; but first and foremost they saw themselves as American patriots determined to defend the American way they affirmed against adverse social developments that accompanied the reconstruction the country was facing. The slogan "Reform so you may preserve" sums up to perfection the conservational and affirmative framework and agenda these activities established for themselves—despite the enormous variety of foci, strategies, and political or religious orientation they represented. Just as slavery had been denounced as an American anomaly by the abolitionists, these reformers regarded slum conditions, extreme labor exploitation, and child labor as aberrations of a potentially perfect Americanness, and they were confident that these problems must and could be solved—and with that, the nation's social and racial stratification maintained, white claims to continued superiority and hegemony defended.[11]

This white reformist agenda and confidence were strengthened by the almost religious faith that most placed in the newly emerging social and natural sciences and the alliance that many reform movements forged with them, a combination of civic commitment and scholarly expertise that was to define progressive reformism in particular. Paleontology, genealogy, anthropology, biology, and philosophy were developing elaborate classification systems and strategies, and these analytical tools, revamped as instruments for social analysis and praxis, were very much in demand as established categories of social stratification failed under the impact of overwhelming demographic upheavals.[12] A nation where slavery and race had been deeply embedded and embattled now had to confront millions of ex-slaves laying claim to the rights and privileges of American citizenship. After the Civil War 90 percent of these freedpeople were living in the South; but extreme forms of exploitation, discrimination, and violence in these regions as well as the promise of better living and working conditions in the North and West, beginning in the 1880s and culminating in the 1920s, initiated the Great Migration, with more than 2 million African Americans eventually relocating from the South to the North and West, and from rural to urban contexts.[13]

In addition, the mass immigration of the period resulted in an ethnic heterogeneity for which these white American reformers were unprepared. Some 4.5 million immigrants entered the country in the 1880s, and another 4 million in the 1890s, no longer primarily from regions the native WASP population could tolerate within their construct of a consanguine white race. They increasingly came from Italy, Greece, Russia, Ireland; a considerable percentage were Jewish, and by 1880 more than 75,000 Chinese were working in California alone—immigrants the race discourse of the day defined as incompatible with exclusive white constructions of Americanness.[14] Small wonder that the classification systems developed in these new sciences were taken up and reductively reformatted to explore, explain, and ultimately legitimize human and social difference and stratification.

The route for this transplantation of categories from natural sciences to social praxis had been prepared in the eighteenth and nineteenth centuries by the work of Linnaeus, Lamarck, Charles Lyell, and Louis Agassiz, as well as the German Romantics; now the process acquired increased urgency and legitimacy through these demographic challenges, and it was accelerated especially by the impact of Darwin's evolutionary theories. As the work of generations of American scholars and scientists from Agassiz through John Fiske, Chauncey Wright, and William Graham Sumner to Charles Davenport documents, evolutionary theory with its reaffirmation of nature over nurture was reconceptualized as both an explanation for human variation and gradation and a tool for scientific projections into the future of humanity. In its reductionist reformatting into a Spencerian synoptic evolutionism or social Darwinism, with its celebration of the laws of human progress, it not only became instrumental in naturalizing human inequality but also paved the way for the biological engineering project that began to revamp American social reformism in the 1880s under the catchword "eugenics."

In 1883 Darwin's cousin Francis Galton coined the term "eugenics," from the Greek *eugenes*, or "good in stock," to propagate what he defined as "the science of improving stock." Arguing that "judicious mating . . . especially in the case of man" must be complemented by a scientific methodology that "takes cognizance of all influences that tend in however remote a degree to give the more suitable races or strains of blood a better chance of prevailing over the less suitable than they would have had,"[15] he laid the foundations for the eugenic program of the following decades. On the one hand, he promised that—through "judicious control of human reproduction," meaning the numerical increase and the improved genetic quality of the eugenically desirable—the racially perfect nation could be bred; on the other, he insinuated that these eugenic measures would ultimately solve all social problems.

In *Love and Eugenics* Angelique Richardson offers a perfect metaphor for the transformational process from evolutionary theory to essentializing biological engineering that took place among British and American reformers during the final decades of the nineteenth century and the opening decades of the twentieth, and that also had an impact on the parlor debates in the James household. "Darwin's evolutionary theory of descent through modification had laid the foundations for eugenics, replacing paradise with primordial slime," she contends. "Man had not fallen from Grace, but risen from the swamps. And, as architect of his own destiny, he might rise even further."[16]

The Carlyle-Marx-Darwin-Spencer-Galton itinerary which Frances James and her friends followed during their nights of reading and debate from the 1870s through the 1890s thus acquires an inner inevitability and representativeness if placed in this larger context of the enormous social challenges of the day and the nation's racialized reformist response. Harriet Haynes had supported abolitionism in the antebellum era, and together with Frances James, she protested anti-black violence and discrimination as the postwar national reconciliation of North and South confirmed the white contract and trampled black hopes for full citizenship.[17] Both were proud to define their America as a haven for the persecuted of the world, as an immigrant nation. Still, during this period of transformation they, too, came to embrace the organic visions of social Darwinism rather than Marx's class paradigm. Their reading inevitably took them from nurture to nature, from class to race, and an ultimate conflation of class and race.

These intellectual quests did not remain in the adults' parlor; they moved to the dinner table and nurseries. They provided Cornelia with her first powerful lessons in race and class matters. As long as her mother was alive, this focus on race would remain uncontested between them, and under the impact of eugenics and the immigration controversy that defined the opening decades of the twentieth century, it would mutate into the complementary dread of racial decay, displacement, and suicide, on the one hand, and their longing for an "Anglo-Saxon civilization," on the other. This fixation on race also laid the foundations for the eugenic feminism that Cornelia James Cannon, her mother's faithful pupil, would live and advertise.

In addition to her intimate reading circle, Frances began to invite between eight and twelve women to "topic luncheons"—her response to the women's clubs that sprang up all over the country.[18] During an elegantly served meal, they would discuss subjects as various as "Favorite Author," "Nation of Greatest Influence on World's Civilization," or "The Ideal Woman, Town or Country." Frances supported the argument of the contemporary women's movement that women's activities outside the home, far from destroying the domestic realm, improve its atmosphere in that they provide women with a substantial sense of self. "The best mothers are always something more than mothers," Antoinette Brown Blackwell, a mother of six and the first American woman to be ordained a minister, had maintained at the Third Women's Congress of the Association for the Advancement of Women in Syracuse in 1875. "Their homes are better kept, their children are more wisely guided, and their husbands are more honored among their townsmen, because this energy of the soul has found expression and tuned the whole nature to a broader harmony."[19]

As she began to carve out her public career, Frances James thus embraced a feminist discourse that legitimized woman's new mobility as service to her family. She became a co-founder of the St. Paul Woman's Club, a supporter of women's rights, and a lecturer who tackled controversial issues such as the anti-black racism of the American women's movement, the impact of socialism on U.S. society, birth control, and, later, Emma Goldman's socialist feminism. These activities beyond the home were possible only because Frances James, like many white middle-class reformers, enjoyed a privileged social position. The Jameses could afford to hire a host of maids, a cook, a nurse, washerwomen; and their work allowed Frances to soar beyond the domestic realm.

Her activities were encouraged by her family. Her husband acknowledged her right to a life of her own, always provided, of course, that his needs were not neglected. A letter of 30 January 1898, which Cornelia

James wrote from Radcliffe, reveals how profoundly Frances's daughters admired a mother who did so much more than run a home. "I always knew you were a genius and now I am sure of it," Cornelia commented. "You were never destined for the humble domestic sphere, you were meant to *shine*. Let the children go dirty and the beds unmade but shine!" The Radcliffe junior encouraged her mother to do what she herself would pursue all her life: go out, make her voice heard, be an agent in the shaping of history, a participant republican. The James children thus grew up in a household in which both parents, staunch Republicans and supporters of midwestern reformism,[20] were not only deeply interested in political and social issues but also determined to participate in the political life of their community. Politics was discussed at the dinner table, and the children were included in the conversations, provided with data and invited to speak up, to read newspapers and magazines—all in accordance with the Jameses' belief that the training of an American citizen begins in the cradle.

Among the James girls Cornelia was the one closest in nature to Frances. When Cornelia was born on 17 November 1876, her elder sister Margaret was suffering from a potentially fatal illness. This, in the words of Aunt Lucy Williams,[21] left "the new baby to get along as best as she could—a good natured child . . . and a satisfactory *cuddler*." Cornelia learned to fend for herself, soothing herself with stories of her own invention, singing to herself. Twin to this early self-reliance was her unwillingness to be a burden. During the frequent bouts of sickness in this extended family, Cornelia was content to lie in bed with her watch and her medicine by her side, confident that she had everything under control. And once she had learned to read, which was long before she started school, she began to regard periods of illness as a special treat—an attitude she maintained throughout her life.

Still, this relative neglect also took its toll: she was almost determinedly her mother's child, and her demands for her mother's attention became even more desperate as additional babies with claims to Frances's love arrived in rapid succession. Cornelia also developed a keen eye for the emotional needs of family members, and she gave generously. Her ability to feel with others was especially strong when it came to her mother, for Cornelia was well aware of the exhaustion that at times threatened to overwhelm this delicate but energetic woman. She became increasingly protective of Frances, slipping into an almost maternal role. But the quality in Cornelia that struck her family most was her efficiency, combined with her absolute certainty that she was equal to any emergency.

An episode pertaining to five-year-old Cornelia's conduct has a near-paradigmatic quality. "One afternoon Fanny was out driving, and as little Ethel was hungry, I said, 'I wish your mamma would come home and give you something to eat,'" Aunt Lucy remembered. But Cornelia was up to the occasion: "'Oh,' replied Cornelia, 'I can do that!' so she proceeded to get ready . . . and when she was stripped down to her shirt, she took a little rocking chair and said: 'Now give her to me!' It was a comical sight, yet very interesting in its assurance." The word "impossible" was never to find a place in Cornelia's vocabulary.

From the family memoirs Cornelia steps forth not as the stereotypical white middle-class girl, soft and pliant. Hers was a personality that adults evoked with respect, even awe. Cornelia, fiercely defending her territory, developed a temper that frightened her siblings and parents. Life with this strong-willed girl was a challenge for all. "Cornelia [is] an incorrigible tease, but the life of the family," Aunt Lucy wrote about her.

At times her behavior was obnoxious, as when she teased the Swedish maids to the point of outright insult. "Cornelia is bubbling over with life and spirit," her grandmother sighed; "she is not bad but jubilant—with perfect health."[22] Suffering most from Cornelia's "jubilant" spirit were her siblings, especially her elder sister Margaret. Thus Margaret's vegetarian diet roused Cornelia to feats of satire. In a poem, accompanied by a pair of felt slippers, which she gave Margaret for Christmas 1891, she wrote:

> To my dear Maguerite:
> Who will not eat meat,
> But will wear on her feat
> The skin of an ox
> In spite of her knocks
> Of her conscience.[23]

"Poor Margaret, what will she do under that tantalizing power," Harriet Haynes exclaimed. She tried to soften Cornelia's edges by bribing her into tolerable behavior, promising a silver watch, provided she cease teasing for three month; two months later we hear that Cornelia had begun to earn her watch all over again.

At times her grandmother despaired: "Sometimes I think she has no heart. She does not mind punishment at all."[24] Difficult as it was for the girl always to know where teasing ended and hurt began—a weakness that burdened her for a lifetime—she also had a keen sense of right and wrong and probably suffered more than her victims once she realized what she had done. She never hesitated to apologize. "I send these little gifts of love because I am so sorry that I ever was mean to you," she wrote to Margaret in January 1887. She was destined to write many forgive-me notes in the course of her long life.

In 1887 the James family, now consisting of Henry and Frances, their four girls (Ethel had died in infancy), grandmother Haynes, and numerous "poor" relatives, moved to Newport. It was a dream come true: a family mansion on the bluff above the Mississippi. Henry James named it Harvard Place, out of devotion to his alma mater. He claimed that a residence in Newport would contribute to his business as a realtor, attracting wealthy clients to the community. Love of family and professional shrewdness were interwoven in this attempt to mask as professional calculation what really motivated him: their old home lacked the glamour his Micawber-like nature craved.[25]

Harvard Place was designed to satisfy this craving. It opened its doors to the family in mid-November. They were enchanted by its elegant rooms, whose large windows provided them with a lovely panorama. The parlor with its pale cream ceiling, olive walls, natural pine woodwork, cherry mantel, and tiles the color of russet apples was Frances's special pride, a perfect expression of her sense of beauty and ease, elegance, and entitlement. And then there was the library—the most important place in a household of bookworms. The house boasted all the luxuries they had missed in St. Paul—a room for each family member and a few spare chambers for others who might arrive, two guest chambers, sunny rooms for the servants, a billiard room, even an elevator.

Cornelia was enchanted with her room, and especially with her window seat; here, in her private nook with a splendid view of the Mississippi, she spent hours reading and writing. For the children, life at Newport was heaven. They were free to roam, to camp out in summer, to go sledding and skating in winter. Theirs was an open house where other children from their milieu were always welcome. They had a dog, chickens, even a lamb. The Jameses kept a stable of fine horses, and the girls, animated by a mother who rode ten miles or more a day, sat on horseback almost as soon as they could walk.

Inside Harvard Place generosity and openness reigned supreme. Although the Jameses employed a host of Swedish American maids, the girls were expected to help with the household chores. Cornelia was in charge of feeding the chickens. "Papa furnishes the feed and pays me five cents profit and ten cents for every one we eat," she reported on 12 November 1889. "I do not think he pays me enough because it is hard work to mix all the feed." Hardships, indeed, in their Garden of Eden! But Cornelia was aware of her privileges. Sitting on her window seat, she constructed an island of rural bliss for her aunt Helen in Massachusetts: "Today is lovely. . . . The clear blue sky, the misty distang [sic] hills, the quiet little village, the soft green of the fields and the darker green of the trees, the sweet clover on the front lawn, the warm winds fanning the woodbine and swinging the hammock gently to and fro, the sweet little birds singing in the trees and the quiet peacefulness of the scene. I wouldn't change this place for a king's palace." Why should she? It *was* a palace, and hers, too, inhabited by strong individuals who respected one another, who offered guidance without too much force, who embraced without stifling, who fought without trying to subdue.

The passage is relevant not only because it illustrates Cornelia's sense of privilege but also because it attests to the self-containment characterizing her domestic realm.[26] The Jameses were an extended family, a family committed to social reform, but the adults moved among people of their own kind—that is, their own class and race—and so did the children. None were aware how exclusivist their world truly was, for each and every one celebrated openness, tolerance, liberality. Yet the new immigrants from southern and eastern Europe arriving in the Midwest and the African Americans settling in the Twin Cities might as well be living on a different planet.

The only Others in this self-contained family were the Swedish maids, gardeners, and stablemen—individuals with foreign accents, some unable to speak English, people relegated to the kitchen, the stable, the maids' quarters. They reminded the children that there was a world beyond their doorstep that they could not access, a world that turned deliciously sinister and forbidden when one of the men drank too much, when a maid was dismissed after strange whispers, when Henry warned off "Jens, our morose coachman,"[27] who drank heavily and beat wife and children. In 1928, in her novel on Swedish immigration, *Red Rust,* these maids and servants of Cornelia's childhood resurface as protagonists promising racial renewal and invigoration to a racially exhausted America. During her Newport childhood, however, they were odd strangers the children loved to tease, in defiance of the respectful treatment their progressive parents requested.

All adult members of the James household were bookworms, and consequently the James children grew up with books as playmates. Grandma

Haynes and Frances spent hours each day not only reading to and later with them but also discussing texts and encouraging critical analysis. *Uncle Tom's Cabin,* the novels of Charles Dickens, Sir Walter Scott, Elizabeth Gaskell, George Eliot, and Louisa May Alcott, Shakespearean drama, and British and American poetry were introduced to a circle of girls eager to have their individual quests stimulated by tales of adventure, romance, and suffering. The family's Unitarian leanings and their admiration for New England Transcendentalism are visible in the careful reading of Emerson and Thoreau, as is Harriet's and Frances's feminism in the girls' introduction to Margaret Fuller's *Woman in the Nineteenth Century* as well as to Mary Wollstonecraft's tracts.

Money spent on books was always regarded as money well spent, and Harvard Place boasted a formidable library which became more important than the parlor. In addition to that, the public library, one of their mother's reformist projects, was as familiar as the playground to Cornelia and her siblings. The children were encouraged to grow intellectually, to find their own itinerary through reading, and, beyond passive reception, to express themselves through writing and performance. Frances challenged her girls to compose poems, which were read aloud in the family circle and then proudly circulated among friends and relatives. Also Cornelia and Margaret began to write plays—a dramatization of Alcott's *Little Women* or a tragedy on Jews in Spain—which were then performed by the children and their friends. The entire family participated, sewing costumes, performing on stage or as audience. Henry James was so enchanted that he hired a photographer to take pictures. Cornelia excelled in these productions, moving grannies and aunts to tears. So involved was she that her enthusiasm often culminated in a nervous fever. She was born to perform.

Cornelia was also the most ambitious writer among the children; she was determined to become a novelist, and several of her early attempts at fiction, among them "A Little Life among the Multitude" (undated, but early 1890s), which she dedicated to her teacher May Newson, have survived. It is a sentimental, thoroughly conventional Horatio Alger tale, but it boasts a female protagonist: a virtuous orphaned beauty discovers love and riches in the midst of exploitation.

These tales were an ambitious adolescent's first naïve excursion into fiction, and they are expressive of Cornelia's unflinching sense of entitlement. More than that, they illustrate her familiarity with the popular narrative strategies of sentimental fiction, and they impress by the calm assurance and unerring accuracy with which she made use of these strategies. These tales pay tribute to Cornelia's skills when it came to adopting and adapting established literary modes of representation that dominated the contemporary literary marketplace. At the same time it is revealing that, in miniature, "A Little Life" and its companion pieces encapsulate the quality that would define a mature Cornelia James Cannon's excursions into fiction and limit her impact as a novelist: unreflective stylistic conservatism, stilted dialogue, conventional imagery, heavy didacticism, absence of humor, reliance on the familiar and the sentimental.

But no matter how precarious the result of these adolescent ventures, the family's response was unconditional enthusiasm. The Jameses firmly believed that praise was a child's strongest incentive, and they provided it lavishly, generating in their daughters a powerful sense of their potential. It obviously never occurred to them that their unconstrained celebration of Cornelia's exercises in writing as such was a kind of support that failed to contain that essential element of creative criticism and intellectual challenge, that call for improvement of skill which alone generates excellence. Nobody in this family consciously affirmed the gendered low expectancy syndrome, the "artsy-crafty" approach that programmed the ways in which woman's intellectual and creative potential was regarded.[28] They would have been appalled at insinuations that their attitude contained elements of sexist condescension.

Under the impact of excessive praise, Cornelia internalized and even celebrated the incomplete, the imperfect, despite her rhetoric of "high thinking." It would always be enough for her to have proven to herself and to the world that she could write a poem, construct a chair, complete a novel, publish an essay; it was for others to compose the perfect. Her family's encouragement to accept as glorious whatever she created, and her internalization of this childhood lesson, became paralyzing as it defined the deficient status quo as perfect and final. Their conduct as a family reflected the state of female education during the final decades of the nineteenth century.

By the time Cornelia was ready to start school, elementary as well as secondary education was no longer a boys' prerogative; most public schools were coeducational. By the time she reached high school age, more girls were expected to graduate than boys, and especially among white middle-class families in urban areas, daughters without a high school diploma were rare. Young women of this class now could even hope to attend college, for not only had several prestigious women's colleges opened, but also a number of formerly all-male institutions had started to invite women's enrollment; by 1880 women "constituted more than a third of the entire student body."[29]

Yet the availability of these educational opportunities was not without drawbacks. Although girls were admitted as equals, the expectations regarding the objectives of education, and especially its application in life after school, were still strictly gendered. Education for boys was designed to empower them for survival and success in the marketplace, whether in trade, manual labor, or the professions; they had to prepare for their role as sole providers for their future families. Education for girls trained them for wifehood and motherhood, for the domestic sphere, and this also held true for higher education, as my analysis of Cornelia's Radcliffe years will document. Despite identical curricula in coeducational public schools, despite the efforts of enlightened educators like Harriet Haynes, despite the egalitarian rhetoric, lower expectations, the "good enough for a girl" formula, was systemic, as the response of Cornelia's kin to her intellectual accomplishments, especially her creative writing, illustrates.

Those young women whose ambition and achievement transcended this sexist reductionism then faced the even more devastating realization that "the chief difficulty . . . was not getting an education, but using it."[30] In addition to this absence of viable professional opportunities, women with aspirations were terrorized by a medical profession that targeted white middle-class women with their racialized eugenic assignments. As early as 1873 Harvard's Edward Clarke warned in *Sex in Education* that as a woman's brain expanded from her exposure to learning, her uterus inevitably shrank and her reproductive capacity diminished. Eminent scientists such as Clarke, R. R. Coleman, and Charles B. Davenport, supported by eugenically programmed politicians, reformers, and the media, criminalized women's educational efforts by associating them with race suicide.[31]

This was the context in which the Jameses prepared their daughters for adulthood; these were the positions, conscious or unconscious, affecting the educational choices they made, the expectations they articulated, their negotiations of contemporary discourses of gender, race, and budding feminism. They saw to it that Cornelia received a solid public school education. Education for the James family was neither a male prerogative nor a rich woman's privilege; it was a human right. Small wonder that Cornelia could read and write by the time she entered elementary school. She was a voracious student, absorbing everything offered to her with enthusiasm and intellectual curiosity. Cornelia's parents were wealthy enough to supply stimuli for her young mind: from her diary we know that she took French, piano, and violin lessons, and she attended dancing school. Her family helped her deal creatively with her enormous energy, but it is revealing that they chose activities of the "artsy-crafty" style deeply embedded in conventional gendered role assignments.[32] Cornelia acquired the decorative, genteel skills expected of middle-class girls and future wives-as-entertainers.

The James daughters began early to imitate their mother's organizational abilities by founding discussion clubs; Harvard Place became the headquarters of the Purity Club, the girls' reinvention of the social purity campaigns organized by the Women's Christian Temperance Union of the day,[33] and they published newsletters. These juvenile ventures paid off when Cornelia entered high school. In no time her fellow students, and especially the girls in her class, learned to appreciate that here was an adolescent who possessed brains and the courage to map out new roads.

In a society that expected women to be seen but not heard, she had the voice to express her ideas as well as the skills to implement them. Cornelia and her schoolmates had been raised in a city with an active women's club, by mothers who often subtly transformed the nineteenth-century cult of true womanhood or even subscribed to the emerging feminist progressivism; they were fed up with boys who took it for granted that the president of the class of 1894 should come from their ranks. They also knew that the girls' academic performance was above that of the male pupils, and that more girls graduated than boys, who tended to drop out as soon as a reasonably lucrative job was offered. This awareness made their claim for participation even more legitimate than their righteous indignation at the boys' macho pose.

But who possessed the courage to make the transition from complaining at male prerogatives to actively challenging them? After all, these girls knew the cost of "unwomanly" behavior: exposure to peer pressure and ridicule during the campaign; hard work and even more ridicule and male resistance if one succeeded. They chose Cornelia James, class secretary, as trailblazer. On 2 March 1891 Cornelia recorded in her diary, "Lots of girls want me to try for the Presidency." From the moment this suggestion was made, the class split along gender lines, the boys rallying behind Arthur Powell, the girls behind Cornelia. And she accepted their nomination: "I *didn't* want him to be president. I would rather be it myself." A vicious struggle ensued, but Cornelia already held the key to success: the unity of sisterhood. She arranged meetings for girls and mobilized all of them to vote. Although she was a controversial figure who made enemies with her teasing and meddling, the public persona she adopted was that of the pioneer of women's rights, thus placing herself beyond personal likes and dislikes.

She was nominated. "I . . . received the most votes so all those 65 girls swore to vote for me except one," she reported triumphantly on 12 March, only to add: "I think it is dreadful. I cannot get up tomorrow and preside. . . . I just *dread* it." Yet the next day Cornelia made her way through the traps the boys had laid, and when she took up her diary that night, she did so as class president. "We have had the most awful time," she confided. "We had our meeting and I was elected by 62 votes. . . . The boys are dead set against me and declare that they will leave the class. Let them!"

Whether it was running for office, organizing clubs, publishing a newsletter, performing a play, or staging a party that lasted from Christmas to New Year's Eve, the James girls could count on their parents' encouragement. Any act of empowerment, any attempt to claim and define their realm was affirmed as a step toward personal autonomy. The Jameses also believed that to educate their children, they needed to expose them to the world beyond their midwestern horizons; they embraced every chance for travel.

Cornelia got her first opportunity at the age of eight. In the early 1880s Frances's sister Helen, Cornelia's "Auntie," married the Unitarian minister Julian Clifford Jaynes and moved to West Newton, Massachusetts. Like Frances, Auntie maintained an open house. Cornelia's initial encounter with New England took place in the summer of 1885. No sooner had her invitation arrived than she started packing for the adventure, so eager, indeed, that her mother could not suppress her jealousy. The girl responded to the promise of travel as the mature Cornelia and even the grandmother in her eighties would: by packing up and enjoying to the fullest. She stayed three months—only a moment when seen in relation to Cornelia's long life, but an eternity from the perspective of an eight-year-old. The Jayneses toured Boston with her, providing her with a keen sense of her country's heritage; they took her to Haverhill to visit her paternal family, the James clan; there were excursions to Cape Ann and Cape Cod, and afternoons when neighborhood girls, proper little Bostonians, were invited to meet the vivacious relative from the Midwest. Enchanted aunts and nieces improved Cornelia's wardrobe and competed to entertain her. It was a summer full of joy, excitement, adventure, a summer also during which she learned to adapt to a new setting, to meet new people, and to define a realm of her own outside the protective fences of the familiar.

Her first visit to West Newton was a pleasure trip, a brief excursion into a new world under the protective wing of an aunt who was like a second mother; her second trip, however, acquired a different quality. In many ways Cornelia experienced it as exile, or what was worse, as a poor relative's humiliating escape into the arms of the more fortunate. When the Jameses moved into Harvard Place, the family could afford a generous lifestyle, but their situation deteriorated as the depression of the 1890s struck. The continued westward movement, industrialization, urbaniza-tion, and mass migration had turned the Midwest, and especially the Twin Cities area, into a veritable boom territory in the seventies and eighties, and Henry James participated successfully in this gold rush. The despair in the (Mid)West at the collapse was boundless because expectations in progress and profit had been so. Although a succession of boom and bust had shaped the nation's economy throughout the century, and although these cyclical waves accelerated in the postwar decades as crises surfaced in 1866–67, 1873–1878 and 1884–1887, the depression of the nineties struck a nation unprepared for its quality, intensity, and lasting impact.

Like no other crisis before, this bust revealed the country's dependence on international economic developments and contexts when domestic problems were accelerated by events in the global market. Not only had overproduction in the farming areas resulted in dramatic price drops; not only had President McKinley's protective tariff of 1890 decreased revenues precariously; not only were steadily increasing veterans' pension claims depleting already destabilized government funds; but also in 1893 the U.S. Treasury was suddenly drained of gold when foreign investors sold their securities. In April the gold reserve fell below the safety mark of $100 mil-lion in May to a precarious $80 million. Panic ensued as banks, businesses, even railroads went into bankruptcy, and the realty market collapsed. Un-employment and labor unrest skyrocketed.[34]

Henry James's hope that his mansion would attract investors to Newport failed to materialize in the eighties and early nineties. Potential customers had proved reluctant to expose themselves to the daily commute; and as a result of the depression, investments in real estate were dropping dra-matically. The profits on which James had counted did not come in, while the costs of maintaining his mansion exploded. Frances and Henry real-ized that drastic changes in their lifestyle were inevitable. One by one the number of domestic help was reduced, and Frances drew up a work plan for family members. Poor relatives could not be dismissed so easily. The James women sewed their own dresses instead of going to the dressmaker, and they turned silks in a sincere but ineffective attempt to cover up the fact that they were waltzing on the brink of ruin. They were still well off in comparison to other American families, but they felt the pain of living on considerably less, and they were aware that things might get worse; a sense of impending gloom permeated the household. Frances communicated her despair to her sister Helen, and in the fall of 1892 Auntie invited Cornelia to spend a full year with her. The proposal was encoded as Cornelia's chance to prepare for college, but it is clear that Helen hoped to ease the family's straits by "adopting" one of the girls. The offer was gratefully accepted. In January 1893 Auntie received a telegram saying: "Cornelia will be with you on Sunday evening at six o'clock. The Lord be with you!"—a tornado warning indeed.

Living in a new social setting as a poor relative forced Cornelia to control those outbursts that terrorized her Minnesota kin. "I have learned lots of lessons not written in books since I have been here," she admitted.[35] Her uncle Clifford actually was the first person in her doting family to censure her. He resented her outspokenness, a form of conduct he despised as unwomanly, and he did not hesitate to upbraid her even in the presence of guests; there was constant pressure to curb her passions in this household of soft-spoken, well-behaved, genteel New Englanders. And yet the lessons she learned were never internalized. Teasing, ridicule, and emotional outbursts were central to Cornelia's sense of who she was and wanted to be, and to repress them would have been a liquidation of self. Her sharp tongue, her "inordinate impulsiveness,"[36] and her irreverent wit survived Uncle Clifford's feminizing endeavors, and they were to keep her husband and children, friends and neighbors on the alert.

Life in West Newton also taught Cornelia that people thrived on much less than she had always taken for granted even during her father's bankruptcy. The Jaynes house felt small indeed, and the polite phrases she used to describe it reveal her sense of amazement that people could be satisfied with so little. "Auntie has a very pretty cozy, homelike house," she commented condescendingly, "but dreadfully cold."[37]

Friends were entertained, but there was none of the Jameses' abundance, only the simple, proud elegance so typical of the bourgeois New England Cornelia eventually learned to cherish. In Newport Cornelia had taken piano and violin lessons, had been exposed to church music and local choirs; in West Newton she learned to listen—to differentiate, appreciate, enjoy consciously. Her aunt and uncle were more economical than Cornelia's parents when it came to praise, more demanding in aesthetic matters; they pointed out weaknesses as well as strategies for improvement where her family had applauded the effort as such—trying to equip their naïvely enthusiastic niece with an appreciation for excellence and the skills of the *connoisseuse*. Cornelia was introduced to a new world of aesthetic refinement, of knowledge and criticism. This was a field where the West could not compete, she wrote to her mother after having heard Paderewski. "How beautiful it is to live where you can hear music and be surrounded by musical people. I do enjoy it."[38]

Cornelia attended high school in West Newton, walking two miles through lushly arbored streets to and from school. As a girl from the much maligned Midwest, she had been afraid that she would not be able to compete intellectually with the young Bostonians. To her pleasure she found, however, that she was "way ahead of the girls and boys of my age and even ahead of the Junior class here," she bragged on 9 January 1893. With that advantage she approached the new setting, making friends, participating in extracurricular activities such as drama and debating clubs, and studying vigorously to prove that the "frontier girl" could measure up to them. And as the number of her friends increased, so did the mobility she claimed for herself. In a jubilant letter to "darling Papa" she reported that she had learned to ride a bicycle. "The first time I got on I just rode a few blocks, the next time about a mile and Monday took an *eight* mile ride and the next day a *ten* mile ride," she crowed on 31 May 1893.

Embracing both intellectual achievement and a healthy, even athletic lifestyle, she transformed herself into a Gibson girl, a complement to the turn-of-the-century New Woman variant of white middle-class womanhood that *Life* magazine was propagating.[39] The Newton year would have been close to perfect had it not been for a problem that was to haunt Cornelia throughout the depression: money. "I wish that Papa would telegraph me some money," she begged on 27 March 1893. "I haven't a *cent!* and I do *hate* to keep borrowing all the time." Her relatives proved sympathetic, but Cornelia felt humiliated, "as if I hadn't a father to support me," she exclaimed on 28 May. Frances had taught her to handle money carefully and make it last; but now she had nothing to handle and nothing to make last. She was for all to see the poor relation, and she hated the situation, for it was utterly incompatible with the persona of the self-sufficient, proudly independent woman she had constructed for herself and others.

As the time for departure from Boston drew near, happy anticipations of the family reunion were overshadowed by the pain of having to leave an intellectually stimulating environment. Part of herself had taken root in New England, and in her last letter home she wrote: "I am afraid Papa we shall have to move East. . . . There is a cultivation and a refinement about the very air one breathes. Well I was an easy convert—wasn't I?" Happily so, for she would spend only a few more years in Minnesota. New England was her destiny, and fortunately she was able to embrace it without reservations.

CHAPTER 2

"Four Years of Unorthodox Study"
THE RADCLIFFE YEARS

I N SEPTEMBER 1895 CORNELIA BOARDED A TRAIN FROM ST. PAUL
to Cambridge. She would spend the next four years at Radcliffe College,
a student of the century's final class—the class of 1899, the "Nineteenth-
Century Limited." Asked in the late 1960s to record her college reminiscences as one of the last surviving class members, Cannon insisted that hers
had been a direct road to Radcliffe: "As time grew near to choose a college,
I collected catalogues of all the colleges admitting women students to see
what they had to offer. Most of them had only one course in a subject such
as Philosophy I, Geology I, etc. Radcliffe, however, thanks to its affiliation
with Harvard, had many courses in all fields. That opportunity made me
decide on Radcliffe immediately, in those happy days of President Eliot of
Harvard; who both admitted women and let them choose their own program."[1] Constructing herself as a feminist seeker in quest of knowledge, the
ninety-two-year-old alumna left no doubt that Radcliffe had always been
her undisputed first choice. By the time she dictated these reminiscences,
her life was so closely entwined with the history of her alma mater that the
old lady could no longer imagine alternative interpretations. Seven decades
had passed since graduation, blurring the contours of a picture that had
been characterized by a more lively intermingling of light and shadow.
Also, the class of '99 was characterized by an intense loyalty which the
alumnae revived in annual reunions. As Marian Cannon Schlesinger remembers, "even in their very old age they would come together for Class
Reunions, leaning on their canes and often still wearing hats left over, it
would seem, from those lighthearted undergraduate days."[2]

For decades Cannon had taken the lead in organizing these reunions, and not only was she a reliable contributor to the class's anniversary reports, but also hers were usually the most self-ironic. For years she had served on the Radcliffe Board of Trustees, and her loyalty to the college was further strengthened when three of her four daughters—Wilma, Marian, and Helen—passed through Radcliffe in the 1920s and 1930s. Her endeavors to set up a scholarship for Filipino women were recognized when a Philippine Room (subsequently the Cornelia James Cannon Room) was established in the graduate center in 1958. In 1954 her loyalty was publicly acknowledged through a citation at the college's seventy-fifth anniversary celebration, and finally, four years before her death, she received one of Radcliffe's first Founders Awards as "one who has for more than sixty years served family and community with warmth and understanding," and for representing "a shining example of illustrious womanhood to your many friends and acquaintances."[3]

By then a remarkable number of Cannon's granddaughters were enjoying Radcliffe, and the proud grandmother never tired of encouraging communication between her generation's genteel women and those young feminists of the 1960s who staged Vietnam War, civil rights, and women's rights protests on campus. "Perhaps the members of the Class of 1968, better educated and no doubt better trained than we were, will help us with new ideas," she wrote, expressing her willingness to learn from the young. "We of 1899 are eager to hear what they have to say."[4] Small wonder that this dynamic member of the "Nineteenth-Century Limited" would portray her relationship with her alma mater as a love affair.

In her desire to reimagine this history in terms of continuity, Cannon ignored the fact that the college for which she had prepared had not been the then still adolescent Radcliffe, with its predominantly local, middle-class clientele. By the time she was ready to enter college, institutions of higher learning all over the country had opened their gates to white middle-class women. There were private coeducational colleges; state universities were inviting women's enrollment; and the East Coast boasted six exclusive women's colleges: Vassar (1861), Wellesley (1870), Smith (1871), Bryn Mawr (1885), Mount Holyoke (1893), and Radcliffe (1879–1894).[5]

Cornelia had opted for the older and more expensive residential Vassar. "I am taking the General Course with Latin and am trying to prepare for Vassar," she recorded in her diary on 1 September 1890. From entries over the following months and in letters she wrote, it is clear that Vassar, with its predominantly female faculty, its large, wealthy resident student body, its impressive buildings, its museum, art gallery, and astronomical observatory, was her goal; Cornelia prepared as systematically for the Vassar admission exams as some of her male classmates studied for Harvard or Yale. But fate in the form of pecuniary problems intervened, forcing Cornelia to redefine her dream. Even after the onset of the depression, and despite the family's strict economizing, Cornelia had no idea how precarious her family's economic situation really was—a sign of how deeply entrenched were gendered notions of the male provider and naïvely secure daughter even in this enlightened household.

She thus was little prepared for the crisis they faced throughout the 1890s, but by the time she was studying to enter college, she could no longer deny that they were on the brink of ruin. In her senior year her letters to her Massachusetts kin reveal her panic lest her college dreams collapse. Desperately she sought alternatives, and the first decisive step she took was to discard Vassar once and for all. It was a compromise that came without too much pain, for by the time Cornelia was forced to make this decision, she had indeed already become aware of an alternative which her pragmatic nature could easily redefine as promise: Radcliffe College.

During her 1893 stay in Newton, Cornelia had begun to collect information about Radcliffe. After its humble beginnings as the "Harvard Annex" in Carrett House at 6 Appian Way, Cambridge, in 1879—with twenty-seven registered students, only three of whom took the full course at a tuition of $200—President Elizabeth Cary Agassiz, her small staff, and students had moved to the more spacious Fay House on Garden Street in 1885. This building would contain the entire college for the next decade: administrative offices, classrooms, auditorium, and lunchroom. By 1893 the student body had increased considerably; Harvard professors and instructors taught at Radcliffe; and citizens devoted to women's higher education, first among them the Women's Education Association, had raised the $250,000 that Harvard's President Eliot had demanded before considering "the Annex a part of Harvard." Now the "Annex would become a separate women's college with Harvard professors as its faculty and as its visiting body. Degrees would be signed by President Agassiz and countersigned by President Eliot to attest that the Radcliffe degree was equivalent in all respects to that of Harvard."[6] In 1894 the Massachusetts legislature granted a charter to Radcliffe College, and President Eliot admitted women to graduate-level classes at Harvard.

Cornelia observed these moves carefully, and she saw the advantages of the Harvard-Radcliffe compromise: an impressive number and variety of courses, teachers of superior quality, and, of utmost importance, moderate tuition fees. Not only did Cornelia's reorientation meet with her father's enthusiastic response, but also she was encouraged by her teacher May Newson, who had coached dozens of pupils for the Harvard admission exams.[7] Newson was impressed by Cornelia's commitment, and she changed her role from observation to active monitoring, preparing Cornelia for the exams to be held in Minneapolis in June 1895.[8] Cornelia studied almost obsessively, though signs accumulated that even her more modest Radcliffe plans might ultimately be defeated by forces beyond her control. She passed, but she could not triumph, for the family's financial problems had reached a state that ridiculed her ambitions. "You don't know how I can't bear to give up Radcliffe after I have passed the examinations—to have to stop for such a small thing as money," she lamented. "We shall have to teach school and be old maids before our time. To settle down as so many girls do and just wait until a husband turns up is too disgusting."[9]

Again a woman—an "old maid"—in this woman-centered family came to Cornelia's rescue. Aunt Lucy, moved by Cornelia's despair, asked to become a permanent member of the James household; the portion of her income thus saved was to pay Cornelia's tuition. The arrangement was gratefully embraced, and in mid-September Cornelia bade farewell to her family. Months of emotional turmoil lay behind the young woman, during which she had displayed her iron will by refusing to be conquered by circumstances. Now, during her train ride from the Midwest to New England, she was torn by conflicting emotions: the pain of separation, relief at succeeding against all odds, the anxious question how she would cope in the new environment. She had grown up in a "self-contained" domestic circle; in this her self-confidence and strength were grounded. At the same time, she had to sever the umbilical cord attaching her to this protective web and was facing the challenge of her individual uprooting as well as the need to forge new social relationships—a reinvention of self.

Although Cornelia saw her move from Minnesota to Massachusetts, from family to college sisterhood, from adolescence to young adulthood as a new beginning, even a rupture, it also spelled continuity. She traveled from a "self-contained" domestic realm to an equally "self-contained" academic and social one. In her history of the college Dora Elia Howells argues that the women "who chose Radcliffe were, in the main, the middle-class daughters of Massachusetts clergymen, teachers, and physicians,"[10] commuting daily between home and college; they were, almost as a rule, Protestant and white. Harvard admitted a small number of African Americans, among them W. E. B. Du Bois, whose doctoral thesis on the suppression of the African slave trade to the United States was published as the first volume of Harvard Historical Studies the year Cornelia arrived in Cambridge.[11] But Cornelia's class was entirely white, a racial exclusiveness of which she and her fellow students were totally unaware, as it was so deeply ingrained in the world they inhabited and the expectations and entitlements that came, almost automatically, with that middle-class whiteness. The year Cornelia entered Radcliffe, *Plessy v. Ferguson* cemented racial segregation and exclusion in its "separate but equal" formula, but this only confirmed the way she and her fellow students were living and would expect to live on a daily basis.

In choosing Radcliffe over Vassar, Cornelia also had to do without the protection that residential colleges such as Vassar, Smith, and Wellesley offered to their students. In 1895 Radcliffe was as yet unable to provide housing, which caused considerable problems for women from outside Massachusetts. They found accommodation in carefully selected boarding-houses, provided they could afford the $11 a week charged for room and board. As Cornelia's financial means were too limited for one of the "better" houses that Dean Agnes Irvin preferred for her charges, Aunt Jaynes found inexpensive lodgings on 49 Wendell Street.

In her first letter to her mother Cornelia was full of praise for her land-lady. "Mrs. Howard is the sweetest, most motherly woman you could imagine. She is a widow with two daughters and she keeps one girl to do the odds and ends of things and *she* does the cooking! I had dinner here today and it was perfectly *delicious!* Just so wholesome and nice as we have it at home," she wrote. "Everything is exquisitely clean and neat, and I am perfectly charmed."[12] A perusal of Cornelia's letters, however, reveals that she was being generous not only with her praise but also in juggling fact and fiction. The picture conjured up what both mother and daughter had envisioned against all odds, but it was deplorably far from reality. Months later, in a letter of 7 April 1896 to Margaret, studying sculpture in New York, we encounter a definitely less enthusiastic Cornelia: "I have come back to the land of *plain* living and high thinking. I could stand it if there weren't *quite* so many cat hairs in the food and human hairs also! and meat that is *touched!*" Cornelia tried to protect her family against anxieties on her account, refusing to exact additional sacrifices. With Margaret, however, she could be frank, for she had been to Wendell Street, and they had agreed to keep mutual confessions from the family.

The seediness of her boardinghouse dampened Cornelia's spirits, but she realized that there were more important issues. After all, she was about to enter a new world—the intellectual life of Radcliffe and Harvard, the society of Radcliffe women—and she had to adapt to unfamiliar rules as she tried to define her place in this community. On 26 September 1895 she faced a "trying ordeal": she joined the line of sixty-three equally nervous newcomers and "*entered* Radcliffe" as a member of the class of '99. "It wasn't so terrible as I anticipated," she wrote in a letter of that day, but her reserved tone suggests that there was little to arouse the kind of enthusiasm she was always willing to work up. Her report contains no explanation for the sober, almost anticlimactic mood.

One possible reason surfaced two years later, when she described the cold welcome address Dean Irvin, who had also greeted her class, gave the freshmen of 1897. "Miss Irvin delivered the most remarkable address of welcome today that I ever heard," she charged. "Not a word of enthusiasm or of welcome but simply rules about behavior, urging us to sleep enough, not to eat too much, and to be unselfish about the library, considerate and thoughtful about other things. If we had been little Sunday School children it could not have been more goody-good. The great opportunities and cultivating influences of college life she has never known." The judgment she pronounced over Miss Irvin was devastating: "She is a curious failure as a woman and as a dean."[13] Though frustrated and angry, she would not allow one individual's shortcomings to mar her enjoyment of college.

Once she had made up her mind to enter Radcliffe, she embraced her school wholeheartedly, determined to appropriate the place by making her presence felt. From now on she would wear her Radcliffe connection as a badge of honor, and her pragmatism made this process of appropriation a relatively easy one. No lachrymose thoughts were allowed to linger, and within a very short time she had convinced herself that Vassar had never been on her life's itinerary; she was, she ultimately believed, where she had always wanted to be. For the rest of her life this was the story she told, a narrative that had become truly hers. There is only one sign that some resentment survived: her ridicule of elite women's colleges. The social realm to which she aspired had excluded her; in response, she banned it from her dreams to a world she now wrote off as undesirable.

Compared to the most elite women's colleges, what Radcliffe offered in terms of buildings was meager indeed. Yet the people who supported the institution, and especially President Agassiz and Dean Irvin, were indefatigable in their efforts to provide the kind of space they felt necessary for young minds to mature. And they were successful; the college expanded rapidly. In 1897 a large, irregular square between Garden Street, Brattle Street, Appian Way, and Mason Street was acquired, and in its new buildings the college provided more and larger lecture rooms as well as a steadily increasing variety of courses for its growing student body. A gymnasium was built; *Radcliffe Magazine*—with Cornelia James as class editor—was launched in 1899. Dean Irvin proudly announced, "For Radcliffe the day of small things is over."[14] Cornelia's comments on these changes reveal a firm sense of identification with her alma mater. There was, after all, considerably more glory in contributing to the construction of a new institution than in enjoying the results of others' toil, more excitement in pioneering than in establishment life. Radcliffe meant movement, growth, challenge—an ideal intellectual home for Cornelia's dynamic nature.

Cornelia was eager to broaden her horizons and was enthusiastic about Radcliffe's curriculum. "I decided to take one course in every possible subject which gave me four exciting years of unorthodox study," she later recalled.[15] Her records reveal that her retrospective evaluation was correct. Her college schedule illustrates her insatiable intellectual curiosity, her eagerness to embrace new subjects, her almost voracious love of information. At the same time there were no endeavors at specialization, at developing skills in preparation for a clearly defined career, at a deepening of knowledge in specific disciplines; instead hers was an attempt to acquire basic information in as many fields as possible.

Among the twenty courses she took were English, German, History, Philosophy, Chemistry, Geology, Zoology, Botany, and Economics. This approach was expressive of Cornelia's lifelong attitude toward knowledge—a longing for breadth rather than depth; a love of playful learnedness. Schlesinger described her mother's mind as "speedy, emotional, full of ad hoc opinions and conclusions, and usually directly on target on a myriad of different subjects and problems."[16] She mentions Cornelia's exasperation at the intellectual sobriety of men. "Why do they not let a poor lady have her ideas without being so severe about it?" she exclaimed in mock despair. "If I had to *prove* every statement I make, I should be stricken dumb for life!"[17] Her idea of a perfect education was to acquire a little of everything rather than everything in a small, specialized discipline. The Radcliffe curriculum suited her to perfection.

Cornelia's attitude toward learning was the result neither of limited intellectual capacities nor of a lack of ambition; it mirrored the progressive doctrine on women's education of the day and was supported even by liberal nineteenth-century advocates of women's higher education.[18] In his inaugural address of 19 October 1879, President Eliot praised Radcliffe's "newly established University Courses of Instruction to competent women," while denying, almost in the same breath, that they were designed for professional training. "In these courses the University offers to young women who have been to good schools as many years as they wish of liberal culture in studies which have no direct professional value, to be sure," he admonished, "but which enrich and enlarge both intellect and character."[19] Nineteen years later, when Cornelia was in her third year of college, Eliot had lost his fear "that, in developing this higher side of the life of women, the beauty and charm of the feminine character may be impaired,"[20] yet he had not given up his dread of white "race suicide"—according to one observer, "a doubt always lingered in his mind lest, as a result of such training, women might be lured from the home and the cradle"[21]—and he still could not envision an education for women that would enable them to compete as professionals with men. Rather, he espoused learning that would render them attractive wives, intelligent, reasonably informed respondents to the male discourse, receptive instead of competitive, encouraging rather than challenging. "Can any greater gift be made to a man than to keep him in the presence of a highly-trained intellectual and spiritual woman?" he asked, defining women's education as a gift to men rather than a response to women's needs. "Can any greater gift be made to human society than to make it possible, generation after generation, for men and women to live together in this quick intellectual and spiritual sympathy?"[22]

It was a philosophy to which Cornelia subscribed fully, with one essential qualification, as an article titled "Science at Radcliffe" documents. It was written in the mid-1920s, when Cornelia Cannon was already deeply entrenched in the eugenic camp. There was one position within this eugenic discourse, however, that she would continue to combat to the end of her life: the connection that especially male supporters of the movement established between a woman's higher education and her reproductive capacities. "Science at Radcliffe" is one of her spirited replies to this charge, evoking images of enlightened domesticity and intelligent white motherhood to make her point.

The ideal Radcliffe alumna she conjures up is the mother of a "growing brood," and the knowledge she acquired at college makes her life in a conventional female realm sparkle. "She greets the stars as beloved friends and points out to her children the course of their wanderings as one familiar with their ways," she admonishes. "Even the everyday housekeeping problems are to her absorbing scientific experiments. . . . When the drafts do not draw, the doorbell gets out of order, the jelly refuses to 'jell,' or the dye-bath corrodes the kettle, she meets the difficulty in the same spirit of enthusiastic understanding she would devote to the larger problems of the conservation of energy and the constitution of the ion."[23] The article reveals how thoroughly Cornelia had internalized the gendered perspective on education, and in that it helps us understand the approach she herself chose. Where male needs claimed absolute priority over a woman's intellectual autonomy, where women's education was denied professional perspectives, education for women was bound to remain dilettantish—tourist-like excursions into the various disciplines, but no process of genuine appropriation, no transformational contribution.

Small wonder also that the Harvard professors who agreed to teach at Radcliffe tended to develop a paternalistic attitude of low expectations toward their pupils—benevolent condescension rather than intellectual challenge. An encounter between Cornelia James and her philosophy instructor William James was symptomatic of this kind of relationship. In an examination Cornelia found herself unable to answer James's questions. Instead of returning an empty sheet, she simply ignored what was before her and wrote an essay on issues (unfortunately unidentified) that interested her. It was a—perhaps desperate, perhaps proud—defiance of the male prerogative of defining what was central and important. Professor James gave her an A, exhibiting not only flexibility as an instructor but also the condescending generosity displayed toward those whose contribution is regarded as marginal, as decorative rather than relevant.[24] That this episode was typical becomes clear when we consider it in parallel with an encounter between Gertrude Stein, Radcliffe class of 1897, and the same instructor. Stein had preferred attending the opera to studying, and in the finals, unprepared, she wrote on her exam paper: "Dear Professor James[,] . . . I am so sorry but really I do not feel a bit like an examination paper in philosophy to-day." He replied via postcard that he understood "perfectly," adding, "I often feel like that myself." Her work was given "the highest mark in his course."[25] Neither Cornelia James nor Gertrude Stein saw anything but generosity and humor in William James's response.

As Cornelia failed to elaborate on which subjects were interesting to her, it is difficult to trace the impact of what she actually learned at Radcliffe on her later life. There is one discipline, however, and one teacher associated with it, that became of utmost importance for her reformist career: zoology, taught by Charles B. Davenport. Davenport, after receiving his Ph.D. from Harvard in 1892, became an instructor in the Department of Zoology until 1898, also teaching at Radcliffe; in 1897 he made a name for himself when he published his course notes in his textbook *Experimental Morphology*. He was a junior scholar in the process of claiming his place in zoology when he taught Cornelia, and nothing about the man and his course intrigued her sufficiently to record his name, but the position he eventually defined for himself provided Cornelia's reformism with the scientific legitimization she required.

Davenport, as his first publication documents, was a disciple of Darwinian evolutionary theory and was especially interested in experimental evolutionary biology and the question of heritability. An early convert to Francis Galton's "science of improving stock," and encouraged by the rediscovery of the Mendelian theory of inheritance and genetic selection in 1900, he devoted himself as a scholar to biological engineering, to the "improvement" of the race. He became one of the earliest spokesmen for eugenics in the United States and, because of the respectability he brought to eugenics as a scientist, its most powerful voice. He was active in the American Breeder Association with its *American Breeder's Journal,* a founding member of the influential Eugenics Committee of the United States, and co-founder of the American Eugenics Society; he would serve as president of the Galton Society, president of the International Federation of Eugenic Organizations, and as editorial committee member of *Eugenic News,* among other posts. In 1910 he established the Eugenics Record Office at Cold Spring Harbor, Long Island, turning the town into "the holy city of American eugenicists."[26]

All of this was in the not too distant future when Cornelia James was attending Davenport's classes, but as the aspiring instructor reemerged as the lionized scholar-apostle of eugenics, Cornelia claimed the old relationship to confirm her eugenic reformism. The St. Paul parlor discussions about Darwin, Spencer, and Galton, her family's serene security in their Anglo-Saxon superiority, had laid the groundwork for her eugenic orientation; her association, however vague, with Davenport at Radcliffe would legitimize her position with the respectability and authority of science.

William James and Charles Davenport as instructors, Gertrude Stein and Josephine Sherwood (later Hull) as fellow students: Cornelia's letters during her Radcliffe years celebrate the privileges of college life, "plain living," and "high thinking." "How thankful I ought to be for this time of intellectual work as separated from the commonness and wickedness of the world as though I were in a convent"[27] is a representative comment of the period—on the one hand formulaic in its banal conventionality, on the other impish in its potential subversion of stereotypical imagery, for after all, she used the open "ought to be" instead of the closed "am." Did college provide the intellectual challenge she claimed to crave?

We hear next to nothing about the books she read and the topics of her term papers. She mentioned that her compositions were praised and read out loud in class; William James was impressed by her lectures for the Philosophy Club; together with only one other Harvard student she received an A in history. But what were the issues she tackled? "The History marks here came and *one boy* at Harvard and *one girl* at Radcliffe got an A and—well modesty forbids my saying who the girl at R was but you can be sure she is the happiest girl in Cambridge today!" she triumphed in a letter of 7 March 1896. "The Freshman class are very proud that it was one of their members that gained the honor because Harvard usually carries off the prize regardless of us." The letter reduces her victory, a sign of Cornelia's academic potential, to a social event with a feminist tinge. She wasted not a word on the subject she discussed. Is it possible that learning as originally designed for male professionals and then boiled down to produce reasonably—but not competitively—educated wives for these men contained nothing that would challenge her to move beyond a gendered competition toward academic excellence? As long as her learning failed to touch a personal harp string in her and involved no professional perspective, as long as she had no clearly defined goal in life, competition as such was all that counted. With her enthusiastic nature she could not help becoming interested in various subjects, yet she never took the time, and nobody ever encouraged her to do so, to delve beneath the surface of things and claim a discipline as her own.

Her attitude appears even more ambivalent in her letters to her sisters. "I am beginning to get rather tired of the study grind," she confessed to Margaret on 14 March 1896. "It is wearing after a time." More revealing still, the excellent student of her letters to her parents admitted to her sisters a panicky fear of examinations which forced her to take recourse to sedatives—"nerve medicine to pull me through the exams."[28] Later complaints multiplied and even surfaced in letters to her mother. "I am tired of studying, I think I had enough of that last year for a steady thing," she wrote on 5 May 1899, and only one week later she reported to Helen that after hearing "dear old Dean Everett of the Divinity School" lecture to the Philosophy Club, she "came to the conclusion then that I had had enough of Philosophy, that it is all vanity and confusion, that I revere it as the staff that has led me up some steep hill, but I cast it aside now, that I have developed my walking legs."[29] To the end of her life Cornelia James would be invigorated by her intellectual curiosity, but she absolutely refused to transform herself into one of those devoted scholars whose "dreadful" fate it was "to make life simply a mental gymnastics"—as if that were the only option.[30]

Most Radcliffe students during the 1890s were middle-class women from Massachusetts; it was not a rich girls' college. Still, Cornelia was keenly aware of the chasm between those who belonged to Harvard and Radcliffe—the golden boys and girls of the Boston Brahmin class—and those who were tolerated, working their way through school, or living on stipends. There were those for whom every door was wide open, and those who were forced to come to terms with the ugly fact that some structures are impenetrable.[31] As a woman from the Midwest, Cornelia was something of an exotic in this exclusive setting, and her letters sparkle with sarcastic comments on the pioneer woman's adventures among proper Bostonians. Yet her self-reliance and remarkable sense of humor empowered her to cope with this potential impediment; she joined every club and activity Radcliffe afforded, "from the Idler down," with the exception, at first, of the gymnasium, "for you have to pay four dollars for a suit"—money she could not spare.[32] Eventually she joined even that, bragging of her success at basketball.

During her Radcliffe years she held just about every office her class had to offer: secretary of her class and of the Philosophy Club, president of the Science Club and the History Club, class editor of *Radcliffe Magazine*, captain of the class of '99 ball team.[33] Her rhetorical skills certainly helped, for she had trained herself to speak freely, enjoying the visibility others dreaded, and she had none of her fellow students' shyness when it came to making her point in controversies with the Radcliffe authorities. Within a relatively short time her love of performance, her energetic nature, and her organizational skills gave her a place and a voice in her new social realm. It was a success story that was all her doing, and perhaps her greatest achievement during her college years. Time and again fellow students asked her to be their spokeswoman, and Cornelia always complied, although this caused friction between her and Dean Irwin.

Most of her energy, however, went into performing with the Idler, the Glee, and the Emmanuel clubs, which had a special quality during those years, since Josephine Sherwood, later a distinguished actress, and Beulah Marie Dix, soon to gain national reputation as a playwright, were members of the class of '99.[34] Radcliffe, the *Boston Sunday Herald* headlined in a feature story, was "A Girl's College Where Any Student May Be an Actress."[35] Twenty-five plays were performed each year: class plays, operettas, vaudeville, as well as French, Greek, Latin, and German drama. More than that, women not only performed and directed but also wrote plays. Dix's play *The Wooing of Mistress Widdrington* and Sherwood's operettas *The Orientals* and *The Princess Perfection* were written for and first staged by the Radcliffe Glee Club. In all performances Cornelia James was in the cast, second only to Sherwood. Her enjoyment was, however, checked by the rules of propriety which the dean imposed on her girls; an enraged Cornelia denounced Radcliffe as "this nest of old maids, where we are not allowed to wear trousers that *touch* in our plays or to dance when a man is within calling distance."[36] She offered the following description of the actresses' tribulations when they produced Schiller's *Der Neffe als Onkel* (*The Nephew as Uncle*): "A number of the girls have to take the part of the army officers in Germany. We are allowed to wear gold laced coats, swords, boots etc. but we have to wear *bloomers* instead of trousers and the worst of it is that no men are allowed to come. The idiocy of such conduct is almost inconceivable."[37] For these productions she worked to the point of exhaustion. Her father feared for her academic performance, and her mother observed that "Cornelia seems to have fallen on her feet most surprisingly and the great danger to her will be in too much social life."[38] But Cornelia's discourse on her social life was one of success and triumph, of assimilation and belonging. It is only two years later, when she is describing her endeavors to make freshmen feel welcome, that we find a hint that the first months might have been more disconcerting than Cornelia cared to admit. "Radcliffe is a desolate place for a girl who does not know anyone and does not make friends easily," she wrote, carefully locating problems in others. "I shall constitute myself a committee to . . . raise their poor fluttering spirits. I remember how a kind word cheered my soul the first year."[39]

Cornelia James was enchanted with life in Cambridge, and she praised Radcliffe and Harvard as seedbeds of culture, but from the very start she also developed a rather critical attitude toward the traditional Harvard student. "These Harvard Swells do make me tired," she complained to her mother on 18 January 1896. "Their calm superiority to the littleness of life and man is so young and so aggravating that it seems as if only a good ducking in cold water could affect them." Like other Harvard "outsiders," such as Walter Lippmann, John Reed, Owen Johnson, Joseph Patrick Kennedy, even Franklin D. Roosevelt, her former schoolmate Walter Cannon suffered from the impenetrability of the university, perceived by outsiders as "a bastion of a bygone era, an intolerant island."[40] Cornelia, too, acknowledged the problem, but she aggressively claimed that she could conquer anybody—if she chose. She admitted to no bitterness and recorded no rejection. Still, she eagerly sought the support offered by a small community of midwesterners at Harvard. For these people, students and faculty alike, the house of the Unitarian minister Samuel McChord Crothers and his wife, Louise, who had served in St. Paul and now lived in Cambridge, became a foster home. Cornelia had admired them in St. Paul; in Cambridge she learned to love them.[41] In addition, Cornelia cultivated a lively relationship with relatives in Newton and Haverhill. She was equally capable of embracing what her new world offered and of holding on to what had been important to her since childhood. Past and present, instead of competing, formed one dynamic and mutually empowering unity.

Of special interest during this period of redefinition are Cornelia's refreshingly irreverent comments on life around Harvard Yard. She was appalled that, particularly among Harvard women, the ideals of plain living and high thinking became an excuse for slovenliness in appearance. In a letter to Helen of 22 November 1898 she wrote about the wives of celebrities such as President Eliot and professors Josiah Royce and William James, among others: "Of all deadly homely women they do take the palm! And Cambridge women anyway are so homely and dress so badly! I got severely sat on for saying that by a respectable woman who said sternly that Cambridge 'went in for' learning and had no time for clothes. Just the same they have no right to offend the aesthetic eye as they do." No, she certainly did not want to look like any of them—not ever, if she could help it! Alas, it was an attitude she would not maintain for long. Once she had acquired a precarious membership in the exclusive community of Cantabrigians through her marriage to the Harvard professor Walter B. Cannon, she competed with the formerly ridiculed Cambridge women in their ideal of plain living, as her daughters' reminiscences as well as photos of a mature Cornelia Cannon in baggy dresses and battered hats suggest. It was a case of the convert, desperate in her need to belong, trying to outdo those who belonged unquestionably.

But the young Cornelia James gazed uncomprehendingly at these aesthetically offensive displays of female intellectuality. Photos taken during her college days document how hard she struggled to look elegant. Her allowance was never enough to keep her dressed decently, but fortunately her relatives helped out. "Margaret Haskell gave me a lovely spring suit that she had last year," she reported to her mother on 3 May 1897. "It is silk lined which fills my heart with joy. Margaret gave it to me with great apology but I accepted it voraciously." In these photos Cornelia (except for hair that would always be unmanageable) looks very much like the popular images of the "Gibson girl," a creation of Charles Dana Gibson that began to appear in *Life* magazine in the 1890s—young, white middle-class women depicted playing tennis and golf, bicycling, hiking, wearing a white blouse or shirtwaist and a dark skirt, the ideal of the healthy, athletic, confident, and pure white maiden. Lois W. Banner calls this type "the American virgin-woman" with "a refreshing aura of health, sensuality, and rebellion,"[42] but it is also a maiden whose health, athletic feats, and racial identity qualify her as fertile mother of the "future race," a living rejection of the increasingly common brain-shrinking-uterus paradigm.

In her annual report of December 1896 Radcliffe's secretary, Mary Coes, complained that, as a result of the depression, Radcliffe College had lost a considerable number of students. Cornelia, whose pecuniary situation had been precarious throughout her first year, suffered doubly: her father's business stood at the brink of ruin, and the situation became desperate when Aunt Lucy, whose money was to carry her through college, suddenly died. "Must I leave school now?" she anxiously asked her mother.[43] Indeed, anxiety became Cornelia's most faithful companion. She worked as a laboratory assistant, thus saving the laboratory fees for her chemistry course; she went into private tutoring; she spent her summers in Massachusetts to avoid the expense of travel. During her senior year the situation became so desperate that she even applied to Radcliffe for a scholarship—successfully.[44]

It was once again the women of the family who managed to keep her in school. Aunt Lucy's sisters gave their meager inheritance to Cornelia, adding to the $220 Aunt Lu had left her. Cousin Lizzy from Haverhill suggested that whenever "I needed anything she wanted me to call on her for it," reported Cornelia.[45] And Auntie offered her home to save boarding-house expenses; Cornelia lived with the Jayneses during three of her four college years. She had to give up her relative autonomy. "Uncle C. comes down on me like a thousand of brick . . . and I am reduced to pulps," she complained on 31 October 1897. Yet this arrangement kept her enrolled in Radcliffe, and for that she was willing to swallow anything. She would later repay her relatives' kindness by keeping her own house open to kin in need.

The extreme financial and emotional turmoil and consequential sense of humiliation Cornelia James suffered in those years also explains, at least in part, the attitude she would maintain throughout her life toward the most famous of her fellow Radcliffe students, Gertrude Stein. Two years Cornelia's senior, Stein had come to Radcliffe to be near her brother Leo, then at Harvard, and it was during this period, under the direction of Hugo Münsterberg, that she "worked out a series of experiments in automatic writing," as Stein remembers in her autobiography.[46] Desperate for money, Cornelia volunteered as a test subject, only to be haughtily dismissed when her mind and hands refused to display the spontaneity the future avant-garde writer expected[47]—this although Stein, as she admitted, "never had subconscious reactions, nor was she a successful subject for automatic writing."[48]

Cornelia James never wrote about this humiliating encounter in her letters home, nor does she mention Stein by name; at the time she may have dismissed the episode as negligible and the older student, who left Radcliffe for Johns Hopkins a year later, "one Latin exam short of receiving her B.A.,"[49] as uninteresting. The episode was remembered and entered family lore only after Stein became a key instigator of American avant-garde high modernism in Paris and was transformed from just another fellow student into a celebrity whom Cornelia James had known before fame struck. And yet this brief and abortive interaction between the two college students is of utmost importance in that it allows us to locate Cornelia James Cannon within the intellectual context of her time and to investigate the position she chose to inhabit in the intricate negotiations of the literary and aesthetic discourse engaging avant-garde modernism, progressive modernism, and antimodernism between the turn of the century and World War II.[50]

As her Radcliffe writing experiments document, the college student Gertrude Stein, a young woman at home in at least three languages and on two continents, was already eager for stylistic innovation. At college she launched her first attempts at deconstructing language, moving toward a writing career that would challenge conventional metaphysics as it signified on established forms, cultural allegiances, and sociopolitical events. Her rootedness in both Old and New World cultures, her situation as a Jew of German descent in the United States, as well as her first lesbian relationships created in Stein an intellectual mobility, fluidity as well as elusiveness that would metamorphose into creative aesthetic iconoclasm. Rationality, hierarchy, order, the cultural hegemony of sense and coherence—Stein discarded them for the immediacy of experience, the nowness of time which she celebrated.[51] Embracing fragmentation as liberation from the nineteenth-century belief in progress and continuity, she would ultimately reinvent herself as the personification of the twentieth century when she wrote in *Wars I Have Seen* (1945), "There is no point in being realistic about here and now, no use at all not any, and so it is not the nineteenth but the twentieth century, there is no realism now, life is not real it is not earnest, it is strange, which is an entirely different matter."[52]

Though just two years older, Stein must have appeared cosmopolitan to Cornelia James, who knew only Minnesota and Massachusetts; her eagerness to embrace the fragment, chaos, the irregular, and unresolved opposition irrational when a belief in orderly human progress, and especially the progress of white Americanness, had been implanted since childhood; her playful feminist deconstruction of language—"her language is english"[53]—foolish to one who believed so firmly in the power of the word and never once experienced linguistic crisis; and her challenge to established form, her reveling in repetition, circular motion, and the epiphanic, socially irresponsible to one nurtured on the reliable formulae of the Victorian novel and American regionalism. If Stein's writing, as Harriet Scott Chessman contends, is accessible only to the reader and critic willing to "read her writing as co-players, opening [themselves] up to its manifold pleasures,"[54] then everything Cornelia James Cannon was and wanted to be banned her from this realm.

Perhaps none of that entered Cornelia's mind during that first encounter, but it defined her reading of Gertrude Stein when the latter reentered her American context via her notorious celebrity, and it was no doubt enhanced by Stein's opting for an expatriate life, a decision utterly beyond the comprehension of Cornelia's fierce patriotism. Jealousy and competition as a writer may also have played a role in the condescending sarcasm that entered Cornelia Cannon's evocations of the original relationship, but what is essential is the utter incompatibility of their views of the world, of writing, of aesthetics, a fundamental clash of personalities and minds. They could not communicate because they adhered to incompatible cosmologies. Though two years younger than Gertrude Stein, Cornelia James was and would always be a woman and a didactic writer of the Victorian age and of American progressivism, a novelist who shied away from even the subtle explicitness of American realism and naturalism. Cornelia James Cannon as writer and reformer would always cling to the racialized hierarchical order, to the programmatics and representational conventions of nineteenth-century British and American literatures. Stein, proud that "Dickens had always frightened her,"[55] claimed for herself and her writing the twentieth century, celebrating the Second World War as the death of the nineteenth century.

Nevertheless, focusing exclusively on the incompatibility of the two women's cosmologies and aesthetics, as Cornelia James Cannon's retrospective rendering of the relationship suggests, blinds us to the fact that in their writing, both shared a deterministic and thoroughly racialized view of American life. In their fiction they would explore the eugenic discourse of the day and renegotiate their progressivist and feminist credo through that lens. For Stein, as Daylanne K. English's brilliant analysis in *Unnatural Selections* documents, it was her medical training and informed knowledge of woman's physical reality that laid the groundwork for (and provided a special touch to) the eugenic theme that permeated her fiction from *Three Lives* (1909) through *The Making of Americans* (1925); for Cornelia James Cannon, as we will see, it was her ambivalence toward immigration and her birth control activism. Thematically, they walked hand in hand.[56]

Despite her financial problems, Cornelia James's determination, energy, and optimism enabled her to render her Radcliffe years a period of mental growth, and her happy disposition won her the friendship of fellow students and instructors alike. Even Dean Irvin began to appreciate her, for Cornelia reported that she "is really getting quite fond of me now. She tries to hold my hand occasionally but I have sufficient agility to escape that."[57] Still, during her last year at Radcliffe her letters were characterized by an increasing anxiety about life beyond college. "I am just beginning to realize wherein the real problem of the higher education of women lies," she wrote on 9 April 1899. "It is the *afterwards*. How to fill one's life with other interests away from hundreds of sympathetic kindred souls is the question." She was in limbo between President Eliot's definition of women's education as decorative and her own longing for a life beyond established gender boundaries. In a ditty written during this period she articulated her despair:

> You grind away from morn till night,
> As hard as any he,
> But if you are a Radcliffe girl,
> You get no Ph.D.
> You get applause, but that's because
> You had the sand to try;
> And echo answers . . . why?

Much as she professed her longing for a career, nothing in her letters and academic choices suggests that she ever looked upon her college years as a period of preparation for professional life. She had discovered no discipline she could embrace as her own, and nothing in this educational system encouraged her to do so. Now, with graduation approaching, she panicked. She hated the very idea of becoming a teacher—to her a "horrid stupid grind."[58] She wanted to be an actress, to metamorphose into a new identity every day, to enchant people. Her progressive family, Minnesota and Massachusetts relatives in unholy alliance, was up in arms. Her classmate Josephine Sherwood had the courage to soar; Cornelia, unable or unwilling to defy her kin, remained grounded. For some time she considered social work, but again the family had different notions of female respectability and usefulness. "I want to go in the Xmas vacation and work a week at Jordan and Marshes as clerk so that I can see what the life of the girls behind the counters is like but Auntie swears I shall not," she complained to her mother on 22 October 1897 and continued: "I will not be balked in it by the petty prejudices of *Aunts!* When I have sent all my sisters through college I am going into the work and live in Chicago where there is plenty of raw, wicked material to work on."

But she *was* balked in. Twenty years later she would ask herself whether she "was never anything but a parlor-radical?"[59] Despite her bombastic rhetoric, she lacked the stamina to stand up to those she loved—and this is exactly what it would have taken to follow the itinerary she claimed was most desirable. Or was it that she had no itinerary, only a grand pose? Years later, in a tribute on her forty-sixth birthday, friends playfully reminded her of the tribulations during those final months at Radcliffe:

> I see the maiden, her parchment in her hand, looking out of her magic casement on the foam of the perilous Mississippi—What is she looking for?
> She is looking for a career.
> What kind of a career?

A career of Universal Usefulness tempered by Adventure. How does she expect to find it? By careering after it.[60]

Reluctantly Cornelia finally reconsidered the idea of teaching but decided that she could stand it only if it meant adventure. She applied for a position in Honolulu, and when this failed, she considered Buenos Aires, where, as she teased Helen in February 1899, women teachers from the United States were usually married off in less than three months. None of these plans materialized. Finally she was so exhausted by her desperately incoordinate search that she gave up.

In June 1899 the sixty women of the class of '99—"the largest class ever graduated"[61]—received their Radcliffe B.A.s. Cornelia James graduated magna cum laude. In her commencement address President Agassiz reminded the "Nineteenth-Century Limited" of the responsibility that the last class of the nineteenth century bore to the twentieth: "I am confident in one thing, however, which is that the largest liberty of instruction cannot in itself impair true womanhood. If understood and used aright, it can only be a help and not a hindrance in the life-work natural to women. It can never impair, but rather enlarge and ennoble, the life of the home."[62] In July a sobered Cornelia James returned to Minnesota. She accepted a teaching position at the St. Paul Mechanic Arts High School, teaching mostly Latin—a subject she had almost flunked in the admission exams.

We have little information about her two years as a teacher, for most of the letters she wrote to Walter Cannon and relatives in Massachusetts are lost. Still, a note to Walter, written only days after she had taken up teaching, tells all. "The first day I was wildly enthusiastic; the 2nd day a little less so; the 3rd day I decided to go on a ranch as a cowboy—anything but teaching!" she exclaimed.[63] "To watch the mind grasp a thought, and to see the children grow in power and in interests is really a privilege," she wrote several months later, perhaps to bolster her own morale. Still, commenting on the need to discipline boys, she also admitted that this role was simply against her nature; she had to punish them "much as I should love to laugh *with* them."[64] The few surviving letters to Aunt Jaynes and Cannon show that she strove hard to work up enthusiasm for her professional life. More important still, the persona she had invented did not admit failure. Yet there remains little doubt that she could not help regarding this career as a personal defeat.

Her disorientation was aggravated by the unsettling realization that there was no simple coming home. "How shall I ever be able to tear up my

Massachusetts roots and plant myself again in Minnesota?" she had asked her mother on 25 May 1899, answering with an optimistic "Probably it will be easier than I can imagine." Well, she was wrong. She had become too independent to fall back in line. Her youngest siblings barely remembered her; many of her Minnesota friends now had families; she missed her Radcliffe acquaintances, her active social life, the theaters and music halls of Boston, the beauty of the New England coastline. She felt somehow suspended in mid-air.

Her need to hold on to the college world was expressed in her attempt to provide a lasting basis for her Radcliffe-Harvard connection: she applied for membership in the Harvard University Club of Minnesota. Her move scandalized the male alumni, but an undaunted Cornelia James appealed to President Eliot for support. His cold reply deprived her of all illusions as to women's rights at Harvard. "Radcliffe students or graduates are not Harvard students or graduates,"[65] he telegraphed, thus settling a conflict that had shaken the Minnesota Harvard men. So much for "those happy days of President Eliot." Cornelia was rejected by Harvard, but she remained loyal to her alma mater. She became a devoted supporter of Radcliffe College, and as her distance from her college experience increased, her reminiscences became more idealized—inventions of what should have been rather than descriptions of what was. But even in that they illustrate the aspirations as well as the conflicts faced by those white middle-class women of her generation who decided to defy established role ascription. They aspired to higher education, but they also remained more entwined in conventional notions of womanhood than they cared or dared to admit. Cornelia's rhetoric extolled the new, the untried, the unconventional; when it came to choosing, to claiming her rightful place, however, she clung to the familiar.

CHAPTER 3

"Walter Cannon Is My Comfort"

MARRIAGE AND FAMILY

I N AUGUST 1897 CORNELIA JAMES RECEIVED AN INVITATION
to the wedding reception of a Radcliffe classmate. This was not the first
fellow student she lost to marriage, and Cornelia was disgusted. "That is
what they do—give up education for men—base men," she sighed, won-
dering "if I shall ever find the man for whom I would be willing to give up
my dear old Radcliffe."[1]

Her outburst of feminist righteousness was somewhat dubious, for it
was expressive less of deep-seated convictions than of personal frustration. The past week had been marred by a clash with one of her admirers,
a Mr. Wakefield. He was a prominent member of Clifford Jaynes's Unitarian congregation and a cherished guest at the Jayneses' Sunday dinners,
a wealthy bachelor, thoroughly conservative, sincere. Small wonder the
family thought him an ideal suitor for their poor, unruly relative. No doubt
Cornelia was duly impressed; still, this man was no match for her. Despite
his education, social standing, wealth, reliability, she just could not take
Wakefield seriously. The more earnest his intentions, the more the imp in
her acted up, rebelling against this prematurely old "proper Bostonian."
Their encounters usually culminated in frustration and dismay on his side,
a wild medley of laughter and embarrassment on hers.

A night at the theater, described in a letter of 1 May 1897 to Helen, is
indicative of this ill-fated relationship. Cornelia had not been enthusiastic
about it in the first place, and she expressed her suppressed anger by as-
saulting him with iconoclastic remarks on religious matters, well aware
that he was "very easily hurt in this respect." Then fate struck in the form

of a broken garter. Cornelia's dramatization of the mishap is so typical of her position in this relationship that it deserves being quoted in full. With her garter and stocking "spreading in white masses" around her feet, the young woman, conscious of how embarrassed her companion was by any reference to the human body,

> said coolly, "I beg your pardon but my stocking is coming off," quite as if it were a usual occurrence. . . . Meanwhile the garter's snapping had unbuttoned my *drawers* and they were slipping down around my feet also! I could not hitch the whole thing up in one grand sweep on the public street so I said, "Can't we go back to the ladies' dressing room at the theater?" . . . [W]e started back, I clutching my drawers with one hand and my stocking with the other and talking in a light, conversational tone. . . . Mr. Wakefield you know is perfectly exquisite about his clothes, and I don't suppose his garters ever break. . . . I had to encourage and cheer him up or I fear he would have fainted on the spot and could only answer me in gasping monosyllables. . . . I got home and laughed for fully an hour by myself.

It was an episode in which Cornelia's gifts showed to the fullest: her sense of humor and self-ridicule, her ability to improvise. In the midst of a most embarrassing situation she was sparkling. It was also an episode that revealed the absence in Wakefield of all those qualities that, for Cornelia, spelled life: laughter, flexibility, presence of mind. The scene is encoded as an oppositional pattern that was stifling instead of challenging. Where she laughed, he gasped; where she performed, he almost fainted; her voice clashed with his silence. A situation that empowered her threw him into a state of paralysis.

Yet no matter how ruthlessly she teased him, he always came back, and she tolerated him, for not only was she pleased at so much ardor, but also she pitied this man for his inability to embrace life, and for his desperate struggle to grasp a glimpse of it through her. The relationship collapsed when Wakefield, not satisfied with nourishing his stifled nature by observing her vitality, tried to establish property rights by reducing her to that state of paralysis in which he made himself at home. Attracted as he was to this vivacious woman, he felt he must tame her before he could claim her as his wife, never realizing that in doing so he would obliterate everything that attracted him. On a boat ride on the Charles River he upbraided her for her uncouth behavior, "telling me," she wrote her mother, "that on my pure lips *slang* was not becoming and asking me as a favor to *him* to drop it. . . . [B]ut then he went from tender to tender feeling evidently that he was chosen of all the world to guide this stray lamb aright and lead her lovingly back to the straight and narrow path. The stray lamb bawled a good deal more than he really liked." With relief she stated that she "came through safely with a genial impression that I was a little duck that had dreadful faults which must be corrected before he could tender me the honor of his genteel hand."[2]

Anger, pride, and ridicule intersect in her evocation of this dressing down, but in a letter to Helen two days later she also admitted to almost total emotional exhaustion. It took her a full week to reclaim enough composure to relate the end of the tale: Wakefield had staged the boat ride to define his position in relation to her. Glorying in the pose of the enlightened gentleman, and "evidently a little abashed at the sweetness and humility with which I received it," she wrote, "in the grandiloquent manner as if he were handing me plentiful of diamonds," Wakefield invited Cornelia to deal honestly with him. He had forgotten that she never hesitated to call a spade a spade. On 15 August she wrote to her mother: "Mildly and hesitatingly as though feeling my way through a difficult labyrinth, with my irreverent orby eyes fixed on his face, I answered, 'Oh! but I haven't the consummate conceit to do it!'" Wakefield was stunned, yet continued to court, and when Cornelia returned to St. Paul, he planned a trip to Minnesota. He stood no chance; after that night on the Charles he was beneath contempt.

Throughout her Radcliffe years names of men appeared in Cornelia's letters—Harvard students, men she met in church, during lectures, or at parties, brothers of classmates, and relatives like Cousin Edwin, who called her his "purring dynamo."[3] None resurfaced more than two or three times. Her irreverent nature made it impossible to see more than silly boys in the men who approached her; after all, most were about her age, and she felt vastly superior to them—more mature, sophisticated, experienced. "Boys are great stupid things anyway!" she summed up her attitude to her sister and laughingly adopted the pose of femme fatale.[4] Perhaps she was more mature than these boys; perhaps she had enough of the feminist in her to reject the role of the swooning lover. But what she defined as sophistication was also the survival instinct of a woman as yet deeply insecure about her sexuality.

The Jameses were liberals in their attitude toward politics, toward social issues, toward race and gender relations; they were Victorians in their attitude toward sexuality. The word "sex" was never used in the presence of the girls; Frances's babies arrived as a sweet surprise, and Frances and her mother were pleased when the girls organized a purity club, promising eternal hostility to male contamination. The feminine qualities propagated by the Cult of True Womanhood—piety, submissiveness, and domesticity—were subjected to critical scrutiny and subtly challenged in the James circle, but a fourth asset was, if not explicitly discussed, implicitly encouraged: purity, "the sentimental ideal of the inspiring, chaste maiden."[5] Although contemporary gendered discourse defined woman almost exclusively by her sexuality, she was spiritualized to such a degree that she became almost "disembodied,"[6] and this attitude impeded frank discussions, even between mother and daughter, of issues touching upon female physiology.[7] By the time she entered college, Cornelia had so internalized this silence that she repulsed even the most cautious attempts to talk about intimate matters. Thus on 9 September 1897 she complained bitterly to her mother that her aunt Lucy "always talks with me about such horrid things. . . . You never told me such things. . . . I do not think it is necessary and it makes me feel sick for days after." She longed for romance; she desired to experience passions she knew about from novels; but she dreaded those aspects of a relationship that remained shrouded in silence. Her solution was escape—rejection, withdrawal, feminist rhetoric, and, as a shield for herself against an outside world not allowed to see her confused, ridicule. All of this surfaced in the few relationships approaching anything we could call romantic.

In the summer of 1896 Cornelia was stunned when her artist sister Margaret announced her engagement to the railroad engineer Aaron Burt. Cornelia was fascinated with this attractive man, who combined the calm assurance of good breeding and education with the gift of laughter and moved with such ease in the James household—a paragon of white American masculinity. Concerned, Frances James watched Cornelia as she drew Aaron into animated conversations and coaxed him into taking walks. She put an end to this by reminding her in the most unequivocal terms that Aaron was Margaret's property. Cornelia withdrew and protected herself by adopting the pose of the unfeeling bluestocking.[8]

A similar ritual of attraction and withdrawal was repeated in the summer of 1898. The St. Paul businessman Arthur Lanthrop, a friend of Auntie's, paid a visit when business brought him to New England. Cornelia was the life of the party, and Lanthrop enjoyed her company so much that he took her out to dinner and asked her to be his Boston guide. Upon his return to St. Paul he sent flowers and candy, and he expressed his hope that she would return to Minnesota after graduation. Cornelia was vexed by his claims on shaping her future, but she was also charmed. In letters to her sisters she displayed undisguised outrage whenever competition surfaced. "I will not have my property trespassed on," she exclaimed on 5 October 1898.

The following spring Lanthrop was back, paying Cornelia a surprise visit when she least needed it: after a bicycle tour, when she "was as unlovely as red, *red* sunburn and peeling skin could make me." He treated her like a beauty queen, and, she told Frances, after he spent "most of the evening alone with me, (O dies, O mores)," they agreed to take a boat ride to Gloucester—"a most romantic trip!" Those who knew her claimed she was in love. "Perhaps this is the case."[9] But only four days later she announced her decision not to pursue this relationship. "I was beginning to be seized with those awful pangs of loathing, which seem to be my demon," she wrote, admitting to a pattern: she was overcome by nausea whenever a partner displayed signs of intimacy. "I do not think he has a doubt that I am to be had for the asking."[10] Even though he sent her mayflowers, she, calling herself "a stone,"[11] decided not to respond. Arthur Lanthrop vanished from her letters.

Deep inside, Cornelia James may have realized that she was not ready for an intimate relationship as long as she had not even made up her mind who she wanted to be. The Lanthrop episode took place as her Radcliffe days were coming to an end, when she knew neither what she would do nor—and this was the more disturbing aspect—what she *wanted* to do. It was during this thoroughly unsettling interval, as relatives balked at her career plans and rejection letters came in, that she began to consider marriage—not as a goal in life but as a viable escape from what she most feared: "spinsterhood teaching."[12] In one of the last letters before her return to St. Paul she went through her list of eligible men, as if to reassure herself: Wakefield; Harry Brown, a hotel manager and distant relative from Maine; her classmate Elinor's brother.[13] Two years later, on 25 June 1901, Cornelia James would become the wife of the physiologist Walter B. Cannon, the one man who had already been around during her high school days in St. Paul and West Newton, who had been a calm presence throughout her Radcliffe years, but who was conspicuously absent from the list of potential husbands she drew up on the eve of graduation.

During Cornelia's second visit to Boston and through her college years, this young man surfaces as the most reliable male protagonist in her letters. He was a frequent guest at the Jayneses' dinner table; he and Cornelia were part of the Crotherses' circle; he took her to lectures and concerts; they went boating on the Charles; he helped her with her studies; and she supported him during his depressive spells. Cornelia, a newcomer to New England and academia, was happy to have somebody who could advise her on the intricacies of college life, and she appreciated the presence of a man who treated her with respect, who made no demands beyond friendship. For a time her family and friends considered him "her young man," and at least in the initial days at Radcliffe she did not protest.[14]

Walter B. Cannon had always seemed to be the one.[15] He was born in Prairie du Chien, Wisconsin, on 19 October 1871, the first child and only son of the railway employee Colbert Hanchett Cannon and his wife, Sarah Wilma. In 1879 the family moved to Dayton's Bluff in St. Paul. Sarah Wilma died in childbirth in 1881, when Walter was only ten; one year later Colbert remarried. The Cannons were a respected family, but all the children—Walter, Bernice May, Ida Maude, and Jane Laura—as well as their new mother, Caroline Mower Cannon, suffered from Colbert's depressive spells. Encouraging their intellectual ambitions, he was unable to respond to their emotional needs, and his own erratic lifestyle as well as his violent temper embarrassed them. The atmosphere in the Cannon home was the very opposite of everything the James household represented. Socially the Cannons stood beneath the Jameses, but class was an issue of minor importance to Cornelia's parents; they were less interested in where their son-in-law came from than in what he promised. And they foresaw a bright future. Encouraged by his teacher May Newson, he had made it to Harvard; working his way through college, he graduated in 1896. By the time the Jameses began to consider him Cornelia's "young man," he had received his M.D. degree. His research on the action of the stomach was published in the *American Journal of Physiology* in 1898, and he held an instructorship in physiology at Harvard Medical School. They subscribed to the characterization May Newson had given, writing to Cornelia: "I knew that you would recognize the essential beauty of his character[,] . . . his sweet homelike way, his unconscious all most [sic] childlike acceptance of people's interest."[16]

Cornelia's attitude toward Walter was ambivalent. She toyed with the idea of his being her "young man" during her first months at Radcliffe, but as her self-confidence improved with her familiarity with college life, insinuations about the potential for romance were replaced by a rhetoric of friendship. He is "a comfort because there is no silliness about him,"[17] she wrote to her sister Helen as early as December 1895, and only a month later she informed Margaret, "Walter Cannon is my comfort in this frivolous world, because we have such a good platonic friendship with no foolishness in it." What May Newson praised as his "sweet homelike way" at times bordered on homeliness, even simplemindedness from the imperiously vivacious Cornelia's point of view; boredom and an undercurrent of condescension crept into her letters as she reported that other women called him "a dear."[18] Walter "reminds me of that poem in the Bat Ballad of which the refrain is, 'It was his duty and he did,'" she wrote in a letter to her mother on 9 January 1898 after he had gone to dinner with a notoriously dull churchwoman "because it was *his* duty." Her conclusion was devastating in its mixture of ridicule and rejection: "As Mark Twain says, 'Be good and you will be happy but you won't have a good time.'" Determined to have a good time, Cornelia realized that Walter would not contribute to that aim.

"I feel about as big as the head of a pin beside him," she admitted in an undated letter of 1895 to her mother; the metaphor she used testifies to the discomfort she experienced in the presence of a junior scientist whose research was already attracting the attention of the medical community, but it also foreshadows the competitive longing for comparative fame that would drive her throughout their life together. Her rebelliousness was aggravated by the fact that he was such a nice man, for how could she defend herself against someone who seemed to be virtue personified? She could not ridicule him as she ridiculed the other "boys"; distancing was the only available protective shield, and by 1898 she even ceased to portray him as a friend. When his article on the use of x-ray technology in the documentation of gastric activity was about to appear in the *American Journal of Physiology,* she saw him moving in a different world. "We shall probably be proud some day that we used to know him years ago,"[19] she wrote, banishing him from her future by removing him to a pedestal.

One way of reminding both Walter and herself that claims to deeper emotional involvement were nonexistent were her attempts to share him with other women. When he bought concert tickets, she sent a friend; they attended a reception, but, she told her mother, "fortunately Miss Bedford was there and I . . . gave her Walter Cannon and devoted myself to Middleton Brown and eating."[20] Attractive cousins were paraded before him and classmates encouraged to invite him to dances—to no avail. Walter had eyes only for Cornelia. In December 1897 she expressed hope that his devotion to Minnesota would make him fall in love with Grace, a relative of May Newson's. "We are hoping against hope that Walter and Grace will find their paths going the same way. Wouldn't it be nice?"[21] she wrote. Walter performed with his habitual politeness—and then returned to Cornelia. It was unnerving!

The relationship was further complicated by Walter's prudery. As an intellectual he had freed himself from his Calvinist upbringing;[22] yet as a man he never overcame the anxiety about sexual matters his father had implanted. Cannon's son-in-law John Fairbank characterized him as torn by guilt feelings.[23] On the one hand, Cornelia James, too, was incapable of dealing creatively with her sexuality, grateful to befriend a man whose reticence guaranteed that there would be no embarrassing advances; on the other hand, his was a degree of inhibition that amazed even her, as revealed in a letter of 30 June 1897 to Margaret. At the Jayneses', Cannon reported on hypnotic experiments he was conducting at the medical school. Helen Jaynes "was tremendously impressed and wanted to be worked upon," according to Cornelia, who captured the scene, "but Walter refused and said he could not do it to any one for whom he cared because he had to touch the forehead and soothe her to the state!! He is fearfully sensitive about such things." It became impossible for her to associate Cannon with love, with marriage, with intimacy; she came close to representing him as sexless.

Throughout their relationship Walter had been Cornelia's mentor whenever she had to write a term paper, sharing her exultation at excellent grades. She in turn spent hours listening to his research plans. Most important, however, was her willingness to be his mother confessor. Cannon was torn by self-doubts. As long as his research went well, he was all enthusiasm and energy, driving himself to the point of exhaustion, but periods of stagnation inevitably led to a sense of failure, to depressions that bordered on self-destructiveness. He became paralyzed with anxiety, caught in an emotional turmoil that was aggravated by exhaustion from his workaholic bouts. An outsider at Harvard, he had few friends to whom he could turn. In Cornelia, however, he discovered a strong shoulder, and Cornelia accepted the role.

His trust flattered her, and his dependence appealed to her maternal feelings; she felt useful and wise, sophisticated and mature. "Walter Cannon came over last night plunt [plumb?] discouraged," she described one of these encounters in April 1897. "The boy has been overworking himself steadily in spite of my warnings and sage advice."[24] Perhaps these bouts of weakness gave her such satisfaction because they allowed her to express some of her deeper feelings for "the boy," which her fear of male sexuality made her suppress for the successful man.

It is revealing that her most autobiographical novel, *Heirs,* which Cornelia James Cannon wrote in her early fifties, involves a protagonist who can respond to her lover's sexual advances only when he displays extreme vulnerability, that is, when he appeals to her nurturing, maternal qualities. Nevertheless, just as Walter's sobriety ultimately bored, his learnedness cowed, and his sexual inhibitions frightened Cornelia, she could not repress a sense of anger as he continued to use her as his emotional dumping ground. "Walter has just been here in a state of mental unrest but our inane conversation has soothed his savage beast," she reported, but she was not flattered. "I seem to serve as a social relaxation to people and I do not like it."[25] Yet this was one of the most important roles Cornelia was to play in this relationship, and her feelings about it remained ambivalent to the very end. His reliance on her strength empowered her, yet she also felt used. Still, even when he most annoyed her, her respect for him remained intact, and there is not a single episode in her letters treating him with the fierce sarcasm to which other men were exposed.

Walter's saving grace was his sense of humor and his modesty. Not only was this sober man a hilariously funny parodist who would gladly entertain his friends with his impersonations of the Statue of Liberty, a skunk, a teakettle—whatever the occasion called for—but also he possessed the gift of humility. No matter how intimate their relationship, at no time would he take her for granted. He respected her powerful need for space, her individuality, her pride. He loved her for what she was, wanted her for herself—her vitality, her sarcasm, her exuberance. Walter felt deeply about Cornelia, claiming that he had fallen in love with her in high school; she kept him in a state of emotional turmoil, forever uncertain about her feelings but absolutely sure about his.

By the time she returned to St. Paul, he considered her his bride, as letters to Louise Crothers and May Newson document,[26] and during his summer visit Cornelia relented, intimating that she might love him. What followed were months of emotional roller coaster rides: in early 1900 she sent him a rejection, written "on a piece of brown paper that had wrapped up the fish."[27] Cannon was numb with pain, destroying her letters and photos in a helpless rage. Cornelia left neither diary entries nor letters from these months; this crucial period of her life remains undocumented. But in April she sent another letter to Cannon in which she apologized. He wrote his rejection in hot anger, only to beg for her forgiveness the next day in a wildly incoherent note: "Cornelia, forgive me, forgive me. I am so miserable. I have never been so miserable before in my life. . . . Can I ever know you again, Cornelia; can I find in you again all I have lost?"[28] With this exchange of letters the die was cast: Cornelia James and Walter B. Cannon embarked on a life together, in a relationship that was based, at least on Cornelia's side, less on romantic love than on respect, less on physical attraction than on deep feelings of belonging, less on proprietorship than on thorough respect for the other's individuality and need for space, in short, a companionship that would sustain both for forty-five years.

The correspondence the lovers exchanged is paradigmatic of the relationship that ensued—Walter adopting the role of the humble supplicant for his maiden's generosity, Cornelia answering with formulaic submission yet also struggling to defend her individuality. There is little that can be defined as intimate; their love talk mirrored the language of sentimental fiction and poetry. Studiously avoiding references to sexuality, they subscribed to prevailing notions of gender and marriage which George Austin, in *Perils of American Women, or, a Doctor's Talk with Maiden, Wife, and Mother* (1883), had prescribed as essential for marital bliss: "The woman, more of a stranger to the practical life, less serious, less strong, becomes the pupil of the husband, who, by his tender relations, initiates her, little by little, into the intellectual and moral world in which he dwells. The husband learns as much as he teaches: he discovers, in the depth of the soul of her whom he loves, treasures of affection, of goodness, of delicacy, before unknown to him."[29] Yet no matter how hard they strove for mutual consent, the correspondence documents creative dissonance. Walter's letters were affected rhapsodies, and his insecurity at his new role found expression in his clinging to the formulaic. He dreaded the response—jokes, perhaps even ridicule—of his acquaintances. He seemed confused at any sign in Cornelia's letters that she might be thriving away from him.

His reports on his daily life focused exclusively on the meaning these activities acquired for their prospective life together. He was only her creature, "all you would have me be."[30] Cornelia cautioned him against placing her on a pedestal. Her letters are a curious medley of submission to conventional gendered role ascription, on the one hand, and struggles to maintain a space for herself, on the other. Thus she responded to his self-deprecating remarks by promising that she would bend her nature to adapt to his needs. "I really believe I should *love* to be ruled by you—perhaps because I know that you would do it in such a heavenly way," she claimed on 31 May 1900. Only two days later, after having been to the Italian theater "under the shadow of your disapproval," she almost begged him to tell her what he wanted. "Do you want me not to be reckless and independent, and instead to use common sense and the more womanly qualities?" she pleaded on 2 June 1900. "There is nothing for me to do but to sit and work to make myself over."

Fortunately she never practiced what she promised—utter negation and transformation of self. She was never in danger of becoming a relative creature, for parallel to her letters' discourse of submission ran one of self-affirmation that undermined her code of acceptance. Cornelia depicted herself as a woman with a life equally directed toward her lover and independent of him. No matter how many vows of submission she made, Cornelia kept her distance. The feelings she expressed bespoke a love based on respect, gratitude, friendship. Many years later she would advise her daughters that it was essential for a successful marriage that the man love unconditionally, that he be more in love with his wife than she with him,[31] and perhaps this best characterizes the way she saw herself in her marriage. It also locates the relationship firmly in the eugenic context of the day and the feminist twist Cornelia gave it.

Cornelia and Walter had been raised in a community that urged women and men to choose "mates according to the highest physical standards . . . and to fulfill their 'duties to society' by reproducing those same standards."[32] American physicians of the period such as George Cook and Isaac Ray charged Anglo-American couples to do their "legitimate work" in mental hygiene and physical morality in order to counteract the waves of "moral turpitude and mental disease"[33] that threatened the nation's racial welfare, evoking a racial agenda that led directly to "programs for the eugenic breeding and sterilization of humans."[34] The hierarchy Cornelia established in her advice to her daughters between the man's passion and the woman's rational love suggests, however, that the eugenic mission to which she subscribed was enhanced by an additional source that confirmed her status as woman within this paradigm of selection: the purity movement, generated by British and American women in the second half of the nineteenth century in response to the sexual double standard and the widespread fear among women of venereal disease as a result of male promiscuity. Under the impact of the eugenic turn, that is, the propagation of rational reproduction, this purity movement acquired a feminist tinge in that it charged the woman, said to be less susceptible than the man to sexual passion, to claim control in the racial selection process. Angelique

Richardson contends: "Given the unhealthy tendency of men to promiscuity and vice, and the natural instinct of women to virtue, social purists and eugenic feminists increasingly emphasized the importance of female choice in the reproductive partner, replacing male passion with rational female selection. Women could become managers of male passion, and agents of regeneration, and so introduce the idea of direction and progress into human development."[35]

Describing the wedding ceremony in the Jameses' front parlor in a letter of 27 June 1901 to her sister Helen, Frances James wrote about a lovely bride—"beauty, grace and divinity were contained in her little figure"—and a devoted groom with "the serious holy look." We have no representation from Cornelia's pen. Walter recorded the day in his diary as follows: "Married at 8.00 PM. Electric Car to Stillwater. Night at Sawyer's House. Hottest night in June—collars and shirts were wet rags."[36] The couple's honeymoon attests to the fact that the foundation of this relationship was indeed companionship. It would have been an almost ideal outing for Boy Scouts. Instead of escaping to some luxurious resort catering to newlyweds, they embarked on a canoe trip down the St. Croix River to the Mississippi, during which they got lost in the woods, their tent was torn in a storm, their canoe floated off, and they were almost killed by a steamboat.[37] They cooked over open fires and slept in a tent. They looked so rugged that they were taken for farm workers, and fishermen called Cornelia a squaw. Then they departed for Glacier National Park in Montana, on a railroad pass supplied by Colbert Cannon, immortalizing their union by climbing Goat Mountain and renaming it Cannon Mountain. Marian Cannon Schlesinger never doubted that her mother was the driving force behind these feats of endurance, "my father galvanized into action by the manic energy of his irrepressible bride."[38] She was right.[39] Whether it was on the canoe trip or on their race up the mountain, husband and wife were testing each other's strength, outrunning, outclimbing, outpaddling each other, defining their bodies as athletic rather than sensual. Their sportsmen's attire disguised Cornelia's female form, neutering their bodies. There was an almost extreme physical quality to their exertions, physicality encoded as the unisex equality of sportsmanship, minimizing sexuality. It was a honeymoon of roughing it rather than loving it.

But then this obsessive display of health, physical endurance, and athletic vigor in woman and man alike must also be read as the Cannons' very personal reply to the cries of alarm that emanated from leading turn-of-the-century progressive reformers, politicians, and especially the medical profession, who diagnosed physical exhaustion among the country's white middle and upper classes, a loss of reproductive vitality in men of that race and class, and a weakening of reproductive capacity in the women. Driven by a panicky fear of what would come to be identified as racial decline and even race suicide, proponents of the progressive reform movement embraced eugenics,[40] according to Mark H. Haller not only "a scientific reform in the age of reform"[41] but also a movement (mis)using natural science to sanction their racist, antimajoritarian claim for continued white hegemony. Theirs was, Peggy Pascoe argues, "a modern racism that was biological in a particularly virulent sense."[42]

This emerging eugenic movement especially targeted white intellectuals—the nation's "natural" leaders according to its elitist social theories[43] and thus endowed with special responsibilities for the nation's racial future—with dire warning of emasculation and infertility. Walter B. Cannon, the aspiring scientist, and Cornelia James Cannon, the woman with a college degree, were among those directly addressed by the eugenic prophets of doom on their responsibility to "the future race," and it was a sense of mission to which they subscribed unconditionally and responded enthusiastically. After all, both had studied with Charles Davenport, who was emerging as the nation's most outspoken and authoritative eugenicist; in fact in his autobiography of 1945 Cannon would explicitly acknowledge Davenport as one of his most influential teachers and intellectual guides.[44] Their honeymoon proved to them, and to those contemporaries fearful of intellectual achievement as a potential detriment to the American racial elite, that neither emasculation nor loss of vitality could be associated with this young couple. Their embrace of American nature as a source of reinvigoration rather than a honeymoon in a decadent resort setting had a programmatic quality.

In September the Cannons returned to Cambridge—Walter to the Harvard Medical School, Cornelia to her new role as housewife. Cornelia's ingenuity turned their apartment at 76 Concord Avenue and later their rented house at 14 Avon Place into a home to which Walter returned with pleasure and was proud to invite friends and colleagues; Cornelia blossomed in the presence of his happiness. Throughout his Harvard years Cannon had felt an outsider; now he and Cornelia made friends among Cantabrigians and newcomers, Harvard colleagues and neighbors alike. Dr. Cannon's biographers list among their friends "George and Florence Pierce, Ralph Barton and Rachel Perry, Gilbert Lewis, Harry and Ella Morse, Ernest and Mabel Southard, Robert and Ada Yerkes, Edwin Holt, as well as Frank and Mabel Hammond, Charles and Isabel Whiting, and Allen and Louise Jackson."[45] All loved to come to the Cannons'—for discussions of the Wicht Club, for stunt parties, for animated conversation. These friendships lasted decades, not only because the Cannons were charming hosts, but also because their friends had learned to have an early dinner at home. Mrs. Cannon's table was known for its meagerness. "George and Florence Pierce dined with us—clambake," a slightly exasperated Walter recorded in his diary on 22 March 1906. "Clambake largely crockery."

The young wife spent exciting weeks making a home, apparently supremely happy within her woman's sphere. A few months into the marriage, however, she was out, as she would continue to be for decades to come, becoming involved in communal reform. If Cambridge was to be her home, it must know that she had arrived. The Cambridge of her Radcliffe years had been the Cambridge around Harvard Yard—large, comfortable houses with well-kept front lawns, streets shaded by chestnut trees, a scene of white middle-class self-containment. This was also the Cambridge where the young Cannons resided and would always reside; this is where they belonged. That other Cambridge, East Cambridge, where immigrants from Ireland and Italy crowded ghettolike in tenements and developers' cheap three-decker homes, had been a world apart for the Radcliffe student, a dark, forbidden netherworld beyond her experience and horizons, vaguely and shadily evoked only in Walter's reports about one of his rare medical excursions.

In her Cambridge memoirs Cornelia's daughter Marian recalled that this other Cambridge remained "as remote as Timbuctoo" even during her childhood days.[46] But by becoming Mrs. Walter B. Cannon, Cornelia had also become a member of a white social and cultural elite which, especially in the age of reform, established a connection between social and racial entitlement, privilege, and responsibility. The well-educated wife of Dr. Cannon could not enter into a professional career, but she could embrace the tenets of social feminism and, as a "public woman,"[47] invest her learning and expertise in the nation's improvement, which began at the communal level. Like many reformist white middle-class women, she never doubted that her "fuller participation in public life would reorient public affairs in a broad, humanitarian direction."[48] Babies in working-class areas, and especially in the immigrant ghetto communities, were dying of diarrheal diseases. As soon as Cornelia heard of the problem from Charles and Elizabeth Whiting, she set to work, enticing a reluctant Walter to join her. Her commitment to the Milk Committee, with Walter serving as chairman, was only a first step; it was also a step of programmatic character. Performing as a couple on this committee, they personified to perfection the progressive and pragmatic ideals of competent citizen participation: Walter as scientific expertise and Cornelia as civic commitment, working hand in hand to improve America through expert social intervention; the nation's elite solving social problems to maintain the existing distribution of power and social stratification.

Cornelia Cannon also became involved in voluntary social work as a "friendly visitor," the twentieth-century version of the Victorian "lady bountiful."[49] During the final decades of the nineteenth century the Boston area was exposed to dramatic demographic changes as tens of thousands of immigrants from Ireland and southern and eastern Europe settled in a community unprepared for these newcomers. By 1900, 66 percent of the population in Massachusetts were immigrants or first-generation children of immigrants, and the non–English speaking outnumbered the English-speaking segment.[50] Old Boston watched in horror as entire sections of its proud city were transformed into slums: the North End, the South and West Ends, East Cambridge, Cambridgeport.[51] As was the case everywhere else in the country, nativist campaigns erupted, with social Darwinist legitimization discourses inevitably in tow.

Reform-oriented individuals like the Cannons were constantly moving back and forth between compassion, a sincere urge to abolish extreme forms of misery, the enlightened citizen's awareness of the social dangers lurking in ghettoes without hope, the scientist's fear of epidemics, the eugenicist's dread of racial contamination, and the social Darwinist's anxiety at strengthening the "undesirable" by a racially unjustifiable indulgence in welfare. The small group of women primarily from the white middle class, among them Cornelia Cannon, who entered the city's pockets of misery were all performing these kinds of ideological balancing acts, torn by conflicting motives. Not only did they feel that it was their duty as Christian women to extend a helping hand to these "forlorn creatures," but also they were invigorated by the hope that their example would support the racially desirable among these strangers in their efforts to metamorphose into American citizens and thus reaffirm the social and racial status quo. Long before social work was professionalized and institutionalized, these Boston women created a network of "friendly visitors" that laid the foundation for the social programs that would follow. Often naïvely proud of their mission, and assured of their cultural and racial superiority, they saw themselves as missionaries of culture to those lacking refinement; they advised destitute immigrant mothers how to economize so as to live on nothing and lectured them on how to bring up their half-starved children—swarthy, but potential Horatio Alger characters for Cornelia Cannon—as competent American citizens, reproductions of, according to Paul Boyer, "the reformers' own image,"[52] always provided these newcomers were regarded as racially compatible with native-born Americans, consanguine whites.[53]

There was little awareness in these philanthropically minded women that the people they advised might experience their "visits" as visitations, their friendliness as condescension, their interest as intrusion, their activities as meddling—a benevolent blindness that Cannon shared.[54] Firmly imbued with the social problem novels of Charles Dickens, Horatio Alger, and Walter Besant and the writings of Thomas Carlyle, John Ruskin, and Arthur B. Bentley, and trained in evolutionary theories, she identified with the role of the educator and savior of the deserving and racially desirable poor, and as an American patriot she harbored no doubt that for these newcomers Americanization was bliss. Urban poverty provided an appropriate outlet for a woman so "programmed for the righting of wrongs"[55] as Cornelia James Cannon.

As a next step she began campaigning for a public library and a children's museum. With her onetime instructor William James she believed that the "world stands really malleable, waiting to receive its final touches at our hands,"[56] and there was in her "the Social Gospelers' faith that in the hands of experts, policies could be set that served everyone's best interest."[57] The city councilors in Cambridge learned that they had better be wide awake when they saw her among their audience. She asked pertinent questions, demanded answers, and offered solutions; and if the councilors sought escape in political rhetoric, in silence, or in evasion, her belligerent letters to the editor of the *Boston Herald* reminded them that they were being watched. That dynamo from the Midwest used her pen like a scalpel, and literally hundreds of her letters are on record. Like her mother, and like many reform-oriented women of her day and class, she took on the doctrine of separate spheres by extending its definition of home to the entire community as the true and new woman's sphere, thus transcending the narrowly defined domestic realm while still affirming the traditional concept of womanhood.

Cornelia loved her new role as Mrs. Walter B. Cannon—for the difference she could make in her husband's life; for the pleasure it gave her to rule over a domain all her own; for her mobility as a married woman; for the status that came with a Harvard professor's life; for her new realm of activities. And she loved it because she was certain this was a transitional stage. Marriage for her was the promise of motherhood and family. The first months of married life, the exclusiveness of being husband and wife were special because they would soon be over, to be replaced by the love of many. She saw herself as mother-in-waiting for their children-to-come, subscribing unconditionally to the linkage between sexuality, marriage, and reproduction, to her racial obligation. In his advice books for women George Austin described physical love between man and woman as "that secret affinity which draws one to the other, enchains them by the sweet sympathies of the soul and the irresistible attraction of the senses, and confounds them in a voluptuous union, indeed, for the perpetuation of the species."[58] Sexual love was no longer the brutish act of Victorian representation to which women submitted for the glory of motherhood, but it was still linked exclusively to reproduction, the "perpetuation of the species" or rather, in the racialized terminology of eugenics, of the race. Disciples of Davenport, the Cannons affirmed the responsibility that came with their racial identity and their membership in the country's cultural elite. Children born to them as paragons of a racially ideal America would be not simply a blessing to themselves but a gift to the nation's future, an investment in a race under siege.

Cornelia's attitude toward sexuality affirmed Austin's reading of womanhood as well as the eugenic call for women of her race and class "to breed freely,"[59] but to her dismay she found herself unable to perform: her marriage remained barren. She faced defeat, the paralyzing realization that she was not in control. What did she feel? Frustration at not being able to deliver "as a woman ought"? Anger at a body that betrayed her? Guilt at not fulfilling her duty to Walter and "the race"? She never doubted that she was responsible for this infertility, and not only because contemporary medical discourse on sterility focused exclusively on women; Margaret, too, remained childless, and this seemed to confirm Cornelia's conviction of her "culpability."

In October 1906 she submitted to gynecological surgery to solve "her" problem. Eugenic theories of racial deterioration among Anglo-Americans, and especially among the educated classes, were the vogue; eminent scientists such as Harvard's Edward Clarke and R. R. Coleman had "proven" to the world that, as a woman's brain expanded, her uterus shrank; President Roosevelt and Charles B. Davenport joined their voices in warning against the weakening of the master race; and physicians railed against sterility as a result of "overeducating" women. Cornelia was familiar with these prophecies and struggled to defeat them by her personal conduct and life-style, but as her body failed her, she could not help drawing connections to her own fate. We do not know what she felt, for the family letters contain not a single word on this issue, letters sparkling with joie de vivre, hope, humor. From reading them we would never guess that anything was amiss. She communicated her pain in private notes to her mother and Helen, but these "appendixes" were destroyed, and it is only in the letters that Helen and Frances wrote when Cornelia finally became pregnant, in the relief they expressed at her ordeal being over after "your six years of waiting and heart-breaking disappointment,"[60] that we get a sense of how virulent her despair was all those years.

And the impact on the Cannon marriage? Did husband and wife ever discuss this situation? How did they feel about each other, about their sexual relationship? Wherever we look, at Cornelia's letters or Walter's diaries, we encounter silence. We do not have Cornelia's direct report; but we do have a retrospective evaluation of their situation, under the cover of fiction, in her novel *Heirs* of 1930. The novel focuses on the effects of infertility on a white middle-class couple, Marilla and Seth Walton, and even though an exclusively biographical reading would be reductive, it seems legitimate to argue that Cannon made use of her personal experience in delineating the impact of infertility on her protagonists' marriage, that she used fiction to articulate her own pain. The first year of Marilla's and Seth's life together is one of bliss, with both partners achieving fulfillment in their conventional gendered roles. Invigorated by his love, Seth modernizes his mills, and Marilla transforms the Walton residence into a home for her prospective family—rejuvenating it by inviting the sunshine in and brightening up its colors, planting its garden, making it ring with the laughter of friends; the Walton mansion is prepared for a new generation. But before the end of the first year Marilla succumbs to spells of "sudden depression," and Seth observes that "her old energy was mysteriously dying down" (*H*, 163). Cannon delineates the deterioration of her heroine's spirit by replacing the metaphors of light, food, and life, which she used to characterize the interregnum of hope, with metaphors of death and stagnation, isolation and silence. The doors of the house are closed as disappointment deprives the young wife of her energy; husband and wife, who had enjoyed their intimate moments together in the midst of an invigorating social life, now are thrown back upon each other, two in one room, imprisoned in their loneliness and frustration. This process of self-isolation is accompanied by a steadily increasing silence: afraid that careless words will trigger depressive spells, they protect themselves by following a carefully developed choreography of evasion. They begin "to seek silence . . . in dread of what speech might bring" (H, 189). Marilla oscillates between periods of extreme anger at her "useless mould" that was "incapable of even the brief of bringing forth new life" (H, 193); feelings of resentment at Seth for finding release in his work while she had to give up teaching; and "a dry and desolate grief" (H, 194) at having failed her husband and her race.

In 1907 Dr. Cannon was confronted with a report published by colleagues from New York, F. Tilden Brown and Alfred T. Osgood, in the *American Journal of Surgery*,[61] warning of a dramatic increase of cases of total azoospermia or oligonecrospermia, resulting in sterility, among researchers using roentgen rays. His diary entries reveal that the news came as a shock. Was he, after all, to blame for his wife's anguish? In a meeting of his research team it was decided that all participants should have their semen examined, and Cannon reported "that his own personal examination had revealed 'many active sperm.'"[62] Did Cornelia know about these debates among the initiate, and if she did, how did she respond? We find only silence. But we do know that she, unlike her protagonist Marilla, refused to crawl away to nurture her pain. She thought about taking up teaching, but her progressive family was outraged.[63]

Cornelia submitted, again. She could not have the family she craved, and middle-class respectability forbade that she embark on a career. She felt, however, that she could support Dr. Cannon's work and gain gratification from that; after all, the role of helpmate was one that many Harvard wives played. She began to assist in the laboratory, performing tasks familiar to her from her Radcliffe studies, and she served as his secretary. It was a minor catastrophe. Walter Cannon was a perfectionist, while Cornelia believed in getting things over with, and she gloried in her improvisational skills. His ideal was that of carefully polished marble, hers that of the quilt hastily assembled, and she did not mind using rags, either. Cornelia's letters are full of accounts of the joy of cooperation, humorous evocations of her adventures in the sober world of research. Walter's diary entries speak a different language: "Mistakes found in final proof, all made by Cornelia! Very blue—inaccurate—irresponsible—careless wife I have."[64] Small wonder that her excursions into the laboratory became rare. In her novel *Red Rust* of 1928 she would return to the kind of hierarchical and gendered relationship between scholar and helpmate, celebrating a mutuality of satisfaction and support that she and Walter never experienced.

No, Dr. Cannon was not eager for his wife to serve as his assistant, and as to discussing his research, he took recourse to carefully selected information or even silence. Cornelia's pride in him, and especially her tendency to proclaim success publicly when he was still debating pros and cons, embarrassed him. Thus the information he shared became screened, constructed, alienated; he continued to treat her as helpmate — but at arm's length. The most important contribution she later claimed having made was hosting his laboratory frogs in her icebox and protecting them against suffocating in potato salad. She knew that her husband did not want her in his professional life, and this knowledge hurt, but again she took refuge in self-ridicule and laughter in representing potential conflict. The ultimate loneliness of the genius's wife would resurface only much later, as a powerful subtext in *Red Rust*.

What Dr. Cannon did share were his self-doubts and depressive spells, which struck him "whenever he found himself dissatisfied with his research or discouraged about the activities of his department."[65] He was a man at times almost paralyzed by his sense of failure.[66] If the college student Cornelia had harbored mixed feelings about the role of confidante Walter had imposed on her, her response as wife was equally ambivalent. She appreciated his trust, but it drained the strength she needed to keep up her spirits in the face of her own deprivation, and it robbed her of what she loved most: laughter. When she complained in notes to her mother, she was reminded of the "rare treasure" she had married.[67] The full extent of her tribulations surfaced only in a letter she wrote to her son Bradford in 1938, when his marriage was threatened by his depressive spells. "Your depressions are as cruel to a wife as beatings," she warned him.[68] Cornelia protected herself by taking refuge in willful blindness. It did not work. She felt guilty for abandoning Walter to his terrors, and she could never suppress her fear that someday his carefully tamed and silenced depressions might get out of control.

These conflicting emotions exploded on the night of 5 January 1907.[69] In retrospect both of them represented the event as an almost absurd combination of mishaps, but Cornelia's actual response reveals the depth of her insecurity. Returning home late from a faculty meeting, Dr. Cannon could not get into his house because he had mistakenly given his key to a colleague. When nobody opened the door, he tried to rouse his wife by calling her from the Perrys', but unknown to him, she was still at the theater with his sister Ida; he spent the night at his friends'. Upon their return Cornelia and Ida stayed up, increasingly nervous as the clock hands moved beyond midnight. "Walter had had a bad cold and was feeling much depressed so I had worried over him a while," Cornelia later reported. Also, the women "were both rather haunted by the suicide of a Harvard instructor a few days before and the fact that Walter did not want to pay his life insurance until Jan. 10 when it was due." Her husband, she wrote, had made her "promise to collect the extra $150 if anything happened to him."[70] The specter of suicide loomed large. In a panic she called friends and colleagues as well as the police about 2 a.m., and all responded. Cornelia was not the only one with dark apprehensions. They—George W. Pierce, Samuel Crothers, and Harry Morse, Cannon's colleagues George H. Parker and Frank B. Mallory, as well as members of the Wicht Club—organized a search party, even going out on the Charles. All was in vain, and at 4:30 a.m. the party returned to help Cornelia through the night. When Dr. Cannon entered his house at dawn, he encountered a group on the brink of despair. The potential catastrophe ended in tears of relief, in suggestive newspaper reports of a Harvard professor's Saturday night out, and ultimately in good-natured ridicule. "All the Wichts were so indignant he was discovered that they swore!" Cornelia wrote to her mother. George Pierce informed everybody willing to listen "that Cannon's the kind of person that might go crazy suddenly."[71] The incident would be passed off as a comical episode.[72] Yet it bespoke a dread that none of them dared put into words beyond making jokes. It is revealing that the always fun-loving Cornelia participated in none of the revelry. "Ida and I were perfectly exhausted by the strain," Cornelia admitted in the same letter, and Ida took to her bed for a full week.

No matter how busy she kept, Cornelia felt lonely in the two-ness of marriage. After all, she came from a close-knit extended family, and she pined for the circle of Newport women. She began to invite her sisters for extended visits, even offering support through college; and when her parents faced financial crisis, Cornelia persuaded her mother to spend months in Cambridge, moves intended to create an alternative family. But all members of the James clan had lives of their own, which made it impossible for them to perform as substitute family, and Cornelia craved more durable relationships. Her capacity for love finally enabled her to construct the domestic circle she hungered for by extending her notion of "us" from the Jameses to the Cannons. This longing for sisterhood and female bonding, on the one hand, and for someone who needed her, on the other, was solved when she persuaded Walter's sisters Ida and Bernice to come live with them. Cornelia had befriended the Cannon sisters, and especially Bernice, in high school. Cornelia's marriage to Walter transformed them into sisters, and when Ida and Bernice found themselves in a situation calling for help, Cornelia was prepared to give from the bottom of her heart.

The first one to be "adopted" was Ida. After a brief career as a nurse at the Faribault State School for the Feeble-Minded, Ida Cannon had begun to study sociology at the University of Minnesota. There a lecture by Jane Addams, founder of the model Chicago Hull House,[73] awakened her passion for social work, and she became a visiting nurse for the St. Paul Associated Charities; yet daily exposure to a misery she could not heal depressed her to the point of inner paralysis. When personal problems—her father's erratic ways and an unhappy love experience—were added, she came close to the breaking point. Cornelia acted promptly: she suggested that Ida, who had just turned twenty-nine, continue her training at a newly established school for social work in Boston, later Simmons College School of Social Work. Ida arrived in October 1906, moving in with the Cannons. Only weeks later she met Richard Clark Cabot, pioneer of social work in New England, and was appointed head worker in his outpatient department at the Massachusetts General Hospital.[74]

The Ida-Cornelia relationship must have been mutually satisfying, for why else would Bernice, who had made a career as a teacher in St. Paul and Michigan and was anything but a dependent relative, have decided to join the sisterhood in 1911? Again it was Cornelia who initiated the move. Aware that Bernice was ready to launch a new career, and keenly aware of her extraordinary abilities as a businesswoman, Cornelia suggested that she study salesmanship with Lucinda Prince in Boston. Bernice followed her advice, acquiring skills that empowered her to make a most unusual career for a woman of her time.[75] Like Walter, Bernice was what contemporaries condescendingly called "homely," with a round, friendly face framed by hair parted in the middle and coiled on top of her head in a no-nonsense fashion, her most beautiful feature, her lively brown eyes, hidden behind pince-nez. Nobody would have guessed that she was a shrewd professional who held the powerful position of personnel manager at Boston's most famous department store, Filene's.[76]

Cornelia, Bernice, and Ida were connected through love and respect, yet the role Cornelia adopted proves that it was by no means a relationship of equals. In an almost paradigmatic way, the hierarchy they accepted as a definer of their sisterhood illustrates the tensions they, like many women of the day, experienced between internalized gender roles and a determination to move beyond the narrow definitions of womanhood. The Cannon sisters made careers as professionals, while Cornelia seemed caught in a more conventional position, yet Cornelia's leadership was uncontested from the start. Her status as married woman and—later—mother gave her authority within a setting that still defined a professional career for women as a second choice and ridiculed the "spinster." Also the fact that she was in a position to invite them to live in her household denoted a power that was lacking in the sisters' lives. Most important, however, would be Cornelia's role as mother and the contribution she made to the childless sisters, the family, "the race."

We get a glimpse of this intricate relationship from the razor-sharp sarcasm of "Reports of Cannon Psychiatric Clinic," which the Cannon clan composed in December 1932 for their absent daughter Helen. Here Bernice's and Ida's tribulations are portrayed as follows: "Quarrelsome children and slovenly sister-in-law complicate home life. Over-talkative sister-in-law dominates table talk. Patient swooned by aggressive family."[77] A sense of condescension, though coated with sincere respect, at times surfaced in the way Cornelia portrayed herself as a liberator of women unable to free themselves, a substitute mother to "girls" in need of advice, and finally a sister providing the joys of motherhood for the childless, a family for the spinster, a home for the lonely. And just as she embraced Walter's quiet ways and depressive states as empowering, on the one hand, and yet tired of them, on the other, Cornelia was at times exasperated at the reliance of her sisters-in-law on her strength.

In that respect, a letter she wrote to her mother on 26 June 1897 was prophetic. Detailing a Harvard Class Day she had attended with Bernice and Walter, she was appalled at Bernice's inability to enjoy herself spontaneously, to laugh and sing with Cornelia. "I know it is not nice to say so but she impresses me as the most *deadly dull* girl I ever knew," she admitted. How did Cornelia feel years later, when the "indigenous" Cannons—Bernice, Ida, and Walter—withdrew to their rooms on weekends to indulge in depressions or "headaches"? In an undated letter to Cornelia of September 1912 Ida Cannon admitted, "I know what our 'dumps' mean to you."[78] Cornelia harbored second thoughts about her adopted family, but sisterhood, respect, and a rich emotional bond were stronger than the frictions to which they were exposed.

The strongest bond among them, however, would be the chidren—children that were not only Cornelia's and Walter's but, within the paradigms of eugenic feminism and "the future race" they affirmed, also Bernice's and Ida's. As Ida Cannon wrote to "Dearest Cornelia" upon Marian's birth:

"How can we ever tell you what it means to have you bring these adorable babies into the world for us to love. . . . Was there ever so a sister-in-love?"[79]

On 29 March 1907, in the sixth year of their marriage and five months after Cornelia's surgery, Dr. Cannon's diary recorded that his wife might be pregnant. What followed were months of pure joy. For a while Cornelia, suffering from bleeding, had to be careful, but as her condition improved, her happiness found expression in the active lifestyle she embraced. The prospective parents moved into a new home at 17 Ware Street; they visited with the Crotherses at their summer home at Silver Lake in southeastern Massachusetts and spent weeks vacationing at Woods Hole, sailing, swimming, and hiking; they entertained with renewed joy. After years experienced as the absence of motherhood and haunted by the eugenic dread of failing her racial mission, Cornelia, eugenic feminist, had to prove to everybody that she regarded pregnancy as the most invigorating event in a woman's life, and her almost obsessive activism—she opened another milk station in Cambridge; she went on shopping sprees to furnish the house and prepare for the baby; she finished her pamphlet "Social Welfare in Cambridge"—and athletic escapades worried friends and relatives, who warned her against "violent exercise."[80] She always regarded her first pregnancy as the best months of her life.

Bradford was born on 2 December 1907. They had planned on a girl;[81] as Walter wrote to his in-laws: "Of course you can imagine my *dismay* when I learned it was a boy! a boy! Lord! what could *I* do with a boy? My plans for meeting responsibilities had all been directed toward the life of a girl."[82] (They would not repeat the mistake: in the following eight years, four girls were born, Bradford wailing at being surrounded by a thousand sisters.) A life defined by innovation and change had begun—a life with a new center, new joys, new responsibilities, new anxieties, and new frustrations. Cornelia and Walter gloried in their parenthood, observing their baby's every movement, admiring every development as miraculous, proudly displaying their son to duly enthusiastic kin and friends. Pride and happiness reigned. And new cares: Bradford suffered from eczema, which made him irritable.

The next ten years were happy but also hectic, defined by the children, their needs, their demands. In August 1908, only eight months after Bradford's arrival, Cornelia knew she was pregnant again, and Wilma was born on 23 April 1909. It was as if a floodgate had been opened: Linda arrived on 18 March 1911, Marian on 13 September 1912, and Helen in February 1915; in addition, Cornelia suffered one miscarriage in March 1914. Every child was celebrated as a personal blessing and—in communion with eugenic definitions—a contribution to "the race" and thus "the nation." Their sense of racial mission and entitlement shaped the way the Cannons raised their children: as Arthur Schlesinger Jr. affirmed, "despite their theoretical 'live and let live' talk," they "bred in them a sense of superiority to all other children."[83]

Disciples of John Dewey's pragmatic concept of "creative intelligence,"[84] the Cannons were determined to guide their offspring on their road to greatness. They studied the literature on child rearing, and every family gathering, every meal, every game, every outing was part of an educational design. Raising their children was a passion they shared, and an issue over which they fought their most extended battles—he agonizing over every childish lie, a bad grade, the first touch of lipstick; she believing in a genius that needed only time and space to develop, even if it took a few painful detours in doing so. "What is the matter with fathers?" she asked her mother after yet another rupture between Walter and a happily lazy Bradford. "They will not let the plant grow quietly but are always jerking it up to see if the roots are secure."[85]

Design—but in the midst of creative chaos. Cornelia had never been an enthusiastic housewife. Now, with five children to raise, the only way to keep her sanity was benevolent neglect; her survival strategy was a generous redefinition of the motto of the Cambridge intelligentsia: "plain living, and high thinking." As a Radcliffe student, Cornelia had been appalled by the clutter at the Crotherses'; but with children roaming all over the place, clutter made sense. And the children profited: they were encouraged to play and experiment; their friends were always welcome—so many at times that some people took the Cannon place for an orphanage.[86] Cornelia preferred to spend her time reading to her children, taking them to the museum, and playing with them rather than cleaning up after them. She had five children, each of them a complex individual, and doing justice to this individuality was demanding to the utmost. Everything else paled beside this great responsibility and the gratification she received from the progress her son and daughters made on a daily basis.

Child rearing for Cornelia Cannon was more than offering maternal guidance, more than feeding, cleaning, and negotiating between warring siblings or father and son; it extended from her domestic realm to the community. Her gifted children were entitled to the best education America could offer, but not by attending private schools. As a progressive and pragmatic, Cornelia Cannon, like her grandmother, fought for the improvement of public education,[87] regarding the school as "the key institution for the nurturing and the saving of souls for democracy."[88] She insisted, "The United States for her salvation . . . must depend upon the training of the children of the land in democratic ideals," her use of "salvation" establishing a link between education and the evolutionary paradigm of social Darwinism. In the anticipated struggle between nations and races, America would survive only if American children were prepared; "and the one institution . . . which places these [ideals] first and foremost in importance is the public school."[89]

This affirmation of the public school was her response to the dramatic challenges the system faced under the impact of mass immigration during the opening decades of the century. More than 70 percent of the children attending school in the Boston-Cambridge area were foreign born or of immigrant parentage, a majority from non-English-speaking households.[90] Critical voices warned that "an ossified pedagogy and curriculum, overcrowded and unsanitary facilities, poorly trained teachers, political influence, and inadequate financing"[91] had rendered the public school system incapable of fulfilling its most important objective, Americanization—to, as E. P. Cubberley wrote, "assimilate and amalgamate these people as a part of our American race, and to implant in their children, so far as can be done, the Anglo-Saxon conception of righteousness, law and order, popular government, and to awaken in them a reverence for our democratic institutions."[92]

The ideas on education that Cornelia Cannon contributed to these controversies on school reform were based on John Dewey's concepts of communities of inquiry and participatory democracy, as he expressed them in articles such as "Ethical Principles Underlying Education" and "Education as Politics." For Dewey, as for Cannon, the "versions of man as a changing and developing being in the midst of an environment which fosters and at the same time threatens his life was decisive. . . . Organism and environment, development and struggle, precariousness and stability—these are the basic ingredients of the cosmic mixture."[93] With Dewey she wanted schools that "cultivate the habit of suspended judgment, of skepticism, of desire for evidence, of appeal to observation rather than sentiment, discussion rather than bias, inquiry rather than conventional idealizations."[94] Dewey argued that the school's moral responsibility, as a training ground for future generations of American citizens, was to society, and this called for producing competent citizens qualified to participate intelligently in forming, running, and supervising the system. As Marvin Lazerson documents in his analysis of turn-of-the century public education in Massachusetts, the state pioneered, though reluctantly, in encouraging this kind of qualified and committed interaction between the private and the public spheres, between parents, teachers, and politicians.[95] The implementation of school committees with publicly elected councilors, especially in the urban centers, provided white middle-class citizens like the Cannons a voice in their children's education and relocated public education from the periphery to the center of communal and state public policy.

Cornelia Cannon was not merely eager to live up to these obligations of what Dewey called "Education as Politics"; she also felt that her college education gave her both a responsibility and an entitlement to claim leadership "in the effort to widen the scope and improve the quality of public education."[96] Most Harvard parents sent their children to elite institutions, avoiding the deplorably bad Cambridge public schools. Hers was a different mission: she, Mrs. Walter B. Cannon, would see to it that these public schools were good enough to receive her children—the most precious gift she had to offer America—by the time they were ready to enter the system. "Now a school system that is not good enough for my child is not good enough for any child," she charged.[97] In creating perfect public schools for her offspring, she would create new opportunities for all American children.

She extended her woman's role as a teacher, nurturer, and healer beyond the domestic realm, taking the step from self-improvement to the improvement of society, from the preservation of her family to preservation of the community. Issues of public health, education, and city politics were there for her to tackle—issues that enabled her, like many active women of her class and generation, to "integrate this newly expanded definition of woman's capabilities and interests with her role as wife and mother."[98] As soon as school began to loom on the horizon, she therefore became involved—attending city council meetings, campaigning for the school committee, serving as its secretary, and writing hundreds of combative letters to the *Boston Herald*. "The best way to make ourselves intelligent servants of public education is to know our local school as we know a beloved neighbor," she wrote, demanding that school and community become as one. "We must drop in for a visit, become acquainted with the family . . . and help constructively to remove difficulties and make improvements."[99] For years her involvement in the Cambridge public schools became all-absorbing, and Cambridge profited.

Cornelia James Cannon's reformist activities, like those of most reform women of the day, were possible only because her family could afford to hire a maid. Shopping, cleaning, cooking were delegated, as Marian Cannon Schlesinger would remember, to a "long-suffering family of 'colored' girls," one at a time, the labor of each enabling Cannon's free flight. For the children, as for their parents, this maid emerged daily "from some vague remote hinterland," Boston's South End, though she might as well "have come straight from the Congo." Schlesinger evokes the kitchen as the black maid's all-purpose realm, which especially "the adored Hortense" turned into a "heaven of fun and warmth" for the Cannon children, "never complaining as we swept through her kitchen like marauding ants"—a mammy scene that seems lifted undiluted from Aunt Chloe's plantation kitchen. How could Hortense complain, with all those "long-suffering . . . 'colored' girls" out there?[100]

Before Hortense came to stay, the Cannons obviously exhausted a whole regiment of African American domestic workers, so many and in such rapid succession that none ever made it beyond the nameless "maid" of Cornelia's letters. Despite Schlesinger's formulaic reference to "girls," they were mature women, with a name, a personal history, and probably with families of their own; none of that was relevant enough to be recorded. Was Hortense married? How old was she? Were there children to whom she returned at night, exhausted from her domestic labor plus the demands of black surrogate mammy-hood? Her identity was reduced to the Cannon kitchen and its requirements, as was that of most black maids in contemporary positions.[101]

Schlesinger recalls the relationship between her mother and Hortense "as of two equals: both were ladies,"[102] but one would always be "Hortense," the other "Mrs. Cannon." Race and class mattered; the "Self-Other binary"[103] of blackness and whiteness remained firmly intact. Boston and Cambridge boasted a large and historically significant African American community, with historic spokespeople including Phillis Wheatley, David Walker, and Harriet Jacobs before the Civil War, and the civil rights leaders Archibald Grimké, William Monroe Trotter, Pauline Hopkins, and George W. Forbes in Cornelia Cannon's day. It was a community that had built its own churches, academies, and schools, had its own newspapers, organized literary associations, women's clubs, and social reform activities.[104] None of those struggles and achievements entered the racially and socially "self-contained" domestic realm of the Cannons or of Cambridge families of comparable status, only the nameless maid from the black "hinterland" whose presence freed Cornelia.

As the family expanded, the house on Ware Street became too small, and together with Ida and Bernice the Cannons moved to a more spacious home at 2 Divinity Avenue, where they remained for twenty-seven years. They would never own a house in Cambridge, but in January 1911 the Cannons purchased a farm in Franklin, New Hampshire—a dilapidated place which they transformed into their haven. Here they could—and did—rough it, for as Arthur Schlesinger Jr. remembers, "Mrs. Cannon long resisted the introduction of decadent modern conveniences like electricity and plumbing."[105] The children roamed all over the hill; they planted more than a thousand trees in their first year. Dr. Cannon displayed his skills as carpenter and plumber, and Cornelia found time for painting walls and shingling roofs, for reading and writing. The summers at their farm became the most precious time of the year, and, like a magnet, this life in the "wilderness" attracted their Cambridge friends. First they came as guests, staying in "The Chalet," and being put to work as carpenters, woodcutters, or cooks. But soon the Yerkeses, the Pierces, and finally Ida and Bernice all bought property on what became known as New Boston Road, a community of Harvard intellectuals turned part-time farmers and carpenters, lumberjacks and plumbers. Franklin would never be the same after the Cannon invasion: it learned to welcome Professor Pavlov, and nobody was surprised at encountering Robert Yerkes's apes in the forest.[106]

The period in which their children were born was also the most demanding decade in Dr. Cannon's career. In 1906 he became George Higginson Professor of Physiology; he was constantly in demand as a lecturer; appointments to committees and professional associations could not be turned down; and he became enmeshed in the vivisection controversy. No matter how eager he was to share the responsibility of child rearing, it was inevitable that Cornelia carried most of the burden. She did so with enthusiasm and skill, and without giving up her precious self. Devoted as she was to her children, she was grateful for the hours when they were off at school and exasperated when bad weather kept them at home; she cherished her morning hours of reading and writing, and every once in a while she indulged in a bout of sickness, the luxury of solitary days in her bedroom. "I am alone in the house, and it is the time in which my soul renews itself," she wrote to her parents on 28 April 1920. "How people bear it to be constantly surrounded by humans I cannot see. It is an outrage on the essential solitariness of the human soul. . . . [W]e must make friends with ourselves to have companionship on the way."

Also, no matter how busy her family kept her, she refused to close the door on the world outside: friends were welcome; there were parties and discussion groups; she attended lectures and city council meetings, visited with old friends and recruited new ones, worked on committees and enjoyed the Boston theaters. And she never stopped writing, sitting at her desk beneath the staircase in a house where too many people lived to provide her with a room of her own: letters to Minnesota, to the press, occasional poetry, stunts and sketches, plays to be staged and performed by her offspring and their friends. Cornelia James Cannon's children were fortunate, for they had a mother who offered fully out of the fullness of her own life.

CHAPTER 4

"The Woman Who Stays Behind"
WORLD WAR I

F AMILY PICTURES TAKEN ON THE EVE OF WORLD WAR I PORTRAY
Cornelia and Walter B. Cannon as a middle-aged couple, dressed and
groomed in a no-nonsense fashion, surrounded by four healthy children—
the prototypical white American family. And an ideal family they were,
by all standards: a husband who, at the height of professional success,
regarded home as haven, was a loving mate and father; a wife happily exasperated by the blessings of motherhood and determined to be the perfect
helpmate to the soaring scientist; children blooming physically and intellectually in the security of their parents' love and status. Cornelia was sincere
when she wrote to her parents on 25 June 1915, her fourteenth wedding
anniversary: "It was a good gamble I took 14 years ago, and the winnings
are all mine. Walter still seems pleased, too. . . . Isn't marriage a discipline
and an education of the most inflexible kind? However gently and lovingly
it may be done, it knocks off the angles, tempers the selfishness."

They were not wealthy but well-off, with a reliable income, sufficient for
the modest lifestyle they preferred. They had a comfortable home, and they
delighted in their farm. A maid shouldered Cornelia's domestic duties, and
in 1914 the Cannons joined the class of the idle rich when they purchased
a Model T Ford. Nothing in their lives prepared them for the separation,
rupture, and transformation that war was to force upon them and their
country over the next four years. As for many American women, World
War I became a watershed in the life of Cornelia James Cannon: she initiated a restructuring process which fundamentally changed her relation-

· 90 ·

ship with her husband and children. The sense of autonomy she developed empowered her to conquer new public territories as a writer and reformer, and it eventually made her a crucial figure in New England's birth control movement.

Nothing prepared the Cannons for this transformation of the world they knew and cherished. What is more important, even after the war had erupted, there seemed to be no need to be prepared; after all, this madness was taking place in another world, too far away to affect life at 2 Divinity Avenue beyond providing topics for patriotic discussion and exercises. As Doris Kearns Goodwin argues, "most Americans viewed the struggle as just another in Europe's progression of internecine squabbles, far away in distance and even farther away in spirit from the primary concerns of their daily lives. The early inclination of the typical American was to turn his back on what seemed to him a barbaric conflict, a senseless quarrel that would surely come to an end before the first winter's snow."[1] It was a widespread attitude of neutrality if not national self-containment and parochialism that was encouraged by the Wilson administration and President Wilson's promise that the United States would not become a party to the European conflict: "There is such a thing as a nation being too proud to fight."[2] In declaring its neutrality, the administration not only affirmed an American foreign policy toward Europe that dated all the way back to George Washington but also hoped to avoid internal ethnic strife.[3]

The Cannons were deeply moved by the violence in the Old World, deploring war as a regression to barbarity. Still, it was not their war, and they could respond only in abstract ways. The family Christmas of 1914, delineated in a letter from Cornelia to her parents of 28 December, is typical of the attitude they adopted: children waking their parents at 4:30 a.m., the noisy enjoyment of gifts, Christmas carols, and the lightning of the tree—every detail signifying continuity. Only at the very end is the world allowed to enter this happily contained circle when Cornelia mentions lighting candles as a token of sympathy with suffering Europe: "We had candles in the windows . . . so we are feeling very festive and Christmasy—but except for the children's unconsciousness, what a sad Christmas it is!"

Throughout 1914, 1915, and 1916 the war continued to have only a symbolic meaning in the Cannons' lives—a cloud on the horizon, which the adults watched with dread, but as yet too far removed to define their daily routine. Cornelia's primary concern was her family, and her letters tracked the banalities of everyday life: Linda's flu, Bradford's teasing his sisters, the success of Dr. Cannon's *Bodily Changes in Pain, Hunger, Fear and Rage* (1915) were more relevant than a self-destructing Old World. The changes that aroused the strongest emotions were those within their domestic realm. In February 1915 Dr. Cannon's father died, leaving him with a new awareness of his mortality: "I have a strange sense of being alone, of being the head of the line with no one in front—of its being my turn next," he confided in his diary on 21 February.[4] On 29 November Cornelia's Aunt Jaynes succumbed to kidney infection; only fifteen months later, on 26 March 1917, Auntie's daughter Ethel Jaynes Macomber died after giving birth to twin boys. Small wonder that the anonymous dying in the trenches of Verdun paled in the face of tangible pain. Death made Cornelia cherish the life her family personified and, even more, her capacity to give life. On 24 February 1915, only days after Colbert Cannon's death and on Henry James's birthday, she gave birth to her last daughter: "Here I lie, peaceful in bed, another beautiful little girl safely in the world, and all's well!"[5]

For almost three years the Cannons succeeded in keeping the war from defining their lives—a response encouraged by the circles in which they moved. Dr. Cannon's pacifism was shared in the Harvard community, with its ties to German scholarship, and the pacifist longing that defined the community was affirmed on a national scale. Though economic considerations, the nation's dependence on open markets, as well as established cultural ties undermined U.S. neutrality, as did huge bank loans and the shipment of arms to the Allied forces, Wilson still won the election of 1916 on the "Peace without Victory" ticket. He could rely on a large and highly diversified antiwar coalition: progressives and Quakers, the socialists around Eugene V. Debs, industrial magnates such as Henry Ford and Andrew Carnegie, African American civil rights leaders such as W. E. B. Du Bois and A. Philip Randolph, the trade unions, and suffragettes formed a unique alliance against the European war.[6]

The Cannons were in respectable company. Still, as the war continued, the interventionist voices increased, as did the administration's admonitions that a changing situation—the German submarine war, the diplomatic alliances with Japan and Mexico that Germany tried to forge, as well as economic considerations—might force the United States to move beyond neutrality. The country was slowly but inevitably edging toward war, and the Cannons began to renegotiate their pacifist positions with the nation at large. As early as January 1915 Dr. Cannon was urged to join the volunteer surgical unit his colleague Dr. Harvey Cushing organized; he refused, claiming obligations to his research and, when approached again in early 1916, his family. In his autobiography *The Way of an Investigator* (1945) he admitted that he dreaded "a sharp break with all my previous habits. I must cease to be a laboratory hermit and go forth into the world for scientific study. I must turn from observations on natural processes in lower animals to observations on grievously torn and battered human beings."[7] Yet no matter how anxiously the Cannons tried to avoid it, the war came to them.

Cornelia, as always, was the one most inclined to invite the world in. From the very beginning her patriotic enthusiasm conflicted with her publicly proclaimed creed that "we women are by instinct peace lovers,"[8] and with every German war atrocity the America press reported, the balance shifted from pacifism toward cries for retribution. Cornelia's ambivalence was tangible in her response to Dr. Cannon's refusal to join Cushing's unit. Was their pacifism legitimate when "thousands" less privileged "say good-bye to their husbands, almost certainly forever!" she asked. And, even more true to her nature, "Germany must be whipped, like a child, for the good of its soul."[9] Only a month later, on 22 February, she called the American position, "this neutrality situation . . . too appalling," for "any war is a crime against us all!"

All doubts ended when a German submarine sank the *Lusitania*, killing 1,198 people, among them 128 Americans. "We are still staggering under this awful blow!" she wrote to her mother on 10 May 1915. "Horror and grief are swallowed up in rage. I find myself full of the most primitive emotions." Her "Must we go to war?" was a rhetorical question: "It seems as if it [the war] might be the only way to wipe out this horrible blot on humanity." Rage and horror defined her response, but also a profound sense of loss: "The awful thought is, where is our Christianity and our toasted civilization?"

Perhaps it was this sense of loss that enabled Cornelia and Walter B. Cannon to reach out to individual Germans in their community despite increasing public outrage. This willingness to differentiate between the group and the individual was illustrated by their loyalty, often against their innermost urges, to Hugo Münsterberg and his wife. Ever since his arrival at Harvard in 1892, Münsterberg, embracing his role as a representative of German culture, had worked for German-American partnership; when the war started, he felt called to defend his country. His "Nibelungentreue," a self-negating, unquestioning, and absolute loyalty to Germany, isolated him, and skepticism turned into hostility after the *Lusitania* incident. The

Cannons continued to invite the German outcasts to their home, and Cornelia paid visits to Mrs. Münsterberg, whose hair turned gray under the stress of harassment.

In December 1916 Münsterberg collapsed while teaching at Radcliffe. The Cannons were horrorstruck and stood by his widow, who in her bitterness excluded the Harvard community from the funeral rites.[10] Cornelia Cannon hated Germany as "the enemy," but as late as 9 May 1918 she wrote to her husband: "We are not familiar with the European Germans and our own are either peaceful and innocuous or among our finest citizens. Perhaps they are the *true* Germans." Yet references to fairness disappeared as the war continued. Cornelia became increasingly outspoken against her country's neutrality, and as a self-styled twentieth-century paragon of republican motherhood,[11] she insisted on active commitment in her domestic realm: when her children complained about their food, they were reminded of starving war orphans; their wardrobe became so shabby that Bernice undermined the war effort by providing from Filene's.

Cornelia's determination to make the war felt at home and her disregard, if not outright scorn, for food and clothes formed a bizarre alliance indeed; war served as a patriotic excuse for weaning the family from those comforts they had always refused to give up. In 1916 the Cannons adopted "their" war orphan, and the children were charged to donate their meager allowance as well as money made on chores. Christmas was perverted into a rite of self-denial—no tree, no gifts, the Christmas goose shrunken to a miserable pot roast. The humor of her family letter of 25 December cannot disguise that her enthusiasm met with outright despair: children deprived of gifts, aunts pitying their martyred nieces and nephew, even Dr. Cannon, his hope shattered for the luxury of handkerchiefs when "even the rag bag is exhausted." But "mortify the flesh and exalt the spirit is our motto," she wrote. Wilma found the adequate image for this domestic tragicomedy: "Mother said we can't have a Xmas tree, we've got to have an orphan."[12]

By the time they staged this deprivation Christmas, a decision had been made that would render the war central to the Cannons' lives in a frightfully real sense: Dr. Cannon, under pressure from the National Research Council and a bellicose Cornelia, agreed to join Cushing's unit. He was to conduct research on the phenomenon of wound shock, which had been puzzling medical scientists for centuries and which gained a terrifying relevancy during World War I. On behalf of the Rockefeller Foundation he had established a physiological committee on shock research, but while most of its members focused on the causes of shock, he hoped to find a therapy.[13]

Dr. Cannon's move received heightened significance when President Wilson asked Congress to declare war on the Central Powers in April 1917. The Cannons, anxious for their children to understand the historical import of this day, staged a "patriotic celebration." Wrote Cornelia to her mother: "We sang the Star Spangled Banner and America and The Battle Hymn of the Republic—then read them things from the first and the second Inaugurals of Lincoln. . . . We met at 12, as the Congress assembled, each child had a flag and I had a big silk one across the book case—We ended with the salute to the flag and the pledge of allegiance. . . . It was a cunning sight to see the little patriots."[14]

The family was ready for war. The Cannons were thus among those eager to discard their pacifism at President Wilson's call to arms; large segments of the nation, however, were not. After years of affirming neutrality the administration faced problems rousing the nation to the kind of national consensus the war required. Congress had to reinstate a draft when too few men volunteered; a Committee on Public Information, chaired by George Creel, was required to boost enthusiasm for the war; the African American community debated whether a segregated army and a racially torn country were equipped to make the world safe for democracy;[15] and the socialists declared the war "a crime against the people of the United States."[16] The Espionage Act of 1917 and the Sedition Act of 1918 document the extend to which the administration had, and was willing, to go to secure its war efforts against fierce internal opposition. But by the time the United States joined the war, the Cannons needed no patriotic enticements.

Cornelia's letters preceding Dr. Cannon's departure were a medley of conflicting emotions: there was the realization that this meant the end of merely playing at war,[17] dread at the thought of "the final offering," anger at the passive role she was forced to play, as well as an almost grotesquely masochistic anticipation of the glories of widowhood: "I sit at home and steel myself. What the women have suffered in this war! The men have the thrill of action, but we can only endure. . . . This war means, to me, the great battle for human freedom and world peace, and in comparison no human life matters." Remnants of her discarded pacifist creed resurfaced, however, in the satisfaction she drew from knowing that "mine is the blessed privilege of offering up my dearest to *save* life, and not to destroy it." But nothing could cloak the truth that the definer of war is death: "I cannot feel to let him go until I have accepted the possibility that he may never return."[18]

As his departure neared, she found herself coping with a mounting sense of dread she could master only by clinging to the familiar, encountering the all-transforming reality of war by celebrating continuity. Her letter of 2 May 1917 expressed a passionate embrace of routine: "He goes to the Med. School to his work, and I go to the school to see how Bradford is doing his arithmetic, or help dear sister Linda buy a spring suit." She accompanied her husband on his parting visits to Harvard presidents Eliot and Lowell; she bought him a wristwatch with phosphorescent numbers and a camera, but there were no stunt parties, only a domestic routine that suddenly appeared precious. "I seize each precious moment like a miser," she admitted on 4 May. Dr. Cannon, by contrast, experienced the delays she embraced so greedily with a mounting sense of restlessness. The scholar in him was eager to start working. "Walter, darling thing, is half lost to me already," she confessed on 7 March. On the eve of separation we encounter the first glimpse of what was to become the definer of Cornelia's and Walter's wars—an awareness that HER story and HIS story were incompatible.

After the suspense of waiting, Cornelia's letter of 9 May, describing her mate's departure, was a discourse on controlled performance. Presenting herself as a self-abnegating female patriot sending her offering to the war gods with a proud smile, it illustrates the degree to which she adhered to conventional gendered roles that froze the man in the centralized pose of heroic masculinity, the woman in marginalized passive femininity. There can be little doubt that the situation appealed to her love of performance, and she embraced the opportunity to display her qualities as actress and director. Yet her letter also documents that her ritualized conduct was a form of self-protection against fears she could not bear to admit: "Walter went this morning at 10 a.m.—There was not a tear except those shed copiously by Dr. Cushing's black chauffeur, who was inconsolable. We had the true Anglo-Saxon horror of showing emotion evidently—isn't it curious?" The control she exerted and its conventional gendering is graphically revealed in the distancing image of the weeping black chauffeur, her twentieth-century reinvention of Uncle Tom. The episode testifies to the degree to which she had internalized nineteenth-century romantic racialism and its hierarchical head/heart dichotomy which associated the Anglo-Saxon nature she so proudly claimed for herself with rationality and the Othered African American with emotion.[19]

At the same time this binary opposition of Anglo-Saxon and African American allowed her to subvert for herself established gendered patterns of order, a kind of cross-dressing via racial assignment. The African American man is feminized through his weeping while the Anglo-Saxon Cornelia appropriates male rationality and control: empowerment through racial-

ized masculinization. She used the black chauffeur to express all she had
suppressed in favor of a heroic pose: love, fear of death, pain, veneration
of the great man. He became her substitute sufferer while she performed
the role she had written for herself. Only toward the end does a ray of
doubt become visible: "Do we suffer more or less for it?" The question is
pure rhetoric, for the racial hierarchy between African American heart and
Anglo-Saxon head has been implemented beyond doubt. The answer can
thus be reduced to another formula of patriotic self-denial: "It enabled us
to send dear Walter off with smiling faces."

The twenty months between Dr. Cannon's departure and his return to
the United States are well documented. Cornelia collected his war letters,
editing them for publication. Also she wrote essays about her experiences,
some for private circulation, some just for herself. And finally, in the mid-
twenties, she started to work on a novel called *The Clan Betrays,* the first
third of which dramatizes the challenges a New England couple face during
the war and its aftermath. These different narratives constitute a multivocal
choir of self-representations that defy closure and invite passage, transformation, and uncharted roads as paradigms of our heroine's war years.
The war violently disrupted Cornelia Cannon's way of life, but she embraced the potential she found in disruption. Like many American women
she shouldered new responsibilities, learning to cope with separation and
death, and she discovered new realms for herself.[20] The months of separation became a period of self-recovery, self-discovery, and self-liberation.

At first sight, her representation of the period appears incompatible with
this reading. She gloried in the role of the patriot woman sacrificing "my
dearest" for the good of all. Her poem "The Women Who Stay Behind,"
written weeks after Walter's departure, is representative of the public persona she adopted:

> Who will speak for us,
> Who will teach us to endure? . . .
> Frail creatures that we are,
> The statesmen take the letters,
> Form great words, democracy,
> The right of nations—
> We only spell a boy's name.[21]

The formula by which she engendered her life as a soldier's wife was one of
sacrifice, submission, endurance, and devotion. Her letters, however, document that for her the war was not simply an event that was taking place on

the other side of the globe. Transcending boundaries of public and private, she insisted that it define their lives on the home front just as drastically as it did in the trenches of Verdun. It sat at the table with them, and they wore its shabby garb for all to see; it entered their yard, and it slept with them.

Financially the family was secure, for Harvard made up the deficit between Dr. Cannon's income as an officer and his salary. But Cornelia believed that any kind of indulgence was blasphemy, and she subjected her household to a dreary war diet; the "meatless Mondays" and "wheatless Wednesdays" that the U.S. Food Administration under Herbert Hoover prescribed as a form of secularized patriotic fasting, turning a family dinner into a site of public contestation,[22] were studiously observed in the Cannon kitchen. During the winters of 1917 and 1918 she adhered slavishly to the public campaign for saving coal and fuel. That her zeal attracted public attention, if not ridicule, even in patriotic Cambridge becomes clear in an episode she inserted into her family letter of 11 September 1917, reporting on rumors "that 'Mrs. Cannon is not going to have a furnace fire this winter but is going to dress the children with warm underclothes and strengthen them.'" Well, she came dangerously close. "I am so ragged now that there is no dress in which I can be spontaneous," she bragged to her mother on 25 March 1918. For the party the Harvard unit wives organized on 11 May 1918, Cannon wrote a poem called "The Day" in which she made fun of her patriotic zeal in a parody of Whitman's "Song of Myself":

> I sing the song of elimination; the
> elimination of the superfluous, of
> the debatable, of the essential . . .
> I behold a manless world, filled with
> old clothes, liberty bonds, potatoes,
> comfort-kits . . .[23]

And just as she observed every call to save, she gave without reservation when invited to serve: accompanied by baby Helen, she roamed the community selling Liberty Loans, setting an example by investing in bonds the money she saved through rigorous domestic economy. On 2 July 1918 she reported to her mother from Franklin: "One barn is fairly papered with Liberty Loan and food conservation posters—it is very patriotic and gorgeous, and I hope will inspire the children." Small wonder that even the children's playtime was transformed; they dug trenches in the yard to recreate the Verdun landscape.

The family's patriotism was fanned by Dr. Cannon's war letters. At home he had been reluctant to adopt a belligerent stance, and was remarkably slow in succumbing to what Randolph S. Bourne called "the itch to be in the great experience which the rest of the world was having."[24] But the exposure to life at the front—mangled bodies, bombed hospitals, villages in ruins, the miseries of fugitives, "men with their bellies torn open, with the sides of their faces ripped out, with brains oozing from skull wounds, with the bladder shot through"[25]—eliminated all traces of his pacifism. The scientist who had been reluctant to join a surgical unit now perceived conscientious objectors as traitors; after the bombing of a hospital he admitted, "I hate them [Germans] . . . with a deadly hate."[26] He developed "a dread that when the war is over there will be a lot of easy-going sentimentalists who will urge us all to forget and forgive."[27] The physician devoted to saving life refused to treat Germans as long as Allied soldiers remained unattended. He ceased to use the word "German," speaking exclusively of Huns, Boshes, Fritzes. His change of attitude influenced his family: whenever a letter arrived, Cornelia assembled her children and sisters-in-law; the text was read aloud and discussed; friends, colleagues, and neighbors were invited to hear the "public" parts of the epistles, and their approval of Dr. Cannon's increasing militancy in turn encouraged his kin. With Walter admitting to and being praised for feelings he had never tolerated before, Cornelia no longer saw any reason to check herself.

She was well equipped to take care of the family without her husband. Her mother had taught her that it was a wife's duty to empower her husband in his professional life by managing family business, and throughout her married life she had lived this doctrine. The important difference now was that Walter was unable to share responsibility for decisions that had to be made. Investments, house repairs, school matters, vacation plans had always been primarily her responsibility; now they were wholly so. She had nursed the children in sickness; now she alone had to decide when to call in professional help. And there was plenty of sickness during these years: the influenza of 1918 that killed 675,000 Americans, sparing the Cannons; minor challenges like measles, mumps, scarlet fever. Cornelia had support in Ida and Bernice, yet the ultimate responsibility was hers—as was the glory. More than that, with Walter in France, there was no need to observe those aspects of daily life that seemed important to him only, and without these distractions Cornelia could give vent to her easygoing, improvisational nature. Family business ran more smoothly than ever under her rule of "wholesome neglect." She rewarded herself by devoting time saved to inventing space for her vivacious, happily expanding self. Who was to stop her now?

Cornelia's and Walter's letters were framed by words of endearment, loneliness, the agony of separation. As a rule it was Walter who focused on intimate matters, while Cornelia tended to fall back on a rhetoric of heroism. She, too, was haunted by images of death, but as always she coped by immersing herself in an activism that left no room for fear. Her response to her husband's departure has a paradigmatic quality; she kept her poise, but she was aware that once he was gone, the incentive for maintaining control would evaporate. Consequently she constructed a bridge that prevented her from falling into an emotional pit: she decided to spend the summer among her Minnesota kin, at her sister Helen Sommers's residence in Hudson, Wisconsin.

Cornelia, her children, and their maid Florence arrived in Hudson on 19 June; they lived in a cottage, and for ten weeks they were joined by the entire James clan. The James sisters decided that it was going to be *their* summer, and they transformed Helen's land into a playground swarming with children, mothers, and aunts. Cornelia's humorous delineation of this female reign sparkles with their sense of ease. "I have introduced some reforms," she proclaimed on 13 August 1917: "less conscientious washing of the diapers, wholesome neglect all along the way, and a girdle to hold the baby down. . . . My theory is that conservation begins with the mother." A soaring of spirit characterizes her Hudson letters.

In mid-July the family was forced to make another war offering: the Jameses' only son departed for Europe. Frances James almost collapsed at the sight of Henry in uniform, but Cornelia expressed only pride. Pleased at the courage of Henry's wife, she informed Walter: "I have suggested to her that she and the two children come and spend the winter with us. We can pool our incomes and I shall not feel so guilty having that big comfortable house."[28] Expediency, the ability to embrace the other as sister: her alternative life-model to the men's war was a community of women and children. Henry's wife chose to stay in Minnesota.

The highlight of the Hudson summer, however, was a trip through rural Minnesota with her favorite sister, Helen. They started out on 31 July on a tour that took them to Newport, Shakopee, St. Peter and the Kasota marble quarry, New Ulm, Alexandria, and Finlayson. In her letters to her husband Cornelia evoked a rather conventional pleasure trip of two middle-aged women whose joy was somehow diminished by the fact that their mature bodies would have preferred a bed to camping out. Nothing in these letters suggests the triumphant sense of freedom that would serve as Cornelia's source of strength in the months ahead. The true meaning of this quest is revealed in "A Middle-Aged Adventure," which Cornelia wrote upon her return to Hudson, and is concentrated in its opening sentence: "My sister and I have just reached middle age, and we plan to take advantage of that fact."[29] Their culture gloried in youth, identifying the middle-aged woman as an unattractive matron with no life beyond the domestic realm; Cornelia celebrated middle age as a period of liberation. Securely married, the mature woman need no longer submit to the dictates of fashion, beauty, and charm; her childbearing years are over, the children old enough to be deposited with relatives; gray hair and well-rounded buttocks render chaperones superfluous.

Middle age, far from symbolizing the end of life, becomes the runway for the quests of women who, after years as grounded birds, long for the exultation of free flight. "Middle age has its compensations. We are free to choose our own path, even if it leads to destruction." She joked: "A Ford, a tent, a camp stove, and the world is ours for the taking. . . . You know that psychologists insist that the cow jumped over the moon because everybody said the old cow couldn't do it" (AMA, 1). The departure scene is typical of the women's determination to soar. Bribing their brood with all-day suckers, they set forth "without plan and without destination." She noted: "Our consciences were wrenched at the thought of our careless irresponsibility—for about a mile. Then anxiety over the children's baths, diet, sleep and salvation slipped from us like a garment, and we turned fresh, untroubled faces to the unknown opening before us. If adventure is merely the mood in which you face experience, we shall out-Crusoe Robinson" (AMA, 1).

"Indirection" became the keyword of this leisurely trip through Minnesota's farmland. They may have had a vague goal in mind, but they were only too willing to forget it as they turned into untrodden byways. Fifteen miles seemed a good day's run as they lay in the sun, next to an unidentified river—a woman's utopia, defined by the absence of contours and men. "Men have not the same capacity for aimless wandering and conversation that women have. They are to [sic] apt to set their hearts upon a goal. We kill the hours so gently, death overtakes them before they are aware of its nearness" (AMA, 4). This vacation became the model for numerous trips all over the world which she would undertake over the following fifty years in the company of sisters, daughters, female friends, or all by herself—but, whenever possible, without men. The vacation came to an end after twelve days when the Ford broke down and heavy rain turned the Minnesota roads into "gummy ridges along which we slew from side to side" (AMA, 9), but by then the sisters had already extended their absence by two precious days. For Cornelia this trip acquired a deep meaning: she became aware of that profound need for space and liberty inside. She would never again suppress it.

The rest of the summer was like its beginning—full of joy, children, relatives, the war kept backstage. It reentered with a vengeance. On 7 September the Cannons departed for Cambridge, and as the train pulled out of the station, Cornelia picked up a newspaper left on the seat. In huge letters the headlines reported that Cushing's unit had been bombed; one doctor had been killed, three seriously wounded. Was Walter already with Cushing? Who were the wounded? What was the name of the dead doctor? Cornelia sat trapped in the train with five children to entertain. It was a nightmare. In despair she drew Bradford into her confidence, only to discover that he already knew: he had overheard the Sommerses discussing the incident and deciding to spare her. In the midst of this tumult she again sought solace in heroic rhetoric. That night she wrote to her mother: "I am calm and ready for it. . . . I have had more than most people's share of happiness already."

When she arrived in Chicago, the papers announced that one of the unit's men had cabled "All well," but that did not answer all her questions. The children became sick and started throwing up. Cornelia was again grounded, desperately so, but not for long. In Cambridge the news that Dr. Cannon was safe awaited her, and Cornelia turned her face toward the future. On 11 September she wrote in her letter to Minnesota: "I realize as I tackle the problems how rested I feel. . . . I feel equal to anything." The role of pining soldier's wife just did not become her, and once she acknowledged that, she carved out another one more true to her nature—the doer throwing herself into a tumult of reform activities.

Suffrage became her first objective. The American women's movement, denied political participation in the Fifteenth Amendment, had never given up its fight for enfranchisement, entering into a tedious, costly, all-absorbing struggle that had to be taken from state to state, a maddeningly slow and exhausting process. As the United States edged toward war, American suffragettes saw a new chance to push their agenda, but the movement was torn by factionalism, the enmity between the Women's Party and the National American Woman Suffrage Association (NAWS) rendering it vulnerable to external manipulation. Still, the protest marches and the violence they met, the NAWS's patient committee and war work, the contributions American women made on the home front by working in industrial plants and on the railroads, in offices and schools, could no longer be ignored. On 10 January 1918 President Wilson called for women's suffrage "as a war measure."[30]

There is not the slightest documentation that Cornelia James Cannon had ever been active in the women's movement, that she had participated in rallies or marches, that she worked up anything like feminist enthusiasm for the cause. The war, however, put the vote on the agenda for her. Everywhere women, including herself, had begun to perform the work that had formerly been a male prerogative, efficiently and skillfully. For Cannon duty and rights had always been two sides of the same coin; the denial of suffrage to women became absurd in the face of their war contributions. She had never doubted her ability to fulfill a citizen's duties; now she demanded it as her right, and no doubt the association President Wilson established between woman's suffrage and the war effort legitimized her new position by transforming it into a patriotic act. After attending a rally with Dr. Anna Shaw at the Boston Opera House, she wrote to Dr. Cannon on 29 May 1918 that suffrage was "a war movement because it was the logical preparation for that democracy we are trying so hard to make the world safe for. . . . [W]e are committed to democracy—why not try it?" Dozens of articles on women's issues published in the postwar decade in journals such as *Radcliffe Quarterly* and *The Woman Citizen* testify to her continued interest.

The projects uppermost in her mind, however, were the publication of Dr. Cannon's war letters and her commitment to the Cambridge Hostess House. Her semipublic readings had convinced her that this correspondence deserved publication. Her own letters document her belief that her individual experience mattered; like Benjamin Franklin, she saw her life as worth imitating. If her everyday activities deserved recognition, how much more did her husband's heroic struggle to save the lives of American boys, the scientist-pacifist's glorious metamorphosis into a scientist-warrior. The idea horrified Walter B. Cannon, a modest man facing the mind-boggling idea of having his private reflections exposed to the public gaze. He also feared that Cornelia's impatient pride might tempt her to edit his remarks in ways that could embarrass him before the medical community. "I fear a tendency to idealize everything makes too much of . . . the work I am trying to do," he warned her on 23 August. But once Cornelia, "opinionated, incorrigible,"[31] had made up her mind, there was no stopping her. So her husband responded in the only way possible short of ending the correspondence: he became guarded about the information he passed on.

Reports on research became scarce; potentially controversial topics disappeared; expressions of self-doubt, criticism of Allied policy, and descriptions of disillusioned soldiers diminished. In their place we find accounts of war atrocities, of trips to Paris and Oxford, expressions of his longing for his family—letters that dared not be deep for fear that the intimate might be perverted into the public. Cornelia submitted the manuscript to the *Atlantic Monthly,* then under the editorship of Ellery Sedgwick; it was rejected. She could not believe that a journal dedicated to the nation's welfare could be blind to the treasure she offered. The letter informing Walter about this defeat was her most discouraged of the war, so depressed, in fact, that he found it "inconceivable that your blithe and gay spirit would cloud." Still, he added, "I was immensely relieved."[32] Unknown to him, however, Cornelia had not given up; she continued to edit his letters as they came in. In 1935, when German militancy resurfaced, she submitted the collection to the *Atlantic Monthly's* nonfiction prize contest—with little success.

School politics, suffrage activities, family business, the publication project, preservation campaigns, Liberty Loans: Cornelia Cannon embraced anything that prevented the horror of the war from taking possession of her. The saving grace, however, was her work for the Cambridge Hostess House. As she admitted in a letter to her mother as early as 11 September 1917, "the work with the Radio boys is really saving me, or I should die of homesickness for Walter, now that I am . . . back where every stick and stone speaks his absence." Within months she became so thoroughly involved that she even canceled her Hudson vacation in 1918. On 17 February she confessed to Helen: "More and more I am obsessed by my responsibilities to these Radio boys. There will be 4000 of them this summer. . . . I feel as if the line of duty pointed me to stay right here." "Line of duty" may have been a convenient formula; "obsession" is the more adequate term to describe what had become one of the most enjoyable episodes in Cannon's life.

When the United States declared war in April 1917 the army was small, but the Selective Service Act of 18 May 1917 raised the number of soldiers from 200,000 to almost 4 million by the end of the war.[33] It was an enormous challenge for a nation with an isolationist policy to prepare thousands of men for warfare, within the shortest time possible. Everywhere training camps were established that transformed farmers, industrial workers, college students, and physicians into soldiers. But as thousands of men were drafted, women's organizations, drawing on their former purity campaigns, began to voice concern at the soldiers' morality.

In June 1917 the Women's Committee, consisting of the leaders of the most influential women's organizations, met in Washington, D.C., to discuss solutions to what they decried as a precarious situation indeed. Two challenges to American purity and "the future race" had to be faced: first and foremost, "our boys," snatched from their protective domestic circle, lonely, adventurous, and ignorant of the evils of the world, had to be protected against the prostitutes sure to besiege the camps. Second, the activists feared for the safety of young women from their own communities who, moved by the men's deadly mission, might feel tempted to commit improper sacrificial acts. The conference applauded the Florence Crittenden Mission's report announcing that more than a thousand prostitutes had pledged not to approach soldiers, and in July 1917 the Women's Commission created the Department of Safeguarding the Moral and Spiritual Forces.[34]

Events in Cambridge paralleled those on the national level. Though silenced by their patriotism, many citizens were appalled when this Harvard-centered, elite white community was chosen to host training facilities. With the U.S. Naval Radio School located on the Cambridge Common, thousands of men in uniform from all over the country changed the face of the community in the summer of 1917. Despite patriotic protestations, for Cantabrigians it was a demographic earthquake. Not only did this influx of soldiers attract prostitutes, but also, even more annoying was the danger that this powerful male presence represented for young white middle-class women susceptible to the glory of uniforms and sentimental notions of sacrifice. "We had been much exercised over the tales of high school girls in trouble thanks to the sailors and the sight of sailors parading the streets with their arms round the 13, 14, and 15 years old girls who flock round the school, infatuated with the uniform," Cornelia complained to her mother on 6 November 1917. A committee of five women was formed, with Cornelia Cannon as a prominent member, to negotiate the situation with representatives from the Radio School, but communication proved difficult. A letter of 11 November illustrates the problem via an episode revealing the incompatibility of interests: "A prominent army doctor reported that the consensus of opinion among the army and navy doctors was that it was best for a man to indulge once in two weeks. When he finished speaking there was utter silence. . . . Then a woman in the gallery rose and said, 'I should like to ask the doctor one question: Whose daughters shall these women be?'"

The triangle of prostitute, soldier, and white middle-class daughter that drove the Women's Committee work on the national level as well as the Cambridge women's local campaigns conjured up—implicitly, but understood by everybody involved—the specter of venereal disease. In that it connected the ensuing reform efforts to the nineteenth-century anti-prostitution and purity activism emanating from the women's movement, the Women's Christian Temperance Union's Social Purity Department, and the American Purity Alliance of 1895, on the one hand, and contemporary eugenic and social hygiene discourses, on the other.[35] The medical profession, progressive reformers, and women's rights activists of the day were in rare agreement that prostitution must be seen as "the major, and, to some the only, source of contagion."[36]

Venereal disease became a women's rights issue because the prostitute as the source of contamination violated class, race, and generational boundaries: through the infected man, she invaded the white middle-class domestic realm and the married woman's body and ultimately threatened the physical and mental health of her offspring—America's future. Venereal contagion became a eugenic issue because, writes Mark Thomas Connelly, it "posed serious threats not only to the public health but also to the integrity of certain conceptualizations of great cultural and psychological value: the 'race,' marriage, the family, motherhood, womanhood, and manhood." The World War I campaign associated venereal disease with President Theodore Roosevelt's warning against "race suicide" and the evocation by Prince Morrow (physician and chairman of New York's Committee of Seven) of "race deterioration."[37] Cannon's commitment to the Cambridge Hostess House thus was deeply rooted in questions of sexual and social hygiene, and it fell in line with her eugenic convictions and her devotion to "the future race."

This eugenic reading is confirmed by the Cannons' war correspondence. Cornelia's concern for "our boys" in Cambridge extended to those overseas: in letter upon letter she quizzed her husband about the sexual activities of the fighting men. Dr. Cannon, reluctant to discuss this topic with his spouse, tried to take refuge in a privatizing interpretation of her questions, assuring her that among his companions he had not witnessed "the slightest transgression of decent living." Yet he also conceded that "there is no doubt that the other things exist on an enormous scale." His letter documents his outrage that thousands of army hospital beds and scores of doctors had to be provided for men who came down with venereal disease, and he was furious that the army command did not "take the same precautions against impairing their forces by liability to such infections as they take with reference to typhoid fever."[38]

In April 1918, after attending a meeting of the Red Cross Medical Research Society in Paris, he called the discussion of venereal disease "a sordid and unpleasant subject, but an important one for the armies, and also for the future race." Acknowledging that the kind of physical morality his eugenic creed required could not be enforced, he opted for pragmatic solutions: "By methods now used the specialists believe that it would be possible to stamp out venereal disease, if methods were uniformly applied."[39] What he demanded in arguments that combined a pragmatic approach to military needs with eugenic considerations was a generous distribution of information on safe sexual conduct as well as condoms.[40] The problem of venereal disease among American GIs finally became so pressing that the army was forced to ignore the still valid anti-obscenity Comstock Law and engage in an aggressive information campaign. Years later the birth control activist Margaret Sanger would claim "that the section on venereal disease in *What Every Girl Should Know*, which had once been banned[,] ... was now, officially but without credit, reprinted and distributed among the soldiers going into cantonments and abroad"[41]—an ironic twist indeed. In an indirect way the war thus contributed to a dramatic change of public attitudes toward sexuality. It also influenced Cornelia Cannon. She shared her husband's eugenic concerns at what both considered violations of morality and a threat to "the race," as well as his pragmatic approach, but she also knew that her propagation of his ideas on sexual hygiene in Cambridge would cause a scandal. The establishment of the Hostess House, however, enabled her to deal with these moral, eugenic, and sexual issues in ways that did not threaten her reputation.

When the Cambridge committee suggested channeling the soldiers' sexual energies by establishing a Hostess House, she was eager to give generously of her time and organizational skills. Harvard, whose president, Abbott Lawrence Lowell, was disturbed by the onslaught on public morality, offered its Phillips Brooks House for sailors to meet with friends and family. The women's committee—Mrs. E. K. Rand served as chairwoman, Cornelia Cannon as secretary, Mrs. R. Daly as head of the hostess house, and Mrs. M. Bailey as chairwoman of social work at the Radio Hospital—organized outings as well as poetry readings, put together a library, established connections with local churches, and staged chaperoned dances; they pleaded with Cambridge families to invite soldiers for dinner or weekends and to host sailors on holidays.[42] Cannon plunged into a volley of activities—meetings, press conferences, promotional events. Even more important, she lived what she preached. The doors of her house on Divinity Avenue were thrown wide open. A sailor's fiancée needed a place for a weekend? Make yourself at home. Soldiers were recovering from the flu? Why not among the Cannon children? Fathers felt homesick for their children? There were five to entertain at the Cannons'.

The Christmas of 1917 was transformed into a feast of joy by Cornelia's willingness to define as family whoever needed to belong. At first sight she seems merely to have extended her role as mother by including in her domestic circle a number of soldiers she insisted on calling "boys." But her deep sense of gratification documents that the needs she expressed through her work transcended this role. As the committee's secretary, she played the social network to which she belonged as a Harvard professor's spouse, and she broadened her social realm. Also, she was responsible for communicating with the media, and this gave her the kind of visibility she craved, a visibility, moreover, that was associated with the highly respected persona of the patriotic helpmate. On a more personal level, she simply enjoyed the company of young soldiers. Her description of her work became a discourse on rejuvenation: "We had a Radio party—a regular orgy—Friday," she confided in her family letter of 4 March 1918. "I bask in my 'war work,' because it is such a happiness to deal with youth in its hours of ease." Her involvement enabled her to extend both her private and her public realm; it empowered as it liberated her.

Cornelia Cannon's metamorphosis into a public figure and *mater communitatis* met with her family's mixed response. Her children were enthusiastic, for not only did it provide them with interesting companions, but also their mother had no time left for school lectures, which relieved them of considerable embarrassment. Ida and Bernice, however, were appalled by this new lifestyle. "Bernice is upset about our open house arrangements," Cornelia wrote to her parents on 5 December 1917. "She . . . stays in her room when the boys are here." Even sister Linda interfered and, Cornelia charged, "talked to me like a Dutch uncle, the other night, about my duty to my home."[43] Dr. Cannon was aware of the changes the war had imprinted on gender relations.[44] Upon arriving in London he wrote to Cornelia on 23 May 1917: "The women mark the greatest change. Women are conductors of the busses—smartly dressed in high leather boots, and very efficient. Women are carting luggage on trucks at the station. . . . Their 'sphere' is clearly no longer home." He accepted these developments as a necessary expedient during war, but when it came to his private domain, his patriotic fervor dimmed.

He had agreed to leave his family because he was convinced that Cornelia could shoulder the responsibilities of both mother and father; he was unprepared for her departure into new realms and her absence from the old. His first response was a mixture of pride and anxiety, but soon anxiety gained the upper hand. A letter of 19 May became a cry of despair: "Fatigue is the root of so many evils. *Please* make *some* arrangement to get a respite this summer," he begged, "*please!* If you really love me, you will do so — there." Almost every letter warned against overwork, but there was also the jealousy of the absent husband at the male company she kept. The full impact of his fear became visible in a letter of 24 October 1918 to Bernice: "Take good care of Cornelia, won't you. If she works too hard or shows any sign of being tired, make her stop! I give you and Ida full authority to do so!" Make her stop? There was no stopping her, and he knew that. Cornelia had not just relearned how to fly; she was soaring, and nothing and nobody would ever ground her again.

The controversy over the Radio boys was more than a struggle over gender roles; it reveals how difficult their diverse war experiences had made it for husband and wife to communicate. The conflicting routes their representations of American soldiers took illustrates this point. At the outset of the war both saw the departing soldier as hero and martyr, an offering on the altar of peace and democracy, New World innocence taking on Old World corruption. After Dr. Cannon's departure, however, their images drifted apart. His first letter from the U.S. Army base hospital in Dannes-Camiers, France, was a narrative of disillusionment. "All the glory of war had dropped out of the attitude of these soldiers — they took their places like automata," he wrote on 1 June 1917. "The whole business of war is a grim and ghastly madness." Men perverted into fighting machines; patriotic enthusiasm stifled by the routine of horror; innocence blasted away by shells; young manhood turned into ugly corpses: the war liquidated the familiar glorification of heroism, ridiculed romantic notions of the sublime. Life at the front and his work in army hospitals forced Dr. Cannon to see soldiers as torn, mutilated, violated bodies, the war as a "maelstrom of tumult and horror."[45] In a letter of 16 August 1917 he warned: "If anyone ever says anything to you about the glories of fighting you'll know something that is an essential feature of warfare and that is only to be described as beastly torment and as ghastly mutilation of our own kind."

Cornelia chose not to understand. In a poem she imagined soldiers as child crusaders offering up their innocent blood to redeem a corrupt world:

> They ever saved this struggling, sinful world,
> The old, old crimes were expatiate in their blood,
> The Child Crusaders, hurrying thousands, came
> And sacrificed their radiance in its bud.

None of her husband's evocations of automaton-soldiers, bloodshed, and nihilism could change the fictions of dedication and purification on which her hope for the future of humankind relied. On the contrary, her work with the Radio boys only increased her need for idealization. She invested them with all the paraphernalia of white male youth and heroism; she invited this idealized white masculinity into her life as substitute sons; and she gained an almost masochistic satisfaction from sending them off to an uncertain fate. No, she would not allow anybody to soil her heroes. Even after the war, when Walter shared his memories, she would cling to her inventions. "Young, gallant, ardent, generous, modest, humorous"[46]—Cornelia's American soldier was heroism frozen in time. Whereas Walter's representations focused on what the war did to these men, on images of death, psychic collapse, and mutilation, Cornelia defended her dream, and nothing would bring these conflicting images together.

The Cannons' war letters were framed by longings for a new beginning, conceived as continuity; the only change envisioned was improvement within the familiar. Husband and wife avoided topics that expressed alienation. Yet as we turn to Cornelia's letters to Minnesota, a different picture emerges. Time and again we come across expressions of anticipation that Walter's exposure to the war would transform him. In the beginning the problem was less the bloodshed he had encountered than his social life, the honors heaped upon him. The Royal Society invited him to give the Croonian Lectures in early 1918; he was elected president of the Red Cross Medical Research Society and American president of the Franco-American Medical Society, and was appointed director of the Central Medical Department Laboratory of the American Expeditionary Forces at Dijon; in March 1918 he became a major in the Medical Reserve Corps and was elected to France's elite Cercle Artistique et Littéraire. He traveled extensively, attending conferences, moving as a celebrity among celebrities. He led the life of excitement and mobility that Cornelia Cannon craved; the woman for whom staying behind came so hard was clearly afraid of being left behind.

On his invitation to deliver the Croonian Lectures she confided to her mother on 4 March 1918, "Just think how Walter is growing away from us!" For her the glories of his social life were more threatening than the transformational impact of war. It was only in mid-1918 that the possibility of this transformation as one of loss and deprivation began to dawn on her. In June the *Atlantic Monthly* published an article titled "The Gulf," preparing the public for the return of men who now had little in common with the individuals to whom they had waved good-bye. The emphasis was not on the physical costs of war but on its impact on the soldier's psyche. Cornelia needed the *Atlantic* article to make her see what Walter had carefully traced as psychological mutation. His first exposure to front life still recorded the civilian's horror when he admitted on 14 July 1917: "I fear there is a little too much of the feminine in my nature. I see these cases of desperate pathos and forget the fundamentals of war." Only nine days later he reported that he was "beginning to get hardened,"[47] to which soon was added "the oppressive ennui of war."[48] A year later he admitted to feelings that "are so much outside the control that one may speak of them without boasting or excuse."[49] In November 1918 his satisfaction at seeing the enemy killed had become such that he asked, "Have I become a savage?"[50]

Cornelia had treated these statements as expressions of a hypersensitive nature and had welcomed his change of spirit as a sign of maturation, of American masculinity reinvigorated and affirmed. Only after she read "The Gulf" did she begin to see a pattern that signified alienation rather than growth. She was apprehensive but also naïvely confident that sincere efforts to understand would heal the wounds of war. The article, she wrote to her mother on 2 July 1918, "makes you feel that something is happening to those, close up to the horror of it, that will set them apart unless we can grow spiritually to meet it. . . . We can, at least, respect the silence and reticence of our returned crusaders, when they come." She had no idea how much silence and reticence she would have to withstand.

During this period Cornelia Cannon conceived of change and its potential problems exclusively as a phenomenon relating to others, to the men who had been to war. She portrayed herself, a representative of the women who had stayed behind, in terms of continuity, the stabilizing element to which these battered men could return to be nurtured and healed. Her writings suggest that she was unaware of the metamorphosis she herself had undergone, or if she was aware of it, her analysis testifies that she refused to perceive her transformation as problematic. And in a way she may have been right, for while Walter Cannon, like many men who shared the same experience, faced fragmentation, disorientation, even dislocation, women like Cornelia Cannon emerged from the war invigorated, ready to push forward.[51]

On 11 November 1918 the Central Powers surrendered; the war was over. Cornelia and her children joined the "innocent, joyous, delightful crowds" in downtown Boston. In her holiday spirit she even embraced President Wilson's call for reconciliation with a reformed Germany. "A democratic Germany is our kin," she affirmed. "The thought of feeding the Germans stirs my imagination."[52] Dr. Cannon received the glad tidings while on a hospital inspection tour with Alexander Lambert, chief surgeon of the American Red Cross in France, and Simon Flexner, director of the Rockefeller Institute. The men drove to Paris, where the crowds celebrating in the streets hailed "les américains."

He later remembered that "the news brought relief, rather than exuberance, and then a sense of wonderment as to how events might move."[53] To his wife he wrote on 13 November: "What an extraordinary world the papers are disclosing to us. Republics springing up in the place of tyrannies; kings shipping away to escape disaster; dynasties, centuries old, abolished in a few hours! As Lloyd George says, it's a time 'when emperors, kings and crowns are falling like leaves before the gale.' What does this all mean, and where may the freed spirit lead us?" Cornelia's response was one of hope and celebration. "There was a full moon, inconceivably looking down on a world that had given up killing as a major occupation," she described the first night of peace. "One began to feel that brotherly love might again have a place on the earth." And whereas he worried about the fate of humankind, she enjoyed the return of the little comforts of life, to which she felt entitled now that the war was over: "We celebrated Tuesday at home by starting the furnace. . . . How you will rejoice in getting back to a warm place to live!"[54]

1

*Cornelia James at
Radcliffe, 1899*

2

*Cornelia James as a member of
the Radcliffe Ball Team, 1899*

3 & 4

*Cornelia James performing
for the Radcliffe Glee Club*

5 *Cornelia James during her Radcliffe years*

6 *Cannon family photo taken in 1917: (left to right)*
Bradford, Marian, Cornelia, Helen, Wilma, Linda

7 & 8

Cornelia James Cannon,
novelist, in the early thirties

9 & 10

Cornelia James Cannon and Dr. Walter B. Cannon in their Franklin summer home in the early forties

11 *The Cannon daughters: (left to right) Marian, Wilma, Helen, Linda*

12

*Cornelia James
Cannon in the
sixties*

13

*1965: Cornelia James Cannon
receives Radcliffe's "Founder
Award"*

CHAPTER 5

"Can Our Civilization Maintain Itself?"

IMMIGRATION, EUGENICS, AND BIRTH CONTROL

THE GREAT WAR WAS OVER. NO NEED TO TREMBLE AT THE sight of the mail carrier, no need for food or coal conservation; you could read the papers without shuddering. For many, life returned to normal in no time. America could not wait to welcome back the men who had fought this war, just as the men could not wait to leave the Old World wasteland to return "to God's own country where plumbing is popular and drinking water can be had anywhere for the asking."[1] For the men, "of course, the top question personally is—when can I go home?" wrote Walter Cannon in the midst of armistice celebrations in Paris on 13 November 1918, but it took a long time for sons, husbands, and fathers to return, even for high-ranking officers. His hopes to spend Christmas with his family and to return to his life as a laboratory hermit were shattered by an embargo on all departures, and on 14 December he complained, "I went into the depth of despair, and became the passive prey of uncertainty."

Cornelia, too, was disappointed, but then she kept too busy to fall into depressions. After all, the Radio boys were still in Cambridge, the Hostess House was still open. There was no room for sadness, only the tumultuous happiness of her busy daily schedule. And now she could fully enjoy her life, for gone were the fears that had lurked beneath the patriotic surface. While Dr. Cannon gave in to his depression during an all-male Christmas in France, his wife and children's was one of pure joy, and they shared their holiday spirit with the Radio boys.[2] New Year's Eve was celebrated at the Whitings's, and again the Radio boys were present. "I dressed as a Radio boy," Cornelia wrote to Minnesota on 1 January 1919. "Fortunately a very fat boy lent me his clothes, so nothing split." No apathy and despair where this woman ruled. But in the midst of celebrations she, too, was eager "for my ship to come sailing home!" as she wrote in her New Year's letter.

The long-awaited day came on 22 January. At the docks in Hoboken, in the midst of hundreds of women, "all sisters in sacrifice and joy,"[3] stood Cornelia James Cannon, determined to embrace a new beginning. Was she also thinking of what she might be challenged to give up now that renewed demands to perform her conventional domestic roles were to be expected? Did she anticipate arguments, misunderstandings, assaults on her dearly loved mobility and freedom, as well as the hurt she might have to cause in self-defense? And whom did she expect? The "dear Walter" she had sent off to war? A hero? A man matured by his exposure to terrors she could not imagine? "The twenty months have fallen away like a garment, and I feel like a radiant bride," she wrote to her mother that night. And like a bride she celebrated their reunion. "I have welcomed the beloved warrior to his native land. . . . Life seems all perfect again." Continuity? Was that really what she wanted? And all perfect? Hardly, for even on that first day he was "tired way inside."

The following days were so hectic that the Cannons found no time to talk and feel honestly. "How quickly and happily the men shift off the whole business and become civilians once more!" Cornelia marveled in her family letter of 6 February, but she also admitted that the exchange of uniforms for civilian clothes was only one side of the coin. What the men carried in their souls could not be doffed so easily. She saw that Walter was determined to live up to everybody's expectations—a loving husband, a playful father, a reliable colleague and conscientious teacher—but Cornelia realized how hard he had to work at it. He was performing rather than expressing his true feelings. "Walter is much changed, older and graver—his gayety gone, and much of his resilience." She had read the *Atlantic Monthly* article on the transforming effect of war; now she had to connect it to their own lives. "His whole response is slowed down—as [if] the grief and agony could never leave him." Still, she maintained an optimistic pose, writing off these problems as transitional. The medicine she prescribed was a summer in Franklin, the children's infectious vitality, her love—and time to forget.

"Every thing that love and devotion can give him, we can offer, but we shall have to wait for the slow process of time to heal the deeper hurts." What she did not anticipate was that things would get much worse before they could improve. And there could be no forgetting.

On the first weekend in March, the Hammonds, Sachses, Jacksons, and Pierces held a stunt party for the returned hero, with George Pierce as the Statue of Liberty, a silver teapot in his uplifted hand, a riotously funny event in which relief at the end of bloodshed and hope for a more peaceful world combined with sheer gratitude at seeing a beloved friend safe again in their midst. Dr. Cannon joined in the frolic, but both he and Cornelia knew what it cost. Only days later the dreaded breakdown came. "He became completely exhausted, became dizzy and faint while lecturing, could not stand up for more than a few minutes, didn't sleep, and became so depressed that life was all black to him," Cornelia reported to her mother on 5 March 1919. Finally she was willing to admit that this war would remain a part of their lives: "We are going to get a lot of results of this war, long after the agony is over."

After this collapse we find few comments on Dr. Cannon's condition in family letters, but from Franklin, Cornelia wrote about resting, doing carpentry projects, reading, and hiking—activities designed to take his mind off war. Slowly Walter regained his grip on life, and Cornelia adjusted to the man who had returned to her. It is revealing that her correspondence contains little information on conversations between wife and husband about those experiences that Walter had ceased to discuss in his letters. Selective silence became the mode on which they based their new life together. Cornelia's chauvinism and his disillusionment clashed in ways that called for silence until time could create a new ground for words to share.[4]

The pain and sense of alienation that came with this silence would resurface as a key motif in her first (unpublished) novel, *The Clan Betrays,* a war novel she wrote in the twenties. In fiction she could express what the construction of self that shaped her correspondence had to hide or explain away. In this novel the New England woman Justine Chase marries the Irish American officer Peter Burns, who embarks for the European theater on their wedding day. Standing on the docks in expectation of his return, Justine tries to control her inner panic by clinging to images of familiarity and continuity, well aware that they never had a life together. Once the exhilaration of the first embrace is over, however, this artificial discourse of sameness is deconstructed in a reunion episode that spells disruption.

Justine's naïvely expressed hope that "you're the same Peter inside" (*CB*, 180) encounters a response combining exhaustion, frustration, even anger. Her smiles meet with his "grave tenderness" and "quiet deliberation" (*CB*, 180). Despite their joy at being together, they cannot communicate, for the war has taught them to speak in different languages. The incompatibility of their perspectives surfaces in their evaluation of Peter's promotion. Justine is proud of the "tribute" to his valor; Peter's response is a harsh rebuke: "It's rotten unfair business, the whole of war" (*CB*, 182). Justine is confronting an impenetrable veil. The enthusiasm, the idealism, the binary images of good and evil which the safety of the Hostess House have allowed her to maintain appear ridiculous, if not openly offensive to the man who fought the war she glorified. "Would victory and defeat, war and peace, ever mean what they had meant before? . . . Justine felt suddenly old" (*CB*, 182). Justine and Peter face gendered patterns of discourse in which the readings of the home front clash with those of the trenches, forcing the participants to seek refuge in a choreography of avoidance and silence. His "You didn't see what I saw" (*CB*, 183) denies the woman access to his male realm of experience, almost blaming her for not having been there while refusing to share the information she craves. It insists that the new beginning will have to be made on the basis of an unquestioning acceptance of this void, the depressive moods, the anger, the silences, without the right to understand. It is a gap that will never close; in fact it widens every time Peter's attempts "to talk of his war experiences" (*CB*, 240) encounter the formulaic response of those who were not there. The ultimate solution for Peter's and Justine's mutual Otherness is silence, the blind submission of the woman to her banishment from a realm defined as exclusively male. The novel's war episode ends on this note of disillusion.

Maybe the Cannons could not articulate what they felt during those first months of their new life together, but they could and did discuss what they hoped for, and in that respect they agreed on one point: peace. Nervously they observed the controversies over the peace treaty and the League of Nations, identifying unreservedly with President Wilson's various moves and despising his most outspoken antagonist, Senator Henry Cabot Lodge of Massachusetts, as a traitor to peace and democracy. When, after a deadlock between Wilson and the Senate, the Treaty of Versailles failed to be ratified in November 1919 and again in March 1920 and the United States declined to join the League of Nations, they were devastated, aware that the alternative to nations unable to work out peace was another war. The sacrifices of Verdun all of a sudden seemed lives wantonly thrown away.

On 19 November, Cornelia wrote her most bitter poem, "The Lost Fruits of Victory":

> False to you their wordy frays!
> False to you their party plays!
> Every day you die again
> In the deeds of selfish men.
> With your blood our pact was made.
> Shall we see your faith betrayed?[5]

The sense of betrayal, anxiety, and anger the Cannons suffered during this period was shared by a majority of Americans, and it had many causes, internal and external. The Treaty of Versailles and the emasculation of the League of Nations shattered the hope for lasting peace. There was, as Dr. Cannon had observed from Paris, a new world order, but as news of civil disorder and class violence overseas was spread by the American media, it seemed to spell chaos rather than democratic progress. Most important, the Russian Empire had collapsed in 1917, and the United States was confronted with the frightening reality of a socialist power.

If the international scenario offered little cause for optimism, the situation within the United States was equally disconcerting, as a nation longing for continuity faced disruption. The soldiers returned to a country in the throes of postwar recession, to which the trade unions responded with coast-to-coast strikes, mobilizing more than 4 million workers. This class struggle, disconcerting in itself, took on a new and sinister quality in the context of Soviet Russia and the specter of worldwide revolution. Then, in the notorious Red Summer of 1919, a bomb exploded in front of Attorney General A. Mitchell Palmer's house. It struck a nation already torn by labor unrest and dread of communist infiltration, to which was now added the horror scenario of anarchism. In the following months thousands of "aliens"—that is, immigrants without citizenship—were rounded up and detained all over the country, the majority of them from eastern and southern Europe; 249 were deported to Soviet Russia. In the Cannons' Boston six hundred "aliens" were arrested in January 1920, and as one federal judge stated, "pains were taken to give spectacular publicity to the raid, and to make it appear that there was a great and imminent public danger."[6] A few weeks later the Italian American anarchists Nicola Sacco and Bartolomeo Vanzetti were arrested in Brockton, Massachusetts. The administration and the media united to evoke the frightening scenario of a nation under siege. The fear conjured up with this Red Scare policy and

activism was not just political; the focus on aliens from southern and eastern Europe also points to race and a racialized anti-immigration agenda
as a motivating force. American eugenicists such as MIT biologist Frederick Adams Woods were quick to point out that immigrants from these
regions were "naturally" susceptible to communist indoctrination because
they were of inferior racial stock; they "identified radicals and carriers of
'deficient germ plasm' with the same demographic groups."[7] The goals of
protecting the nation against anarchy and communism and saving "the
future race" came together.

White American soldiers received a hero's welcome, although that
welcome would quickly be marred by the recession and labor unrest.
Returning black soldiers paraded through a proud Harlem, but they faced
a hostile white America. In the years leading up to the war and during the
war years, racial violence and segregation in the South, the promise of
work in the northern industrial centers, and the hope for improved living
conditions had triggered a massive migration of southern blacks to the
North—the Great Migration. It was a demographic shift just as dramatic
in its impact as the mass immigration from southern and eastern Europe,
and the response among mainstream Americans across boundaries of class
to what they perceived as an internal racial peril was equally violent. The
country experienced a tragically perfect example of what Étienne Balibar
termed "crisis racism," that is, a "'social consensus' based on exclusion
and tacit complicity in hostility" toward foreigners that results in a "consensus which makes the difference between classes only relative,"[8] with
the fundamental difference that these "foreigners" were American citizens,
"Other-from-Within."[9]

The St. Louis massacre of 1917 foreshadowed the racial violence that
would transform postwar America. As black GIs in uniform were lynched,
as race riots erupted nationwide, as a revived Ku Klux Klan attracted millions, the convenient white northern myth associating anti-black violence
and racism with an archaic South was shattered. W. E. B. Du Bois, who
had urged a reluctant African American community to join the war for
democracy with his controversial "Close Ranks" editorial of July 1918,
now retaliated with his agonized "Returning Soldiers" of May 1919. It
culminated in the battle cry "We return. We return from fighting. We return fighting."[10] That same year Claude McKay's sonnet "If We Must Die"
formulated the famous black call to arms: "Like men we'll face the mur-
derous, cowardly pack,/Pressed to the wall, dying, but fighting back."[11]
The specter of race war and racial displacement loomed larger than ever

among mainstream Americans. Eugenicists were quick to conjure up the horrendous scenario of inferior blacks and eugenically deficient immigrants breeding new "racial hybrids and some ethnic horrors that will be beyond the power of future anthropologists to unravel."[12]

"The new order is upon us, but where is my eager, welcoming spirit?" a Cornelia James Cannon on the brink of despair lamented to the *Atlantic Monthly* in November 1919. "The walls of my faith are falling in upon me."[13] Cannon succumbed to utter disillusionment, a feeling she had in common with many who had shared her naïve patriotic enthusiasm for this "war for democracy," this "war to end all wars," embracing it as the cleansing fire from which new life could grow,[14] only to see all hope ridiculed. But while large numbers of American intellectuals began to see themselves as a "Lost Generation," even opting for an expatriate exile in the Old World, and while many of her acquaintances abstained permanently from political involvement and withdrew to the private realm, Cannon did not. For her, the politicians' betrayal would never be an excuse to fail in what she regarded as every citizen's duty and privilege—to be involved on that level where she could effect change. Her belief in the war as an instrument for peace had been undermined, but that did not mean her enthusiasm for other causes would suffer the same fate. After all, the title of her *Atlantic Monthly* piece had been "The Reaction of a Radical," a weird choice during the Red Scare.

"A Radical": this was indeed how she had perceived her antebellum reform activities, "radical" here reductively and naïvely defined as pushing for reform in a resistant and blind community, and extending the boundaries of gendered role ascription. It was a curious application for a position that had always been in essence one of white mainstream reformism. Her revival of the terminology in the Red Scare context was programmatic, however, in that it reflected the self-defensive appropriation of the concept in an era of frightening social and racial tensions. Cannon's use of "radical" was (unconsciously) identical with that of George L. Record, a friend of President Wilson's, who in a letter of 1919 had urged him to "become the real leader of the radical forces in America, and present to the country a constructive program of fundamental reform, which shall be an alternative to the program presented by the socialists, and the Bolsheviki."[15] Cannon would have agreed. More than ever before she felt called upon to defend her exclusive white middle-class Americanness against external and internal foes, and as in her prewar progressivism, reform was the medicine she prescribed to maintain the social and racial stratification she affirmed.

With her children still young enough to make heavy demands on her time and her husband back from France, Cornelia must have felt overwhelmed, but not only did she refuse to give up the public work which had become so important during the war years; she also defined new missions in accordance with her conservative reconceptualization of radicalism. She could do so because hers was a privileged class position: there was always a maid to do the cooking and cleaning, and the Cannons could pay to have their laundry done. By hiring help, Cornelia bought time and mobility for herself. There was no lack of causes in a country resounding with social and racial problems, and with reformist movements and social Gospel schemes for attacking these issues: public schools, local politics, welfare, birth control, and immigration, to name only a few. She "flung herself manically into one agitation after another," the historian Arthur Schlesinger Jr. remembered of his mother-in-law, "writing, speaking, reforming, lobbying, traveling," transforming herself into a "novelist and all-purpose reformer."[16]

Especially writing. She had always loved to write: plays, sketches, essays, letters, poems. But now, as the wife of a famous scientist, a mother of five, a woman who had participated in the transformations of war, she felt she had substantial things to say, important contributions to make to that redefinition of American destiny which the nation faced as it emerged from the postwar recession and violence and entered the "Roaring Twenties." The medium she chose for the great task, "the organization of a workable democracy,"[17] was the essay; the topic—inspired by William McDougall's *Is America Safe for Democracy* and James Bryce's *Modern Democracies*[18]—the perfection of her beloved America; her panacea a Deweyan participatory democracy and community of enquirers.[19] She entered into the controversy over the future of public schools;[20] she launched an attack on philanthropy while clamoring for social reform;[21] she challenged fellow Americans to acknowledge that "our complex civilization cannot be kept up apparently for all alike";[22] she fought for minimum wage laws for women,[23] and against a bonus for war veterans;[24] she called upon women to support the League of Nations[25] and public health programs;[26] she ridiculed a nation whining at the high cost of domestic service[27] and at "youthful defiance of Prohibition."[28] There was a pamphlet celebrating the Women's Educational and Industrial Union.[29] And as her children entered adolescence, as first traces of lipstick or cigarette smoke caused Dr. Cannon to panic, as Bradford's mediocre school performance led to ruptures, Cornelia, evoking their evolutionary creed, even used her pen to remind that "agonizing, reproachful father,"[30] via yet another public article, that "modern civilization insists above all things upon the capacity for change. Only so can those who live by mutation be saved from mutations."[31]

The medley of topics Cannon took on in her essays seems to invite the labels "manic" and "all-purpose reformer" that Arthur Schlesinger Jr. applied; she obviously felt moved to comment on every social problem that made the news as well as competent to prescribe a solution. And yet there is a pattern, a core message, a focus: an antimodernist affirmation of change as reform, with the objective of preserving the nation's racial and social status quo. The themes uppermost in Cannon's mind and permeating the argumentative structure of her articles were eugenics and immigration, themes she perceived as intertwined. It was a focus that once again positioned her firmly within mainstream America and the xenophobia and racism that defined this mainstream especially in the postwar decade—years in which the revived Ku Klux Klan attracted membership, North and South, of more than 3 million, among them approximately 300,000 women.[32]

The Cannons, like many liberal-minded reformers, were aghast at this eruption of anti-black racial violence, and they equally distanced themselves from the extreme propositions of a reemerging nativist movement.[33] Yet it was a distancing from crude extremism only, not from the race discourse as such. The patriotic fervor of the war years and the "alien" hunt of the Red Scare had left them and many of their reformist contemporaries more susceptible to a race discourse that, while avoiding open violence, was all-pervasive: mainstream America spoke as if with one voice when it came to regulating immigration by setting quotas that radically reduced the number of racially "undesirable" aliens—southern and eastern Europeans, especially Jews and Slavs, as well as Asians and Africans—while privileging northern Europeans and especially Anglo-Saxons. They united behind prominent spokespeople for eugenics such as Charles B. Davenport and the eugenic twist they gave to the racialized immigration panic of the twenties, just as they provided unanimous support to the institutionalization of eugenics that permeated American reform activities of the twenties and thirties. They embraced the rise of eugenic intervention: the restriction on marriage that twenty-six states imposed on citizens infected with venereal disease; marriage restrictions for those defined as "imbeciles" or "feeble-minded" in forty-one states; even the sterilization laws passed in twenty-seven states.[34] They were as one when it came to condemning philanthropy and aiming to restrict welfare in eugenic terms, out of fear that "maudlin sentimentalism" would encourage the racially "undesirable," the socially "unfit," the "defectives" to "breed" even more profusely.[35] This is the reformist context in which Cornelia James Cannon located herself, that supported her and drew her support, not an extremism of the social periphery but opinion that was firmly mainstream in ways that often transcended political orientation and class differences and even permeated the debates of African American intellectuals of the day.

In the midst of the fierce nativist arguments erupting after the war, Cannon never ceased to remind her readers that they were a nation of immigrants, that even the most belligerent nativist was of immigrant stock. American prosperity, progress, and social stability were based on the regular supply of foreigners willing to take up any work the country offered: "We could indulge our theories of equal opportunity for all . . . without menace to our comfort and well-being. The silent thousands from across the seas were always coming to fill the places of those who had moved up," she lectured the anti-immigration camp. Encoding the newcomers, whom the nativists denounced as carriers of disease and anarchy, as peaceful and humble supplicants without a trace of subversive class consciousness, she continued, "They asked no questions, made no complaint, accepted with humility what God and the great American people visited upon them" (COC, 633). The focus of her immigration discourse in "Can Our Civilization Maintain Itself," an article she published in the *Atlantic Monthly* in November 1920, was exclusively on gains to her America. This very exclusiveness of focus on American interests enabled Cannon to perform the discursive acrobatics that rendered this pro-immigration stance compatible with the eugenic, racialized positions that became all-pervasive in those postwar years. In her essays on immigration, integrationist and exclusivist discourses intersect: on the one hand, Cannon subscribed to the myth of America as a place of refuge; on the other hand, she affirmed the Victorian differentiation between the "deserving" and the "undeserving poor," as well as its Marxian variant of proletariat and lumpenproletariat, Americanizing this differentiation by combining it with eugenic theories such as the differentiation between the racially "desirable" and "undesirable," and the chimera of racial homogeneity.

During World War I her adherence to eugenics—already a defining feature of her midwestern reformism, equipped with the authority of science from her studies at Radcliffe, and further strengthened in the Roosevelt years—gained fresh impetus and a powerful justification as scientific "truth" through the defining role that one of the family's closest friends, the devoted eugenicist Robert Yerkes, played in the development of army intelligence tests.[36] These tests, developed by "a group of hereditary determinists"[37] and given to approximately 1.8 million officers and enlisted men in 1917 and 1918, were officially designed to guarantee proper assignment for the individual soldier and thus improve the troops' efficiency. When the results were published, they became ammunition in one of the most aggressive immigration debates the country had ever witnessed and which culminated in the racially exclusive National Origins Act of 1924.[38] Under the impact of both this research and a rapidly escalating, increasingly racist immigration controversy, Cannon experienced a cooling of her original melting pot enthusiasm; all of a sudden, she wrote, "the pot seems full of ugly and menacing lumps," and, like so many fellow Anglo-Americans, she identified signs of "racial decay" (WI, 808, 810). Her response illustrates how intimately optimism and fear, democratic commitment and racialized perceptions intersected in the progressivist motivation.[39] The multiethnic and multicolored face that the nation increasingly displayed, the dramatic changes she observed in Boston's demographic structure,[40] began to frighten her, and consequently she sought refuge in an exclusivist national origins policy. As Peggy Pascoe has argued, this policy strove to redefine the United States "as a white republic," to divide "white 'ethnicity' from nonwhite 'race,'" and to "draw the boundary of whiteness around American citizenship."[41] It was time for Cornelia Cannon to act.

The army scientists around Yerkes developed two different sets of tests—the Alpha exam for men who were able to read and write English, and the Beta test for the illiterate and the non-English-speaking. On the basis of their test results, the men were grouped into five grades from A to E, A and B representing, in the lingo of the day, superior, C average, and D and E inferior intelligence. The results were devastating indeed: only 12 percent of white draftees made it into grades A and B, while 66 percent fell into grade C, and a total of 22 percent ended up in grades D and E, identified with the mental age of seven to twelve. The results were even more alarming when the tests focused on foreign-born men: while the entire white draft contained 22 percent of so-called inferior mental ability, the corresponding figure among the foreign-born totaled 46 percent; in the Polish draft it came to 70 percent, in the Russian draft 60 percent, and in the Italian draft 63 percent. African Americans, in a move illustrating that they were perceived as internal aliens, were studied separately and divided up into test groups based on, as Yerkes confirmed, "intensity of color";[42] 80 percent were relegated to grade D.[43]

The white results stunned a nation convinced that, racially, they represented the very top of the human scale, and the media responded accordingly, never bothering to question the quality of tests that produced such a rate of outright imbecility; the cry of "race preservation" was raised. "Rome had [misplaced] faith in the melting pot, as we have," the *Boston Herald* cautioned in an editorial of 1924. "It lost its instinct for race preservation, as we have lost ours. It flooded itself with whatever people offered themselves from everywhere, as we have done. It forgot that men must be selected and bred as sacredly as cows and pigs and sheep, as we have not learned."[44] The *Washington Post* warned against "hyphenates" eager to "play politics with the nation's blood stream."[45]

Cornelia Cannon joined those who cried out in panic. In February 1922 the *Atlantic Monthly* published her "American Misgivings," a fierce defense of American racial exclusiveness, justified by the tests. In his autobiography Dr. Cannon listed the most dangerous errors scientists committed: untested assumptions, incomplete tests, omitted controls, and faulty techniques, combined with neglect of detail and neglect of multiple causes, all of which culminate in unwarranted conclusions.[46] In her public campaign for racialized immigration legislation, Cornelia Cannon eagerly committed all of these errors. Like the majority of her fellow Americans, like the researchers responsible for the intelligence tests, she tolerated no doubts about the validity of the exams as such and consequently accepted their results at face value. She, too, was shocked at the high percentage of white men classified as intellectually inferior, and even more so at the results of the mental age classification that defined 47.3 percent "as morons," meaning adults "below the mental age of thirteen" (AmM, 147). There is nothing, she sighed, that America can do about the stock of "defectives" already on its territory,[47] but the nation must develop protective measures against the "morons" knocking at its gates, for "such individuals form the material of unrest, the stuff of which mobs are made, the tools of demagogues; for they are peculiarly liable to the emotional uncontrol which has been found to characterize so many of the criminals who come before our courts," she warned. "They are persons who not only do not think, but are unable to think; who . . . become a drag on the progress of civilization. . . . They are a menace which may compass our destruction" (AmM, 151).

The menace was all the more frightening in that this kind of immigrant did not merely endanger the social and political well-being of the American nation in its present state; the real threat was to "the future race." America had to be protected against that "ever-widening circle of his descendants, whose blood may be destined to mingle with and deteriorate the best we have," wrote Cannon, waving the eugenic red flag. Her solution rested with the uncontested power of science: intelligence testing through immigration officials will reduce the nation's "intake of defectives" (AmM, 151). Even more important, these tests will empower the country to keep the gates wide open for racially "deserving" and "desirable" immigrants—that is, those racially compatible common folk, those consanguine whites from abroad whom Walt Whitman had celebrated as "divine average" (AmM, 145), as well as those superior minds eager to escape from postwar Europe.

But what was the nation to do about those foreign-born "morons" already on American soil, those aliens from within whom the tests identified for all to see? Cannon was ready with a solution even for this problem when she reminded her readers of the difference between a right and a privilege. "Should not the goal of membership in the great Republic be attainable through special effort and distinct merit?" she challenged, evoking the American democratic definer of meritocracy. "Has not the time come to withhold the privilege and responsibility of citizenship from the majority of the new immigrants . . . whose intelligence is so far below that of the ordinary American, and bestow it only upon carefully selected members of the group?" (AmM, 154–55). The woman who bombarded her contemporaries with editorials on the duties of republican citizenship had no second thoughts about reconstructing civil rights as racially defined privileges for the "desirable" and "deserving" few as far as immigrants were concerned, as well as that other un-American element, "the negro," whose relegation to separate schools, thanks to the tests, acquired "justification other than that created by race-prejudice" (AmM, 156). No need to raise the question of criteria for belonging or exclusion, for as a result of science and objective testing, white America owned the truth. From Cannon's perspective—a combination of racialized perception and progressive faith in science and statistics—this was identical with the end of doubt: "Indeed, we may have to admit that the lower-grade man is material unusable in a democracy, and to eliminate him from the electorate, as we have the criminal, the insane, the idiot, and the alien" (AmM, 154). Her dread of racial decay caused her to take the exclusivist potential of Dewey's communities of inquiry[48] to a racialized extreme; she was, as her vocabulary illustrates, only a small step away from recommending sterilization, as my discussion of her birth control activities will confirm.

Only a few months later, in "Selecting Citizens," she escalated the argument: calling upon the nation to protect itself against the influx of racial "undesirables," she banned such immigrants from the human family by transforming them into essentially dangerous Others, a "poison against which we have no antidote" (SC, 325). In the past, immigration had been a blessing for the country because it "was of closely allied racial groups" (SC, 330), she contended, primarily of Anglo-Saxon and "Nordic" stock, people "like us" who guaranteed that America's destiny would continue to be white. The new immigration, however, was racially diverse, and Cannon felt so threatened by that racialized Other she constructed that she ceased to associate such people with humankind. In a deindividualizing process, she reduced them to dark hordes endangering Western civilization, to vermin infecting the body politic: "They come in far greater numbers, vermin infested, alien in language and in spirit, with racial imprints which can be neither burned out nor bred out, packs on their backs, leading little children by the hand. And like the hordes of old they are destined to conquer us in the end, unless by some miracle of human contriving we conquer them first" (SC, 330). There was no way in which she could extend notions of human progress and perfectibility to these essentially undesirable Others; she removed them from her concept of history as progress by denying them, on racial grounds, the very capacity for development: "There are certain races that show a somewhat similar incapacity for growth and development, even under conditions which produce marked alterations in other races," she insisted (SC, 331).

Her list of nonwhite, nonprogressive, and therefore undesirable sub-humanity included "the Tartar" as "a race which has always been barbarian," as well as "the Mexican, the South Sea Islander, the African negro [sic]" (SC, 331). A few paragraphs later "the Jew"[49] and "the Asiatic" (SC, 332)[50] were added to this panel of "unassimilable elements," to be excluded because they "bring in social disease" (SC, 333). Succumbing to her racial hysteria, Cannon left no doubt what the answer to her rhetorical question "Are we not justified in exercising discrimination before adding such strains to our social blood" (SC, 331) would have to be, and she lauded the nation's moves to fortify boundaries of whiteness around "her" America by passing racially restrictive immigration legislation as "the greatest social advance of the last decade" (SC, 330). The Coolidge administration realized her white American dream with the National Origins Act of 1924.

The racialized eclecticism of Cannon's constructions of Americanness is further illuminated if we read her articles parallel to semiprivate comments made during this period. While her immigration essays classed "the negro" with other undesirable and "alien" elements and explicitly justified school segregation, she was appalled when Harvard's President Lowell, in 1923, banned African Americans from freshman dormitories, accusing him of throwing "us back into a wretched past." On the one hand, her critique was based on her respect for intellectual achievement; after all, these men had passed the Harvard admission exam. On the other, it reflected the debate on the eugenic underpinnings of the black improvement discourse of the Harlem Renaissance and New Negro intellectuals—Du Bois's call to "train and breed for brains, for efficiency, for beauty."[51] It is, however, important to keep in mind that for Cannon these students, whom black intellectuals and writers celebrated as personified challenges to the white supremacist paradigm, were by no means representative blacks; they were always and most definitely men of genius who had moved beyond "their race," exceptional blacks. She could support their intellectual endeavors without questioning her abhorrence of the "undesirable" and uneducated "negro." Even her outrage at Lowell's segregationist stance revealed her biases. "In such a heterogeneous democracy as ours, we must face association with all kinds!" she lamented, Americanizing the "white-man's burden." For "they are here, we are committed to a trial of democracy and, as Tom Perry says, 'we must pray for strength to bear democracy when we get it!'"[52]

Her anti-emancipatory and racialized discourse intersected effortlessly with her abhorrence of Klan violence and of racial segregation practiced against the black elite, that is, people "like us"—almost. The philosopher Kwame Anthony Appiah explains the all-pervasiveness of race-defining readings like Cannon's as a problem of hermeneutics: "The truth is that there are no races. . . . The evil that is done is done by the concept and by easy . . . assumptions as to its application. . . . What exists 'out there' in the world—communities of meaning, shading variously into each other in the rich structure of the social world—is the province not of biology but of hermeneutic understanding."[53] Cornelia James Cannon, the progressive voice determined "to remove the causes of human despair,"[54] reiterated what the silent Euro-American majority of her day thought, and the public response was encouraging indeed. America's major magazines—the *Atlantic Monthly,* the *North American Review, Harper's Monthly Magazine,* the *Radcliffe Quarterly, The Woman Citizen, Child-Welfare Magazine*—competed for her essays[55] and were eager to publish the comments and readers' responses her articles evoked. She was completely swamped with invitations to lecture. While her friend Robert Yerkes was beginning "a strategic retreat"[56] from the army research project and its conclusions, she embraced her eugenic mission. She traveled and talked, invigorated by the praise heaped upon her, jubilant at the controversies she triggered; elated that, with her husband lionized as one of the country's pioneer scientists, she, too, was making a career. Hers was a name people recognized; hers was a voice to which they were eager to listen. Friends and family stared in wonder. "But has the maiden no philanthropic doubts?" they asked in mock despair at her forty-sixth birthday celebration. Their answer: "Not a doubt!"[57]

No, she harbored no doubts. In fact the success of her articles invigorated her to a point where she decided to move beyond magazine publication and bring together her ideas on "the future race" in a book. She worked on it for almost a year during 1922 and 1923. This time, however, she faced disappointment: even publishers who clamored for her political essays refused to consider *Social Builders.* "I had a very pleasant interview with Mr. Sedgwick [Ellery Sedgwick, editor of the *Atlantic Monthly*], but my book is apparently too *heavy*," she complained.[58] The problem was not that the book was "heavy"; it was fragmented, eclectic, lacking in sustaining argument. Cannon did not understand that, in approaching the book form, she would have to take a qualitative leap. For this, however, she was unprepared: why improve on a style, on a discursive strategy that was immensely successful in the magazine market? Rather than taking a critical look at her approach to the enterprise, she blamed the publishers for lack of political stamina, and once she had discarded *Social Builders,* she simply raided the manuscript for a whole series of individual articles; many promptly found publishers.

It is possible that the decision to abandon *Social Builders* came easily because Cannon was in the process of negotiating for herself a position on one of the most fiercely contested reform movements of the day: birth control. It was a complicated, at times painful process because it brought to light the conflicting motives of her reformism: memories of her mother's suffering, her commitment to eugenic feminism, her racial anxieties, her role as the scientist's helpmate, her dread of "race suicide," her love of performing as rebel.

When Theodore Roosevelt in 1913 denounced a race as "worthless and contemptible" if its men are no longer capable of working and fighting hard and "its women cease to breed freely,"[59] his harangue not only articulated the widespread Euro-American fear of racial displacement and launched a powerful assault on the emerging American birth control movement but also had a side effect he did not anticipate: suffragists, advocates of voluntary parenthood, and feminists, whose attitude toward birth control had been rather ambivalent, were appalled by the president's assault on woman's autonomy. For the first time women activists spoke up publicly for every woman's right to practice birth control.[60] In 1916 the battle reached Boston and with that Cornelia James Cannon's front yard.

Margaret Sanger came to Boston to spread the birth control message in lectures one of her biographers describes as a genuine mixture of "soapbox provocation" and "a quieter approach based on scientific and sentimental arguments."[61] That same year the Fabian socialist Van Kleek Allison was arrested for distributing Emma Goldman and Ben L. Reitman's eugenic pamphlet *Why and How the Poor Should Not Have Many Children,* defined as obscene by the Comstock Act. His defense committee was a heterogeneous group, bringing together people with radical leanings as well as liberals, social workers, scholars, ministers, and physicians, individuals drawn to the organization by such diverse motives as the defense of free speech and women's rights, even eugenicists. Among them were acquaintances of the Cannons, including the Reverend Paul Blanshard, whom Cornelia admired for his vigorous protests against the influence of the Catholic Church and whose *American Freedom and Catholic Power* she was to distribute when it came out in 1949; their neighbor Dr. Mabel A. Southard; the Harvard eugenicist Edward M. East and his wife; and the suffragist, birth control activist, and botanical illustrator Blanche Ames Ames. This committee was reconstituted as the Birth Control League of Massachusetts (BCLM); its constitution of November 1916 identified its main objectives: "To educate and organize public opinion in order to secure the repeal of all laws which make it a criminal offence to print, publish or impart information regarding the control of birth by preventing conception through harmless scientific methods [and] . . . to aid in the development of the best methods by which those qualified to possess such knowledge may be given instruction under proper auspices."[62]

Cornelia Cannon's name does not appear in the League papers, and her family letters of that year contain no sign of involvement. For a woman whose sense of independence must have been offended by Roosevelt's misogyny, she was curiously silent in the war of words over birth control that raged in the country as well as in her hometown. Can her silence be read as tacit support of Roosevelt's position? After all, Cannon saw herself primarily as a eugenicist, and the eugenic movement of the prewar period "damned birth control for its dysgenic effect. The best people were already limiting their families too much," its proponents argued.[63] Its leading representatives, among them the admired Charles Davenport, put up loud opposition to Sanger. Also, the position Cannon later adopted in the Massachusetts birth control movement invites this reading, and her family correspondence reveals that she embraced birth control only after it took a eugenic turn in the twenties.

To explain her abstinence in 1916 we must also recall her personal situation—her memories of years defined by childlessness, and her attitude toward her husband's professional situation. Cornelia's uppermost concern during the first years of married life had been not birth control but infertility. The despair she had experienced made it impossible for her to perceive childbearing in other than positive terms. How could she join the ranks of those who, to make their point, used metaphors of bondage, pain, and suffering for what she had desired most: motherhood? Cannon had little personal interest in promoting birth control before the birth of her children, and she had no time to participate once they arrived in rapid succession.

Of equal importance was her concern that public activities in support of birth control would be detrimental to her husband's career. After all, he was a highly visible member of the medical profession, and she was painfully aware of its hostility toward a movement it identified with radicalism and feminism. In 1917 the *American Journal of Obstetrics and Gynecology* denounced birth control activists as "radical socialists" and "anarchists," wincing at the "unrestrained harangue of the reformer, usually a lay person with little conception of the medical aspect involved," who spread "the spirit of license."[64] The reasons for this belligerence were manifold. Gynecologists and obstetricians were still struggling to establish their authority as members of the medical profession, and they feared that any association with a movement of dubious political standing would lose them valuable territory. Also, many physicians of the day shared the eugenic apprehension over declining birthrates among the white American middle classes. Cannon knew that her involvement with birth control would embarrass her husband, and her loyalty was strong enough to keep her at home. As John K. Fairbank remembered, she was convinced "that a husband's work is sacred and he must be given his chance to accomplish it."[65]

The most powerful deterrent, however, was her firm rootedness in eugenics, including her dread of race suicide and racial displacement, her classist fear of "stone-age individuals" breeding excessively, and her belief in the salvational power of positive eugenics. Each of these fears, each of these hopes, was confirmed by the allies from the eugenic camp among whom she moved, first and foremost scholars from the Harvard community such as the biologist Edward East, the climatologist Robert De Courcey Ward, and Robert M. Yerkes, to name a few. Only her new definition of self acquired during World War I would eventually liberate her from both domestic and outside concerns and inspire her to take up birth control as her new mission. It took Walter B. Cannon's war research and his postwar activities on the Committee for Research in Problems of Sex,[66] on the one hand, and Cornelia's work with the Radio boys and her deepening interest in eugenics and immigration, on the other, to convince her that birth control was an issue inextricably interwoven with her nation's racial fate. And above all it took the eugenic turn and commitment of the birth control movement.

On a very personal level, Cannon's interest in birth control was originally inspired by her mother's pioneering dedication. In a memoir written for the family in 1965, Cornelia recalled listening, as a teenager, to conversations between Frances James and her friends "on limiting the size of a family."[67] Even more important were her memories of how her mother, afflicted with a heart condition, had suffered during her pregnancies, and she never forgot how frail this always vigorous woman had appeared after the birth of her last child. She knew that her mother loved her children, but she also knew that she chafed under her biological bondage. The memory of these tribulations, combined with her belief in a woman's right to take control over her life, sanctified her decision.

Yet another experience provided moral support: her exposure to the conditions of poor women in East Cambridge and Boston. Walter B. Cannon's work among the Boston poor during her Radcliffe years had aroused her awareness that there were women for whom motherhood was nothing but a burden. Years later, when she was doing volunteer work among Portuguese immigrant women in East Cambridge, this abstract awareness was translated into ugly reality when her sentimental response to the death of a baby, "as beautiful as a waxen image," clashed with the exhausted mother's stoicism. "Remembering my own mother's agony of grief at the death of my baby sister, I tried to think of something comforting to say," she wrote, "but she did not listen to me. She did not shed a tear, but she said, stonily, 'I have had eleven children and this is the fourth to die. . . . I had no money for a doctor or for milk, so they died.'"[68] Cannon felt it was her duty to use her talent as an organizer, her rhetorical skills, and her privileged status as the wife of a prominent Harvard professor to help these women gain control over their lives. Contraceptives could no longer be a privilege of the well-educated and wealthy. For Cornelia Cannon, reformer, the poor needed birth control to improve their lot; for Cornelia Cannon, eugenicist, American society needed the poor to limit their fertility for the sake of social and generic stability.

On 12 November 1921, Cornelia wrote to her mother from New York: "Here I am, enjoying what Wilma calls 'Mother's Sabbatical,'" the First National Birth Control Conference of November 11–13, which Margaret Sanger held at the Plaza Hotel, in parallel with the convention of the American Public Health Association. Finally Sanger had gained the endorsement of respected sociologists, all associated with the eugenics movement—among them Thomas Nixon Carver, Edward M. East, Irving Fisher, F. H. Giddings, Ellsworth Huntington, Raymond Pearl, Lothrop Stoddard, and Warren Thompson.[69] It was a special triumph indeed that Sanger's meeting on contraceptive techniques "was so crowded that late-comers could not squeeze in," and she was amused to see so many doctors, each one "apparently surprised to see his confrères there!"[70] As a highlight Sanger scheduled a mass meeting at Town Hall, where Harold Cox, former British MP and editor of the *Edinburgh Review,* was to deliver an address on the topic "Birth Control, Is It Moral?"

When Cox and Sanger arrived, the entrance to the auditorium was barred by police. Sanger succeeded in slipping in and was hoisted up to the platform by Stoddard but could not make herself heard; the police dragged her from the stage.[71] Cannon was among the indignant crowd, thunder-struck when a Captain Thomas Donohue of the New York City police ordered the meeting closed "at the order of Monsignor Joseph P. Dineen, Secretary of Archbishop Patrick J. Hayes."[72] What she witnessed was to her an ugly, intolerable conspiracy of the Irish American political machine and the Catholic oligarchy to undermine the most fundamental American rights. She was so enraged that she could not even wait to get home to inform her mother. "I am sitting in the train," she wrote, "after a night of tremendous excitement. . . . That is what our land of freedom has come to under Irish Catholic control. I am becoming a fanatical anti-Catholic. The whole thing is terribly serious." That night she made up her mind that from now on friends and family would just have to get used to seeing her in the front line: "I am going back to put the matter to the proof, in Mas-sachusetts, and see if freedom of speech there is in control of Cardinal O'Connell. The blood of my Protestant forebears is boiling in my veins!"[73]

In November *The Woman Citizen* published her article "Freedom of Speech," in which she denounced the archbishop's interference as "an in-fringement of the fundamental rights of American citizens to freedom of assembly and of speech that should rouse every thinking American to the danger to our liberties such an encroachment implies." The article was Cannon's call to arms, for "if we fail in this responsibility," she rebuked her readers, "we accept the yoke and become slaves in spirit, perhaps in time in the flesh."[74] Mobilizing her acquaintances, she was, in her words, "speaking at every meeting at which I have a chance, telling my experience of the conference."[75]

Cannon's was not a moderate temper, and her love of performance found ample outlet in her dramatization of Sanger's martyrdom. It is easy to envision her, a small but energetic woman—John K. Fairbank said that she "radiated energy like an atomic pile"[76]—with her hair always in disarray, reenacting the terrors of this New York night before a distinguished Cambridge or Boston audience, trying to inspire them with her fury as well as with her determination to fight the enemies of Americanness. From a letter to her mother we get a glimpse at the nature of her performances: "I am still burning with rage. I know how Latiner and Ridley must have felt when they were burned at the stake, *glad* that they could testify for the truth and against tyranny in their suffering. I wished I too could be burned or flayed for freedom." The letter culminates in an impassioned paraphrase of Claude McKay's "If We Must Die": "It may be we shall be snowed under and vanquished by ignorance and bigotry, but let us at least die fighting."[77] Eventually her rage calmed down, but the experience transformed Cannon's relationship to the movement. She realized that its advocates were in for a long struggle, and it would have to be fought against forces that were among the nation's most powerful. "I am getting back to 'normalcy' since my liberty frenzy and see that the battle will have to be fought to all eternity and probably never won," she admitted a few weeks later.[78] Cannon's life was devoted to many causes—school reform, charity, women's rights, the Loyalist struggle in Spain, opposition to McCarthyism—but to the very end of her life her interest in birth control and eugenics never waned, and she would have been delighted to see that the *Boston Herald*, in its obituary of 12 December 1969, celebrated her as a "Birth Control Proponent."

Though a mother of five and certainly not, as Linda Gordon puts it, a "leisured wife," Cannon was an almost perfect representative of those "relatively privileged women" turned reformers in the 1920s and 1930s who joined the eugenic campaign,[79] and whom Gordon evokes as important birth control supporters in *Woman's Body, Woman's Right:* "Whether themselves 'career women' or, more commonly, leisured wives able to do volunteer work, they were a generation reaping the benefits of a relative social emancipation, one that applied only to their class [and race]. They could have 'help' with the housework or at least with the children; they could get effective contraceptives to reduce the number of their children; they enjoyed social acceptance for their work in the public arena."[80]

When Cannon began to attend birth control meetings, Margaret Sanger, the movement's most controversial spokeswoman, had not yet discarded all her radical connections, her working-class sympathies, and her feminism, and Sanger's American Birth Control League (ABCL), as well as its local Massachusetts chapter, were still small and heterogeneous; but the fundamental, largely conservative reorientation, which would result in the withdrawal of its radical clientele, was already under way: its professionalization, the replacement of feminist values by family values, an alliance with the eugenic camp. It was this very reorientation that made it possible for women like Cannon to join. Sanger's early feminism, her involvement in the free love debate, her association with Emma Goldman and Ben Reitman's anarchism, had conflicted with Cannon's sense of morality and her progressive patriotism. As Sanger's approach became more pragmatic, however, and she began to narrow down birth control from the right of any woman to manage her fertility to the right of married couples to decide on the size of their families and, ultimately, to an instrument of positive and negative eugenics, Cannon saw her belief in the need for biological engineering and her visions of the ideal white American family confirmed and decided to cooperate.

Despite her personal longing for space and mobility Cannon never ceased to affirm the family as the vital center of American society, the domestic realm as a social microcosm, and despite her sexual inhibitions, she realized that a happy marriage is intimately related to a fulfillment of sexual needs. Margaret Sanger's early writings confirmed this dictum: in both *Woman and the New Race* (1920) and *The Pivot of Civilization* (1922), which Cannon read eagerly, Sanger decried the practice of abstinence, for physicians and the Catholic Church the only legitimate form of birth control, as destructive to marriage and an outright "absurdity."[81] In addition, Havelock Ellis's *Studies in the Psychology of Sex* (1897–1910), of central importance to Sanger's evaluation of sexuality,[82] strengthened Cannon's interpretation of sex as a positive good in marriage and thus in society.

Yet how could a free expression of mutual love take place if women were denied the right to protect themselves against the consequences? Birth control thus was more than a woman's right to claim control over her body; for

Cornelia Cannon it became the ultimate precondition for a good marriage and a happy domestic life, which again was the precondition for a stable society. Her attitude found confirmation in her husband's postwar work on the Committee for Research in Problems of Sex, which Robert Yerkes chaired and on which Dr. Cannon served for twenty-five years. As during his service in France, his primary interest was certainly not birth control; it was venereal disease and its disastrous effect on "the future race," but he supported the dictum of the American Social Hygiene Association that sexual fulfillment in marriage was the best guarantee against men seeking adventures in red light districts, where the chance of contracting the disease was great.[83] His expertise added the scientist's authority to what his wife knew to be true, thus strengthening her determination to work with those forces within society which she had come to perceive as the true champions of the American family they affirmed: birth control advocates.

In *Woman and the New Race* of 1920 Sanger defended birth control against Roosevelt's charge of race suicide by arguing that its true objective was supportive of his program in that it propagated the use of scientific knowledge to improve the genetic structure of American society. By adopting eugenic and neo-Malthusian doctrines, she attracted a powerful new clientele to her ranks: the disciples of eugenics. Sanger's activities had impressed leading American eugenicists such as Charles Davenport and Edward M. East from the start, but their initial response had been ambivalent, if not outright negative. On the one hand, they shared the fear of Anglo-American race suicide and dysgenic population trends which Roosevelt painted so graphically, and they realized that birth control was most likely to be practiced by those they were encouraging to have large families: the white middle and upper classes, educated Americans, the best of "the race." On the other hand, they believed in the different fertility of races and classes, and they warned against the rapid increase of non-white immigrants, the black population, and the so-called "unfit," such as paupers, criminals, or the physically and mentally impaired. This demographic trend confirmed the need for active regulative interference. These "undesirable" segments of the American population must be discouraged from "breeding excessively" by providing them with effective contraceptive devices, by teaching and, if necessary, forcing them to practice birth control, they argued; even compulsory sterilization became an option and would be implemented in many states in the twenties and thirties.

The solution that the eugenicists and birth controllers finally agreed on in the 1920s was a dual program of positive and negative eugenics, encouraging the reproduction of the "fit" while discouraging that of the "unfit." It was a thoroughly racialized and classist program, and the Cannons embraced it unconditionally as a dogma that harmonized with their progressive and pragmatic notion of the role science was to play in shaping their perfect America. For them, eugenics was, to adopt Donald K. Pickens's definition, a program of "scientific genealogy by assisting the direction of human evolution toward efficiency and more effective social control which were twin values of American progressivism."[84] Yet the Cannons, like Margaret Sanger and Emma Goldman, would have been horrified had anybody attached the label "racist" to their eugenically defined birth control activities.

The association that post–World War II scholarship would make between eugenics, the extreme right, and especially the atrocities committed by the Third Reich in the name of eugenics must not blind us to the fact that in the late nineteenth century and the first three decades of the twentieth century, eugenic doctrines in the United States had disciples in all political camps—among conservatives as well as liberals and progressives, socialists and anarchists, even transcending the American racial divide between black and white, as Daylanne English's *Unnatural Selections* illustrates. Conservative pseudoscientists like Lothrop Stoddard stirred racial phobia through books such as *Revolt against Civilization: The Menace of the Underman* and *The Rising Tide of Color against White World-Supremacy*—publications that were favorably reviewed by radical birth control advocates such as Henry Havelock Ellis.[85] Emma Goldman's oeuvre contains a solid core of eugenic assumptions; Jack London fathered a race of superman socialists in his novel *Iron Heel* (1908); and W. E. B. Du Bois, Nella Larsen, and other Harlem Renaissance intellectuals dreamed of improving "the race" through careful mate selection. In *American Eugenics* Nancy Odover argues that "the hard truth is that science, and even mere scientific conjecture has often functioned as consensus builder. The divide between reactionaries and reformers, nationalists and leftists, conservatives and feminists has not been the yawning chasm we suppose." Citing Loren Graham, she maintains that "the 'natural alliance' between eugenics and conservative and fascist sentiments 'was not logically preordained . . . and was not perceived in the early twenties by large numbers of radical social critics.'"[86]

Cornelia Cannon moved closer to advocating birth control after witnessing the dramatic event at Sanger's New York mass rally in November 1921, but throughout the 1920s the contributions she made were of a nature that equally enabled her to support activities she perceived as important and to maintain that kind of relative invisibility essential to protecting her husband's position within the medical profession. As late as 1924 she complained, "I want to get into the fight but Walter shows a grave reluctance to having me take part in anything inviting such unpleasant notoriety."[87] This problem evaporated when transformations within the movement—in particular its shift from feminism to eugenics—attracted increasing numbers of doctors. Also, the League ceased to offer contraceptives through volunteers and instead directed women to sympathetic doctors. Once this reorientation was accomplished, physicians began to join—a professionalization and a new respectability that Sanger endorsed. It was in the late 1920s and in the 1930s—that is, in the decade when the League responded most directly to the demands of this new professional membership by adopting "a quiet but steady concentration on a doctors-only bill"[88]—that Cannon finally transformed herself from a quietly active fellow traveler into a trailblazer with a clearly defined eugenic agenda.

The eugenic enthusiasm that formed the seedbed for Cannon's birth control activities found its strongest expression in the form of positive eugenics she practiced in her domestic realm. She herself was a proud mother of five and would have liked an even larger family had not health problems interfered. The way she celebrated her offspring, and the ways she presented them to the public once she had become a celebrity, make it quite clear that this was more than just an expression of maternal infatuation; at its core was a powerful sense of eugenic obligation and entitlement. This became even clearer when her children married and had families of their own. Cannon praised the beautiful, bright mates they chose, and each new grandchild was presented to the world with an enthusiasm that was embarrassing even for her children,[89] but which makes sense when we remember that she perceived each baby her family produced as an invaluable contribution to "the future race."

CHAPTER 6

"Stone-Age Individuals"
The Clan Betrays

THE RENEGOTIATION OF SELF THAT CORNELIA JAMES CANNON performed in the 1920s found an outlet, as we have seen, in intense reform activities and a volley of essays on major social and political issues of the day. Their common denominator was the racial composition of the future America, and the racial phobias she expressed, the eugenic solutions she prescribed, brought her widespread public acclaim. This enthusiastic response of so many fellow white Americans encouraged Cannon to move beyond the essay toward the genre she most admired: the novel.

Novel writing had always been on her life's itinerary. Now, in this difficult and inspiring postwar decade, she remembered this dream—during these years when, on a personal level, she and her husband were struggling with their memories and silences; when Cornelia's need for mobility clashed with family duties; when, on a broader scale, dread of racial displacement, fear of political and social disruption, the longing for continuity, and progressive reformism coexisted side by side. "Privately, I confess the world is moving so fast that I am terrified to find myself on the conservative side!" she admitted to her mother on 7 August 1919. It was an expression of self-doubt exceptional in her correspondence, for as a rule her letters of those years continued to affirm her role as the manager-woman. But obviously there was also a powerful urge to move beyond that smooth surface; consequently she needed to develop modes of communication that would enable her to deal with issues she found incompatible with the persona of her construction. Adhering almost naïvely to a nineteenth-century differentiation between fact and fiction, she felt that, under the guise of fiction, she could roam freely in new territories. Not only would fiction enable her to raise issues too intimate for her correspondence, but also it would attract an even larger and more heterogeneous audience to the vital eugenic message she had to convey. As it was for Charles Dickens, Elizabeth Gaskell, and Charles Kingsley in the England of the Industrial Revolution, and Harriet Beecher Stowe in the slavery controversy, the novel would be her medium for warning the nation of racial decline and designing viable alternatives to the dreaded race apocalypse. The historical earthquake which had transformed her and her world provided the material for her first exercise as a novelist. In the early 1920s she began to write *The Clan Betrays,* a text she continued to rework for more than a decade. It remained unpublished.

Cannon set out to write a novel on the tribulations of an American couple during the war and its aftermath. Approximately half of the manuscript's 427 pages center on this issue. The narrative she produced is a thought-provoking, multidimensional representation of war and its transformational impact on women and men. Unfortunately Cannon made the beginner's mistake of trying to say all that was important to her in a single text. Instead of concentrating on the war novel, she actually ended up juggling four potentially different novels: a novel on World War I, a novel on intermarriage, a novel on machine politics, and, unavoidably, a novel on immigration and Americanization. She could not help losing control over her material, and finally, after several vain attempts at rewriting—the last one in the 1930s, after the success of *Red Rust*—she gave up. The manuscript ended up in the attic in Franklin, unknown to her heirs, and perhaps forgotten even by herself.[1]

As we saw earlier, the novel's heroine is Justine Chase, an educated white woman from New England. During the war she volunteers in a Hostess House, where she meets Lieutenant Peter Burns, an officer of Irish descent. When Peter receives his deployment orders, they marry, and after the war Justine finds herself the wife of a virtual stranger. They move to the city where his Irish kin live; problems of class and differences in religious background and education surface, and husband and wife must face these issues in the midst of a hostile Irish American Catholic environment. The Irish ward boss manipulates Peter's leadership qualities, popularity, and skills, but when the leaders of the machine force on Peter conduct incompatible with his values, he defies them. They destroy his political career: the clan betrays.

The first novel within *The Clan Betrays* is an ambitious attempt to rewrite World War I from the perspective of a white middle-class American woman. It not only constitutes a reply to a public discourse that defined war as a male domain,[2] but also questions the widely held assumption that as war was male property, the war novel must be written by men, deal with the male business of fighting and violence, and focus on male protagonists.[3] The awareness of killing, mutilation, and destruction is ever present in Cannon's narrative, but these events take place in another world, as dark background music. What Cannon delineates is how people, and especially women, on the home front coped with events that changed their lives in every respect imaginable. War, she insists, cannot be defined in military terms only. Though experienced differently, its transformational power is just as dramatic at home as it is in the trenches; it alters the women who stay behind, the children left without fathers, as fundamentally as it does the soldiers. Cannon's novel is based on the awareness that history—even the history of war—is a composite of HIS stories and HER stories.

As with every writing project she tackled, Cannon enjoyed researching her material extensively, but for this novel she also relied heavily on personal experience. Her preparatory reading focused on studies dealing with the impact their exposure to violence had on men, and with the psychological predicaments they encountered on their return. Her friend Robert Yerkes, who was to conduct research projects on these issues during World War II, was quizzed relentlessly. She fell back on her husband's war correspondence, and she absorbed his every remark, just as she listened to conversations between him and fellow veterans. But at the center of her text are her own experience and the strategies she developed: the pain she suffered at parting, the fear that beset and the uncertainties that besieged her, her community activities and the joy of service—and especially the frustration at finding the returning man a stranger, the anger and pain caused by self-protective silence. Not surprisingly she set the plot in an environment that had been of utmost importance for her: a Hostess House in an unidentified New England town.

Although Cannon's protagonist is a young, unmarried woman at the beginning of the novel, it makes sense to see her as the writer's idealized self-portrait. Justine has none of the attributes that characterize the heroine of contemporary popular romance—that slender girl of striking beauty, vulnerability, and innocence. Justine's is an attractiveness defined as stability, health, endurance, strength, and common sense; she is less the playful lover than the reliable helpmate, the model white woman of eugenic discourse, the distillation of "an American phenotype."[4] Justine's beauty "was not of a type to excite sudden emotion. The graceful poise of her head possessed dignity as well as beauty. Her hands . . . were beautifully formed but they were the tools of service. . . . Her skin had the pallor which is . . . the beautiful white of perfect health, and the red of her lips was the brighter by contrast" (*CB*, 5). Though she is only twenty-four, Justine's body is that of a fertile woman: "rounded and full, [it] seemed designed to carry burdens and to do the work of the world without too much nervous friction or physical fatigue" (*CB*, 11). The maturity of her form mirrors that of Justine's personality; in that she can represent the emotional turmoil to which Cannon, a woman in her early forties, had been exposed. Justine thus personifies Cannon's ideal of white womanhood, and the author so identified with her invention that she became unable to move beyond the ideal; Justine is Cornelia minus her sharp tongue, her ability to hurt, her unbridled spontaneity, her self-irony, and her sarcasm.

Justine grew up in rural New England, a life of reading and contemplation, security and continuity, disrupted by war. She "had been caught up, like a feather in a hurricane, by the monstrous effort of a republic to turn its men into fighting machines in a few brief weeks" (*CB*, 2). Although Cannon uses metaphors of contemplation in delineating her protagonist's background, the choices she has her make once the war destroys her solitude are those of an active, creative mind: she joins the Hostess House, where she can do work that is "a part of the same gigantic effort in which [her father and her brother] were engaged" (*CB*, 24) while it adheres to traditional female role ascription. The Hostess House becomes a supra-home, and Justine not merely a mother for all but a *mater dolorosa*, a paragon of service, devotion, and suffering.

Cannon experienced her Hostess House activities as personal liberation; the representation of this episode in her novel, however, confirms conventional gendered notions of work and service, the "separate spheres" doctrine of the day: the men carry the burden of defending democracy, and they can do so with confidence because they know they have reliable helpmates in their women. Men and women in *The Clan Betrays* move in different, clearly defined worlds, and the novel never questions the legitimacy of these gendered realms. Cannon encodes them affirmatively as male heroism and female self-denial. What she challenges, however, are hierarchical definitions ascribing higher value to the work of men—fighting and killing—than to the work of women: healing and nurturing. To make her point, she relies on the authority of a male voice, that of her model officer and man, Lieutenant Burns: "Thank God they've let the women help in this man's war. . . . We'd be in a bad way without them" (CB, 51). He uses the term "help," thus defining the women's contribution as auxiliary to the soldier's, but he also insists that it is as essential to the war effort as the men's fighting—a statement in which the contradictions of Cannon's creed surface. Affirmation of established gender constructs intersects with subversions of gendered hierarchies, deference to male authority with egalitarian feminist rhetoric.

The Clan Betrays perceives disruption as the defining quality of war. War is the destroyer, a force beyond human control that brutally interrupts the life plans people have constructed. But war is also the revolutionary breaking down of established barriers, the unifier negating social conventions, the enemy of stagnation. Cannon illustrates this social Darwinist reading of the First World War by dramatizing its transformational impact on courtship and marriage. Justine, who grew up in a class-conscious, ethnically homogeneous community with firmly established norms, is thrown into a world that defies this sense of organic growth, stability, and homogeneity. People who might face death tomorrow have no time to waste on the rituals of the past; they grasp the moment, and in that they challenge the old order—carpe diem as an act of survival and a motor for change.

The full meaning of this revolution strikes Justine when she meets Lieutenant Peter Burns. She is attracted to this tall, "handsome man with dark heavy hair and deep-set blue eyes," aroused by a voice of "a rich vibrating quality which gave Justine a start of pleasure" (CB, 13–14). Her interest is increased when she discovers in him the natural leader of men, the American meritocrat who unites integrity, joie de vivre, a good sense of humor, skill, and devotion, the ability to command and the willingness to nurture, a strong sense of individuality and responsibility for the other. These qualities endear him to his fellow soldiers, who gladly submit to his guidance. He embodies Justine's ideal of white American manhood.

Justine and Peter are thrown together in an artificial world not really theirs; time is a phenomenon over which they have no control: "So many of the bars of convention were down that men and women of widely different race and culture could look at each other with a frank simplicity which ignored social barriers as though they were non-existent" (CB, 61). Peter is Irish American, working class, a Catholic; he is familiar with neither the books Justine reads nor the music she loves. But the war renders social divergence irrelevant—or, perhaps more adequately, the pressure it exerts leaves no space to reflect on class and ethnicity. The day Justine hears of her father's death on the battlefield, Peter is informed of his imminent deployment. All they can think of is to protect each other against these terrors by defining a space for the two of them in the here and now: they marry.

Cannon portrays her heroine's turmoil at these developments in detail—only to subject her to a solution that is stunning in its banality. Instead of taking on Justine's inner chaos as her artistic challenge, Cannon has her seek closure in the most passive of female roles, again, the *mater dolorosa*. The lovers who had no past together will have no future: "In the confusion of her thoughts one certainty remained, the clairvoyant picture of . . . the tall figure fallen, with arms flung out, and the deep-set, insistent eyes sealed over with the glaze of death. There could be no children. Something infinitely tender and profound stirred within her. Let her say whatever words would close those eyes in peace" (*CB*, 147–48). Justine agrees to marry Peter, but not because she loves him; she sacrifices herself to a man doomed. "The American women have got to show how they take loss" (*CB*, 124), she declared when news of her father's death reached her; will she now show the world how an American woman loves? A terrifying lesson indeed. Cannon transforms her into the ultimate woman as victim, into a sexless sacrificial lamb. The marriage is not consummated after the priest has performed the rites; the pure American soldier leaves a virgin bride to wait for his return—or his death. Justine's is the patriotic American virgin-woman's act of heroic self-denial. Yet Cannon denies Justine the fulfillment of this patriotic dream, just as her visions of heroic war-widowhood had failed her. Peter returns to claim his property, and Justine has to deal with a husband with whom she never expected to live. More important, the Peter who returns has little in common with the Peter to whom she waved good-bye; the relative stranger she married comes back as the absolute unfamiliar.

The war episode ends on a note of disillusion. Justine's sense of contribution, which characterizes the Hostess House chapters of *The Clan Betrays*, is replaced by images of exclusion and submission to the male itinerary that define the postwar episode. The sense of disempowerment Cannon creates mirrors the situation in which many American women, Cornelia Cannon included, found themselves after the war: once the men reclaimed their prerogatives, women were expected to return to their domestic realm and forget what they had learned while being out there, a withdrawal that did not come easy.[5] Cannon illustrates this point through Justine's self-protective response to Peter's stifling possessiveness, to his reluctance to grant a moment that is still all hers: "Justine was breathless under his wooing. She found no opportunity for her own emotions. They were overwhelmed by the surge of his" (*CB,* 183).

Yet Cannon seemed unaware of the potential that her protagonist's insight contains for her novel. Instead of focusing on Justine's quest for a postwar self, Cannon simply dropped this issue and developed a second narrative line by unceremoniously dumping Justine in the midst of an Irish American community. The second part of the novel deals exclusively with a topic that would resurface in most of the novels Cannon wrote during the next decade: the relationship between native-born (for her identical with Anglo-) Americans and the country's immigrant population, and the implication of this interaction for "the future race." Justine's struggle for self is forgotten once she becomes Peter's savior from the pitfalls of Irish anachronism, as she transforms herself into a spokeswoman for Cannon's exclusive white melting pot, a missionary of privileged Americanization.

"I went to an Americanization meeting, the other day, and I never heard such loud bands, such energetic singing, or smelled such strong smells!—I felt like a pale shadow of a person in the vigor and potency of that body of immigrants," Cannon reported in a letter of 2 February 1919 to her mother. Her description evokes those images of difference, of the dark, uncivilized Other that also characterized postwar nativist discourse. Yet her report does not close on the xenophobic note one would expect after these introductory remarks; it celebrates the vigor and rejuvenation those new citizens represent for America: "It was like dipping into the fountain of eternal youth—Our country is in no danger [of] petering out or becoming effete with all that potential in the background." The New World, Cannon never ceased to exclaim, would be protected against the ultimate biological exhaustion of the native Anglo-American population, provided it kept the doors open to those Europeans who were both racially and intellectually capable of dreaming and thus reinvigorating her white American Dream. *The Clan Betrays* was Cannon's first attempt to use the novel as a medium to teach her eugenic melting pot doctrine, and for her lecture on "choosing citizens," she focused on that group of immigrants against whom her ire had long been aroused: Irish Americans.[6]

Although her husband traced his family's paternal line back to the province of Ulster in Ireland,[7] Cannon's attitude toward the expansive Irish communities of Boston and Cambridge must be described as ambivalent at best and hostile at worst. Her response to the strike of the predominantly Irish American Boston police in September 1919 illustrates my point: Cannon chimed in with the public outcry at what Henry Cabot

Lodge condemned as a "sovietization of the country"[8] and applauded the mobilization of the Massachusetts National Guard and a citizens' militia of Harvard students and athletes. When Governor Calvin Coolidge supported the police commissioner's decision never to allow any of the strikers back on the force, Cornelia Cannon was jubilant: "We are at last in a state of victory in the police situation. . . . Gov. Coolidge has asserted the conscience of the Yankee as against the Irish clannish spirit." The issue was not social unrest; it was the Irish colonizing "her" city and the "genuine" America successfully fighting back, "the people" against the Irish mob: "That is really what the whole issue boiled down to—the whole people asserting their rights against the clan-spirit which is the breath of life to the Irish! They are a pernicious influence in our public life."[9] To this diatribe she added, "and as individual humans so attractive!"—the "some of my best friends" formula in which appreciation of the individual Other and bias against the "masses" intersect.

Cannon's Irish phobia was partly rooted in the pervasive anti-Catholicism of the Protestant mainstream, in her Unitarian upbringing and progressive leanings, that is, in her parents' affirmation of individualism, and in an antiauthoritarianism that clashed with everything Roman Catholicism represented for them. Cannon's attitude was further nourished by the xenophobic arguments the women's movement habitually employed in its struggle for suffrage. Thus Carrie Chapman Catt, in a speech in Iowa that was reprinted in the *Woman's Journal* of 15 December 1894, warned that the nation faced anarchy if Americans continued to blind themselves to the "danger" that lay "in the votes possessed by the males in the slums of the cities, and the ignorant foreign vote." For her, Irish Americans were "hoodlums" intent on reproducing "the horrors of the Old World when their numbers are sufficiently increased, and every ship load of foreigners brings them nearer to their object."[10] Finally, and most important, Cannon's anxieties about Irish Americans and Roman Catholicism were transformed into an increasingly aggressive hostility in response to the church's stand in the birth control controversy and its outspoken opposition to the eugenics movement and eugenic policy.[11]

When she first moved to the Boston area, Cannon entered a milieu where anti-Irish sentiments had been virulent and respectable for decades.[12] As early as 1894 the Harvard professor of climatology Robert De Courcey Ward had co-founded the Immigration Restriction League, which targeted Irish and Italian immigration to Boston.[13] Cannon began to associate Catholicism with the city's booming Irish population, and she felt personally threatened by a combination of three forces: the growing number of lower-class Irish Americans in the city, the political power they acquired through machine politics, and finally the influence of the Catholic Church on Massachusetts politics. She saw a Catholic Church not only determined to claim special prerogatives by maintaining its own schools,[14] social institutions, and hospitals but also extending its influence to what Cannon defined as genuine American property, such as public schools[15] and welfare organizations.

The city apparently had fallen into the hands of Irish American politicians, supported by their ward boss system and Irish machine politics.[16] The mayors of Boston and Cambridge, school committees, the city council: the Irish, and with them the Catholic Church, appeared omnipresent. Had not William Cardinal O'Connell, in a sermon preached on the centennial of his archdiocese in 1908, proclaimed the victory of the Catholic over the Puritan? Had he not boasted that the unwanted had taken possession of this once proud and hostile city? Whenever she became active in the public realm, Cannon had to deal with Irish administrators, principals, and mayors; whenever she advocated change, representatives of this network turned out to be her most powerful foes. No law could be passed, no reform program enforced, no school committee elected without Catholic meddling. She felt victimized by an Irish Catholic conspiracy. "I am becoming a fanatical anti-Catholic," she admitted.[17] Her misgivings were affirmed by the circle in which she moved. A family letter of 4 October 1920, describing a party with the Pierces, Perrys, Jacksons, and Whitings, reeks of the anti-Irish sentiments that were virulent in Anglo-American Boston, as in the country at large.[18] "We had a violent discussion about the Irish; Isabel [Whiting] for them and the rest thinking them utterly useless and abominable," she reported. "Allen [Jackson] said he thought we ought to have the slogan 'Ireland for the Irish,' embroidered on our collars. . . . I preferred 'To Ireland with the Irish.'" She concluded with outright condemnation: "No, the Irish Catholics are the worst and most hopeless element in our country." Such violent anti–Irish American sentiments were respectable wherever Cannon turned.

It is possible that she chose Irish Americans to illustrate her ideas on immigration in *The Clan Betrays* because she knew that the readers she hoped to instruct with this novel, educated Euro-Americans, were likely to share her anti-Irish phobia—readers who had been prepared for Cannon's narrative by the fierce anti-Irish stance of Stephen Crane's *Maggie, a Girl of the Streets* (1899), a model for Cannon's evocations of lower-class

Irish domestic and street life. On the basis of this accord she could then move toward the true objective of her novel's Irish American theme: a detailed delineation of her exclusivist "white" melting pot stance. To focus her readers' attention, she structured her narrative as a dialogue between mainstreaming and Othering discourses. On the one hand, Cannon celebrates the relationship between Justine, representative of Anglo-Saxon America, and Peter, the exceptional Irish American, as a tribute to a eugenically sound future America: on the other, she evokes the clash between this couple, idealized personifications of white melting pot eugenics, and the Irish American community—personification of inassimilable, essentialized, nonprogressive difference—as her warning of an American future that could spell political chaos and racial decline.

From the start the reader knows that Peter Burns is of Irish descent, but to sustain her integrationist discourse Cannon's characterization abstained from anything evoking difference from the Anglo-American norm. After all, Peter is an officer in the U.S. Army, and army life was expected to transform the Italian Giovanni, the Greek Alexis, the Russian Boris, the Irish Peter into all-American boys. In the face of that unifying challenge of war, Cannon's heroine never perceives Peter's Irishness as a problem; the idea that ethnic, religious, and class differences might resurface with a vengeance never strikes her. Her confidence in the war as the Americanizing force sustains her even when her brother reminds her that Peter is "not our kind" (*CB,* 164).

War as the great assimilationist: this is the formula imposed on Cannon's war chapters; but it is a discursive pose she could not and would not sustain. The novel teaches that Americanness is not an open category, a matter of choice. Consequently Cannon's mainstreaming war discourse has to be superseded by an exclusivist discourse: accessibility to Americanness is based on the exceptional white Other's racial compatibility with and his unconditional submission to the Anglo-American norm. To render her Irish American protagonist desirable for her New England maiden (and, with that, for herself and her reader), Cannon took recourse to a shift of paradigms: she raised him above the common crowd of Borises and Giovannis, thus distancing him from what she had just celebrated as representative American boys and reinstating him as exceptional. Whether it is his physical appearance—tall, dark (not red!) hair, blue (not green!) eyes—or his conduct as an officer, Peter Burns is a man of superior vigor, intelligence, and morality. Cannon could imagine him in intimate embrace with an Anglo-American woman and as father of "the future race" only after she

had deprived the Irish American of all traces of Irishness; her mainstreaming reconstructed Peter as "one of us."

The novelist makes her exclusivist-integrationist point by sending her
protagonist on a quest that takes him through the Slough of Despond—his
encounter with Irish separatism and machine politics—to the Heavenly
City of enlightened Americanness, and Justine metamorphoses from a faithful travel companion into a guide toward racial conversion and salvation.
Cannon invents a journey that leads from an artificially constructed
homogeneity—the Americanness imposed on the soldier—through a de-
tour of the exceptional ethnic—Peter's immersion into his ethnic community—to an arrival at a genuine American identity, which is earned
as a privilege in a demanding process of learning and adaptation, and
embraced as the superior mind's inevitable choice. At no point in the novel
does Cannon envision Americanization as a process of cultural exchange;
Americanization is always and exclusively reserved for the most advanced
segment of an inferior culture, personified by Peter, aspiring to the lifestyle
of the superior,[19] personified by Justine. As Cannon had contended in the
North American Review in 1922, "no civilization worthy of the name can
be a patchwork quilt. . . . The more promptly our new citizens throw off
the beliefs that kept them apart from the rest of us, the sooner they can
begin to make their individual and characteristic contribution to the bet-
tering of our civilization. Nevertheless there is upon us a special responsibility to help the immigrant through that transition" (WI, 816). In the war
episode Peter and Justine pose as equals, that is, as patriotic Americans in
service to their country, but the postwar narrative undermines this posture. Peter's modesty toward Justine bespeaks his awareness of his cultural
inferiority—another way for Cannon to document his qualifications for
Americanness.

The narrative laments as regressive any expression of Irishness that re-
surfaces in Peter. In the novel's identity quest sequence, an appalled Justine
watches as her all-American warrior husband sheds this shell to reemerge
as a second-generation Irish American: he takes her to his parents' home, a
place she finds "ugly and tasteless in the extreme" (*CB*, 197); he is reclaimed
by his Irish buddies; and he submits to the dictates of his Catholic mother.
From Justine's perspective the Peter who merges with the Irish community
loses his individuality as he betrays his Americanness; for her, his Irishness
is an anachronism he imposes on his true American self, a medieval clan
spirit defending itself against enlightened American individuality. "Why
should Peter belong to an Irish society?" she asks herself. "Surely he was

completely American if anyone was. Why should he be interested in per-
petuating an ancient allegiance which was never rightfully his?" (*CB*, 201).
The blame for Irish separatism is laid exclusively on the Irish, who reject
ethnic self-liquidation in the American melting pot; mainstream anti-Irish
sentiments, on the one hand, and legitimate pride in Irish culture, on the
other, as causes of what Cannon denounced as "clannishness" are never
mentioned. Justine is in the position of the tourist observing people who
belong to a different world; it is Benjamin Disraeli's two nations theory all
over again, redefined in terms of Boston's specific ethnic situation. Cannon
imagines a condescending Justine as an almost obstinately sympathetic observer who struggles to reach out to people who are Peter's kin.

She adopts none of Peter's Irish ways, however; the relationship survives
only because Peter, despite his relapse, continues to aspire to what she
represents: "The differences in their personal habits . . . might have been a
source of genuine unhappiness to Justine, if Peter had been less affection-
ately ready . . . to believe that all her ways were superior to his and asked
only to be shown how best to follow them" (*CB*, 235). She trains Peter,
and she is happy when he finally denounces his mother's parlor wallpaper,
with its huge pattern of purple roses, when he admits that he no longer
feels a stranger in their own elegant home. But then this is a home to
which he dares not bring his friends. She entertains his business partners
and family, but in their company she longs for true companionship—for
people of her culture. Peter eventually lives in two worlds, commuting
between them spontaneously, but for Cannon this is not enough. Justine,
Peter's teacher, lives in foreign territory, exiled, in a wilderness in which
her hermeneutic tools are rendered useless. Her love sustains her, but "for
the life to which he had brought her . . . she felt a mingled repulsion and
boredom" (*CB*, 292).

Cannon underscores her belief that Peter's return is a regressive move by
involving him with Irish machine politics and the dangers that Irish "clannishness" posed for her kind of America. In the context of Irish American
machine politics the novel's title, and especially Cannon's use of "clan,"
achieves a programmatic quality. After all, the novel was conceptualized
during the years when the Ku Klux Klan, profiting from widespread postwar social disruption and disorientation, on the one hand, and from the
racialized controversy over immigration and the African American Great
Migration, on the other, resurfaced nationwide, and triumphantly so,
boasting almost 4 million members in 1925. The Cannons were appalled
and especially enraged at the Klan's success in the North and Midwest;

they associated these new Klansmen with archaic pre- and anticiviliza-
tional backwardness as well as with the pseudo-medievalism of southern
slavery. The term "Klan," as the original Ku Klux Klan used it and which
its full name revealed—Knights of the Ku Klux Klan—referred to family groups among Scottish Highlanders claiming a common, often mythic
ancestry, a concept popularized in nineteenth-century America with the
commercial success of Sir Walter Scott's historical novels. "Klan," as appro-
priated by the Ku Klux Klan, stood for racially defined exclusiveness and
closedness—confirmed by the *kyklos*/circle reference—but it also evoked
the clandestine, the hidden and illicit, secret rituals and dark initiation
rites.[20] It was exactly this association with secret societies, a medieval clan
spirit, slavery, historical anachronisms, and antiprogressive terrorism that
Cannon manipulated through her choice of title and the novel's identification of Irish America with clannishness. In eugenic terms, southern Klansmen and Irish Americans alike became representatives of "the lower grades
of humanity" she had conjured up in 1922 as the nation's contaminated
contaminators in "What Ideals Do We Wish to Preserve": Klanspeople as
inferior racial stock poisoning the nation from within; Irish Americans
as representatives of the immigrant threat; and both determined to "re-
people" her America "with stone-age individuals" (WI, 808).

The clan as polluted polluter: it would be difficult to find a nobler objective for the racial rescue mission of Cannon's Anglo-Saxon heroine. Peter's
leadership qualities render him a "natural" leader for the Irish American
community. At first an enthusiastic Justine believes that the uneducated immigrants need politicians like him; she realizes, however, that in this ethnic
setting Peter will make a career only if he plays by the conspiratorial and
clandestine rules of the ward system—personified in the novel by the ward
boss Sullivan. It is not merely that Peter begins to use the manipulative
rhetoric of Irish stump oration; he condones election fraud, and his business prospers because he has become a part of the Irish machine. Machine
politics were widespread in the nineteenth- and early-twentieth-century
urban United States; they not only marked a professionalization of city
administration but also came to stand for corruption, violence, misuse of
power, conspiratorial networking, and patronage, undermining the definers of American democracy.[21] For an aspiring novelist like Cannon to take
on the machine was an important and legitimate objective, and it required
courage; Cannon had the stamina to do so. Her approach to corruption in
city politics was influenced by her progressive notions of civic responsibility, but also by her familiarity with the muckraking tradition in American

literature. Like the muckrakers she believed "in the ventilation of wrongs" through literature and in "the beneficent impact of an awakened public opinion."[22]

For many of her contemporaries this potential of literature was documented by the Roosevelt administration's investigations of the meatpacking industry after Upton Sinclair's novel *The Jungle* (1906) had exposed the scandalous conditions in the Chicago stockyards. *The Clan Betrays* takes on a serious sociopolitical issue; the problem is its monocausal approach: Cannon's argument is strictly biological. Rather than analyzing machine politics in the American context that served as its seedbed, she makes the machine the product of an essentialized anachronistic and contaminated Irishness, un-American by definition, but in its essential rottenness also immensely dangerous to the American body politic. Machine politics institutionalizes the Irish contaminated contaminator, perverting the American city hall into a source of contamination. Cannon's willful xenophobic blindness and biologistic reductionism are also implicated in the solution she designed for her protagonists: withdrawal.[23] And from her eugenic point of view there could be no other solution, for contact with the contaminated contaminates. What she contrasted was enlightened progress and corruptive stagnation, the ability of the exceptional individual to improve and the racialized inferiority of the nonprogressive Irish masses as mob, essentially beyond reform.[24] While Peter is physically and intellectually equipped for Americanization, the Irish as a group personify "the morons," the "defectives"—a menace, in strict dysgenic reading, to "our racial stock" (AmM, 147, 151).

This monocausal biologization also informs the revelation episode in Peter's Americanization quest. Peter's political mentor Sullivan, the stereotypical rogue of contemporary pulp fiction—feisty, ugly, a bully, lascivious and lewd, unscrupulous and ruthless—sexually assaults Justine. This is more than an individual act of violence; it is symbolic of the dangers lurking beneath the surface of Irish clan rule—brutality, violence, uncontrolled sexuality. It is an episode that reveals the racial intricacies of Cannon's Americanization discourse. *Clan* evokes the Ku Klux Klan in its secretive anarchism and thus, on the surface and in its rhetorical gesture, performs a distancing move. But in her depiction of the Irish folk as essentially inferior, and especially in her representation of the Irish ward boss or Grand Wizard Sullivan as the sexual predator and violator of white American womanhood and purity, she works with the defining images of anti-black Klan racism, newly refreshed and legitimized for mainstream

America through D. W. Griffith's *Birth of a Nation* of 1915. Her Clan = Klan analogy relies on powerful anti-black racist images she knows to be firmly implanted and treated as established fact in white mainstream race discourse: the myth of black male sexual prowess and the threat it poses to white womanhood. Without the slightest misgivings she manipulates racial biases against African Americans, and thus also the racial polemics of the very Klanspeople she disavows, to mark essential, criminal, and racial Otherness—as Nancy Ordover maintains, "a recurrent tactic in the eugenicists' arsenal."[25] Through the rape scene Cannon blackens the Irish—the worst racial verdict she could devise. Gender, nationality, and race intersect as definers in this Irish Othering process.

Peter proves his successful mainstreaming when he knocks down the aggressor-as-alien and race spoiler. By defying Sullivan he defies archaic male-defined hierarchies in which power has been perverted into violence, and by defending white American womanhood against the "black" Irish predator he also affirms progress and an American civilization encoded as white womanhood. He transforms himself into an all-American hero. Sullivan becomes Peter's implacable foe. The Irish American community ally themselves with Sullivan—the ultimate proof that Peter is dealing with "material unusable in a democracy" which ought to be "eliminate[d] . . . from the electorate, as we have the criminal, the insane, the idiot, and the alien" (AmM, 154). Cannon uses this melodramatic, racialized, and sexualized episode to implicate the entire group; everything the Irish American setting represented for Peter is exposed not just as sham but as downright dangerous to the purity of true Americanness. In order to claim him for her America, Cannon must racially blacken and morally destroy his world.

Parallel to the discourse on alien male despotism, on Irish American clannishness and threats to "our racial stock," Cannon develops a salvational eugenic discourse of atonement with Anglo-America. Just as she relied on canonized literary strategies to open her hero's eyes to the errors he had committed, she also took recourse to literary convention in drawing the itinerary for his escape—the deus ex machina motif. While Peter makes his career within the ward system, Justine is approached by "people like herself" (CB, 332), in particular the sophisticated Mrs. Wheaton, who recruits her for local health committees. The Wheaton episode is autobiographical, based on the Cannons' recruitment to social work by Elizabeth and Charles Whiting during the early years of their marriage. Just as this commitment had opened Cambridge doors for the midwestern Cannons, Justine's health work becomes the gateway for her reentrance into her old—the true—America, enabling her to guide Peter into her world which can now also be his. "I think you've got to help your husband through a difficult transition period. He's in the process of change that the individuals of his race must go through before they are completely absorbed into American life" (*CB,* 422), Mrs. Wheaton admonishes her. Her use of "race" affirms the Anglo-American status quo: it reconfirms the ultimate Otherness of the Irish as it renders the acceptance of the exceptional Irish into her exclusive Americanness an act of racial rationality and an expression of the superior race's racially informed tolerance. The solution Cannon offers for the interaction of Anglo-America with Irish America is purely individualistic but has wider implications through its eugenic dimension: America graciously embraces the individual of racial compatibility and merit; it offers a comfortable home to those who are able, from a eugenic perspective, to assimilate, just as the Irish Carnahans had reinvented themselves as the American Cannons. As in Crane's *Maggie,* those who remain rooted in archaic biological distance and difference—the Irish masses—are left behind as not only insensitive to reformist integrationism, not only undeserving of the gift of America, but also as both racially incapable of transforming themselves into Americans and, from a eugenic point of view, contaminated and contaminating.

Why spend time on the discussion of an unpublished first novel whose flaws are so obvious? Because its ideological contradictions, its inconsistencies—whether we turn to its representation of social and political change, to Cannon's wavering between a liberal melting pot rhetoric and essentializing racialized Othering strategies, or to its position on women's roles and immigration—and even more so its consistencies—its eugenic discourse, its biologistic monocausalism and racial xenophobia—mirror to perfection the turmoil that many white Americans of Cannon's leanings experienced in the postwar decade. The war had turned their world upside down, and they were reluctant to give up their old ways because they could not yet envision promising alternatives. The longing for change within the established national system was there, in fact had been tangible for decades; it found expression in progressivism, in reformist activities, in literature, art, and music. But of equal importance was the need for stability, the desirability of the status quo in this time of rupture, the fear of transformation after the revolution in Russia, and above all else, the white dread of racial displacement in the face of the African American Great Migration and the "New" Immigration.

CHAPTER 7

"I've Got a Little Fame Myself"
THE PUEBLO BOY AND RED RUST

E ARLY IN 1925 CORNELIA CANNON DECIDED SHE NEEDED TO recharge her batteries; together with her sister Helen she planned her first tour of the Southwest. It was time to depart when a telegram arrived: their brother-in-law Aaron Burt had died of pneumonia. The sobered travel companions met in Hudson that April, stunned by the sudden imprint of death on their lives, and yet determined to embrace adventure. Expectations ran high. Cannon had roamed libraries for literature on the Southwest, and she considered herself quite an expert. Reality soared beyond anticipation: their letters home portray two adventurers succumbing to the enchantment of a world whose bizarre rock formations, deep canyons, vast open desert spaces, azure skies, blinding sunshine, and flashing color patterns shamed the static visions of sublimity and beauty their culture had implanted in their minds. Their first encounters with cliff paintings and Pueblo cultures shocked them into the recognition that American history had not begun with the arrival of Europeans, that culture was not a European prerogative. A tour designed as an escape from domestic routine took on the character of a revelation; time and space, categories always taken for granted, lost familiar contours, assumed new meaning: magic. It dawned on Cannon that the trip was a call for her to renegotiate Americanness. She returned to Cambridge determined to share her insights by writing a children's history on the encounter between the Pueblo peoples and Coronado's invasion. Barely wasting time to unpack, she rushed to the Harvard libraries and the Peabody Museum, collecting every bit of information on "the chronicles of the early Spanish explorers, and . . . studies of the history and customs of the Pueblo Indians in the publications of the Bureau of American Ethnology."[1] For months her children were served Coronado's adventures with every meal. "Have you ever read about Coronado's expedition into New Mexico?" she chirped. "It makes the Pilgrims look like sybarites!"[2]

As soon as school was out, a unique caravan departed for Franklin: Cornelia, her four daughters, her niece and nephew Helen and Lloyd Williams, the maid, boxes of notes, and "one of those featherweight Corona typewriters that danced all over the table with the touch of a finger."[3] Never had the children been freer to enjoy their summer at the farm, for their mother withdrew to her "Chalet" even before breakfast, focusing exclusively on her writing project. The days were bliss for the children and for the writer in their separate spheres, the evenings hours of reckoning. "My mother used us children as guinea pigs," Marian Schlesinger remembered, "trying out each chapter as it was written to find out whether it was to our taste."[4] She encountered fierce criticism. "It's perfectly awful," they complained. "No child would ever read it."[5]

Her critics were blessedly unaware that their mother was by no means free to roam spontaneously. She was forced to labor under the severe restrictions that publishers of the day placed on books for children. We know about these strictures from a letter one of her editors wrote to Cannon in the 1940s: "no dialect, even with colored characters; no colored characters as main ones; no mean remarks; no coffee drinking . . . ; no tea; no smoking by any character under 16 . . . etc." Even this censor could see how restricted the writer's realm had become. Tongue-in-cheek she continued, "Now, when you take out these limitations and the important ones about no heavy tragedy, shootings and blood-and-thunder, you may see that there is a good deal left in American childhood, after all, that is wholesome and yet dramatic."[6] Cornelia Cannon was undeterred. On 21 July she declared the piece "done"—"46,000 words in 23 days . . . like the product of a book factory"[7]—and sent the manuscript off to a publisher. Her children were stunned when only a few weeks later, on 15 August,[8] an acceptance letter from Houghton Mifflin arrived. *The Pueblo Boy: A Story of Coronado's Search for the Seven Cities of Cibola*,[9] published by the Riverside Press of Cambridge in 1926, was a family venture, for not only had the children served as sounding boards, but also the "map, the cover design on the book itself, and the first chapter heading are [Wilma's] work."[10]

The title reveals Cannon's intent: to represent Coronado's quest from a Native American boy's perspective, and in doing so, to rewrite American history from the bottom up. It was a strategy of representation that, at least on first sight, clashed with a defining feature of the American conquest myth, that is, the assertion that the continent had been vacant, uncultivated wilderness, virgin land.[11] The "Indian" as a construct within this firmly established legitimization myth is reduced to the binary of the bloodthirsty savage masses—Cooper's fierce "Mingos"—as part of this wilderness, on the one hand, and on the other the noble savage, that is, the exceptional "Indian"—Cooper's Chingachgook and Uncas—who guides the white pioneers into this wilderness. It is a legitimization myth that ultimately relegates both the bloodthirsty savage and the noble savage to a distant American past through the construct of the "vanishing Indian." As these are essentially static figures without potential for cultural adaptation and transformation, their extermination is "naturalized" as inevitable; they have to make room for Euro-American civilization.[12] American destiny is white.

Cannon's narrative critically reflected and negotiated this claim that history and civilization had entered the American continent only with European colonization. Her hero is twelve-year-old Tyami from the Acoma Pueblo. The story opens on 22 April 1540—a routine day for Tyami; a historic day for Coronado and his army as they depart on their march of conquest; a historic day also for the Pueblo people, whom the conqueror would claim as subjects of both the Spanish crown and the Christian cross. A salt-gathering expedition, on which Tyami accompanies the Acoma men, catapults the boy beyond the static, closed world in which he grew up and into an encounter with the terrifying white Other—with history as rupture and change. Thanks to his intellectual curiosity and personal courage, he is able to acquire the skills that ultimately enable him to negotiate a precarious truce between the Spaniards and the Acoma people, thus saving the Pueblo from destruction. In the end, initiation rites make him a full-fledged member of the male Kiwa community and, as the eagle imagery of the final paragraph suggests, a chief who will lead his people into a new age.

The Indian as savage is absent from Cannon's narrative. Her Pueblo Indians are modeled on the "good Indian" convention of American mainstream literature, a domestication of the admirable noble savage—peace-loving, self-sufficient, frugal, family-oriented. More than that, like Jefferson's and Crèvecoeur's idealized American farmer, they are tillers of the soil with whom Cannon's adolescent readers can identify because they have been mainstreamed. They stand for a work ethic and a value system these readers recognize as genuinely American. There are no enemies except marauding bands of Apaches—the novel's absentee bad Indians—and, every once in a while, harmless skirmishes with other Pueblos. They are people of peace. The community has a static quality, with clearly defined hierarchies and gendered spheres accepted by all. Cannon's Pueblo protagonists are tangible proof of a pre-European history, of pre-European civilizations in the New World. Her narrative shows how eager she was for her young readers to learn about this history and to appreciate the cultural achievement of these civilizations.

Yet the narrative also reveals how thoroughly Cannon was rooted in the Euro-American cultural myth and its assumptions, a rootedness that ultimately clashed with the writer's revisionist intent. In analogy to James Fenimore Cooper's and William Gilmore Simms's representational strategies, *Pueblo Boy* ultimately defines history and civilization associated with the Pueblo people as cyclical and nonprogressive, and thus as essentially incompatible with the Euro-American concept of linear progress. Cannon's "good Indian" is a timeless being who exists outside of history as movement, disruption, transformation. She could not imagine beyond the imperial-eye perspective of European and Euro-American fiction and travel writing; she, too, Othered the Pueblo people racially and culturally by fixing "the Other in a timeless present where all 'his' actions and reactions are repetitions of 'his' normal habits."[13] They are a nonprogressive race, and as such are doomed by the Darwinian creed to which Cannon subscribed. Their extinction was naturalized as inevitable, and how could Cannon, with her progressive's faith in science and evolution, challenge the laws of nature and science? She imposed on Pueblo culture a racialized program of separate history that spelled doom.

In this narrative, history as transformation and progress is the white man's prerogative; he alone possesses the technology, the skills, and the ruthlessness to impose this kind of history on the static Pueblo culture. Even more important, he is racially programmed by a longing for progress as well as a powerful will to effect change which the Pueblo are lacking. His power is based on the elimination of "impossible" from his vocabulary. Cannon confirms the white man's essentialized superiority through her protagonist Tyami and his admiration for the Spanish expedition to the Grand Canyon: "'The power of the god who withholds the rain, the spirit of the lightning which strikes men dead, the anger of the rattlesnake which carries death in its mouth, the voice of the cliff which calls men to leap to the jagged rocks at its base, the magic of the mirage in the desert which lures men to destruction, had not been able to keep this man from going where he would, . . . ' Tyami marveled. 'The white man is indeed a god,' he said to himself" (*PB*, 186). The colonized legitimizes his colonization by worshipping the white man as a new divinity.

It is a perfidious representational move that had already become a defining feature of the American frontier romance during the American Indian removal debates of the 1820s and 1830s. In these removal narratives—Lydia Maria Child's *Hobomok* of 1824, Cooper's *Last of the Mohicans* of 1826, and Catharine Maria Sedgwick's *Hope Leslie* of 1827—the novelists unanimously chose noble Indians to proclaim their culture's doom, a strategy that granted the subaltern an authoritative voice only to legitimize displacement and genocide, to stabilize white hegemony. Cannon's revisionist tale adhered to the same potent tokenist formula, for who could doubt the "good Indian" voice proclaiming the right of the strongest? Power becomes self-validating. True to the metaphor of the "vanishing Indian" and to her Darwinian creed, Cannon perceived the Native American displacement as tragic but inevitable, and her affirmation of this imperialist myth found expression in the paradigm of normalization and naturalization to which she submitted this process. There was no need for her to contradict a Pueblo man's warning that the conquerors, "children of the sun" and "gods," are also "despoilers and robbers" (*PB*, 109); we look in vain for signs that would undermine Tyami's god imagery. The distance between the colonizer and the colonized becomes essentially qualitative and, with that, absolute.[14]

The ultimate—though deliciously tragic—legitimacy of the Spanish conquest is further affirmed by the conspicuous absence of bloodshed and white atrocities from Cannon's plot, an absence that cannot be explained away by the fact that this is, after all, a children's book. The absence is strategic and has defining impact on the text's myth-making strategy. The novel's very subtitle speaks of "search," thus carefully avoiding any reference to conquest. True, the Spaniards raid the pueblo, but then the skirmish is the result of a cultural misunderstanding; the soldiers force the Pueblo people to seek refuge on the mesa, but this also happens during "Indian" warfare; the invaders claim the Pueblo people as Spanish sovereigns, but Pueblo people, too, invade other communities and enslave prisoners. There are violent encounters, but the only wounded are Spaniards, and there are no fatalities. There is neither Spanish torture nor rape, only an exhausted though wildly determined army that takes recourse to violence only if it must and gladly moves on once the indigenous population has offered "gifts" and ritualized gestures of submission. It is revealing that the only war atrocities happen offstage. They surface in memories of Friar Marcos's vain search for the Seven Cities of Cibola; one of the friar's men, the black slave Estevan, robbed, tortured, and raped as they moved from village to village, and not even the disapproving friar could stop him: Shakespeare's Caliban or O'Neill's Emperor Jones in the garb of the sixteenth-century killer-slave. "As he went through the villages, he stole turquoise and treasures from the men, and he was cruel to the women" (*PB*, 94). Thus the real villain, the ultimate brute of the Spanish conquest, is an African slave; he is killed by the Pueblo men, leaving the New World to "the lovely White and Red,"[15] to quote Cannon's founding hero Benjamin Franklin.

The relative "softness" of the Spanish conquest and his personal intelligence and fortitude enable Cannon's hero Tyami to develop into a translator between the Spanish invaders and his people. Through this constellation Cannon could move beyond the totalizing "vanishing Indian" metaphor to celebrate the encounter between the Old World and the New as progress for both the conquerors and the exceptional among the conquered, a strategy she had already employed in *The Clan Betrays* by adopting Peter into her Americanness while relegating the Irish mob to a stagnant periphery. From the very beginning she depicts Tyami as a precocious child, defined by his mature sense of responsibility. That he is more than a bright youngster becomes clear when the men encounter warriors from a neighborhood pueblo who inform them of the Spaniards' approach. Tyami's response is one of eager curiosity. While the others can think only of flight or warfare, he devises strategies for avoiding violence; he grabs the first chance to learn the conqueror's language, arguing that "if he could understand the white men's words, he would know better how to protect his people from their evil magic" (*PB*, 96).

His linguistic skills and his openness toward change empower him as mediator between the conqueror and the conquered, and he uses his power constructively to guide his Pueblo people into a new age. But he can acquire these skills, he can become an American Ariel, only because Cannon subjects him to a rhetoric of mainstreaming and assimilation[16] that automatically distances him from the Pueblo people, just as she had Americanized Peter Burns by depriving him of his Irishness. While the majority of the Pueblo people are associated with the tragic fate of all nonprogressive "races," Tyami as an exceptional individual is extricated from this racialized fate and subjected to an integrationist discourse, transformed into a progressive American hero, familiarized as "one of us." As such he has nothing in common with the homogenized, essentialized, and tragically doomed Indian Other—the novel's deindividualized "they." "Indian" progress and survival, an option only for the exceptional few, are defined as the ability of the indigenous genius to adapt to the superior European culture. In another context and decades later Frantz Fanon would deplore the road Cannon's protagonist and all the other colonized protagonists of Euro-American literatures have to travel as the colonized psyche's tragic choice to "turn white or disappear."[17]

Pueblo Boy is a Darwinian Horatio Alger story in the garb of a historical novel for children. Boasting a Native American child protagonist, it relies on the authority of an indigenous hero to affirm Cannon's white Manifest Destiny approach to American history. Small wonder that the book was a remarkable commercial success. Houghton Mifflin almost begged Cannon to write sequels—*The Pueblo Girl: The Story of Coronado on the Rio Grande* (1929), *Lazaro in the Pueblos: The Story of Antonio de Espejo's Expedition into New Mexico* (1931), and *The Fight for the Pueblo: The Story of Onate's Expedition and the Founding of Santa Fe* (1934)—all narratives modeled on the popular *Pueblo Boy*. Cannon was eager to comply, for these texts enabled her to endorse the definers of the American myth and thus help educate a new generation of enlightened American patriots.

Taken together, Cannon's Pueblo novels trace a process of "Indian" displacement and European imperialist success in which Native Americans are transformed from agents of their separate cyclical history into victims; that is, the "vanishing Indian" becomes the "dying Indian." Tyami, the translator between the Old America and the New, is replaced by white child protagonists, American Kims who, after having lived in the pueblo, come to pity the natives and accept their personal responsibility to protect them against extreme forms of exploitation. The "Indian" perspective is relegated to the periphery, and the white eye is in control. Finally and inevitably, the novel stands for a processual disappearance of the "Indian" voice. The Pueblo people are perverted into voiceless objects of the white colonizer's talk and gaze, Othered, silenced, and "homogenized into a collective 'they.'"[18] Like Child, Cooper, and Sedgwick in the nineteenth century, Cannon deplored the white man's misuse of power and "Indian" victimization, yet she naturalized this displacement in Darwinian terms as inevitable, subscribing to the white imperialist normalization myth.[19]

In 1928 one of Cannon's most cherished dreams came true: her novel *Red Rust*[20] was published by Boston's Little, Brown, and Company in association with the Atlantic Monthly Press, and it became a national bestseller, according to Marian Schlesinger, "at one time being preceded on the list only by *Winter's Moon* by Hugh Walpole and Thornton Wilder's *The Bridge of San Luis Rey*."[21] "I am rather planning to tackle a novel now," Cannon had announced to her kin. "Why not? Stupider people have done so."[22] The first draft was written during the winter of 1925–26. Cannon wrote in the bathroom, "the only warm room in the house"[23]—and perhaps also the only private space. When spring came, she found another place of refuge: the family car. Small wonder that the manuscript cried out for revision, and with relief Cannon welcomed the approach of her Franklin summer. She withdrew every morning, after she had written out the orders for the maid. "No one," she wrote to F. M. Clouter from Little, Brown, "was allowed to approach my retreat except in case of a sudden death."[24] By mid-August she could report that the "book is up to 70,000 words, only 30,000 more necessary."[25] She was writing "two to three thousand words a day of fairly finished material," she reported to her mother on 18 August. As always, quantity and speed mattered. Still, it was a tedious process, and by the time the manuscript was ready for the publishers, the whole family was relieved. "Dear Mrs. Cannon, I wish you wouldn't always nag us about everything," an exasperated Marian complained in a note she placed on the Corona. "We sure will be glad when you've finished that old 'Matts' of yours."[26]

The setting of *Red Rust* is a Swedish American village in Minnesota. Neighbors regard the novel's protagonist, Matts Swenson, as weird because he is more interested in reading than farming. Ever since he came across Darwin's essays on cross-breeding and selection, he has been possessed by a dream: to create a variety of wheat resistant to red rust. He experiments for years until he produces the perfect grain. Yet Matts dies before the harvest. Parallel to Matts's story Cannon developed that of Lena Jensen, a mother of five suffering from her husband's abuse. After Lena's husband, dies, Matts marries her although she is ten years his senior. She becomes his most important helpmate, and after his death she sees to it that his achievement is acknowledged by the Department of Agriculture.

Red Rust sparkles in those passages in which Cannon invites her readers to follow her to territory that is truly hers, the rural Minnesota of her childhood, sharing with them her delight in the land. But then she also forces them to accept the starkness of that land, which brutalizes those who try to subdue it, that terrorizes its inhabitants with desert heat and fierce arctic winters. Cannon's rural Minnesota is a protagonist in its own right. *Red Rust* moves back and forth between the nostalgic gaze of the regionalist tradition to the naturalist's unflinching confrontation with the forces of nature, with a harshness of life that threatens to obliterate individuality. This negotiation between reverence for the midwestern landscape—its beauty and its terrors—and respect for the pioneer experience reveals how closely Cannon modeled her novel on the writing strategies of the region's most powerful contemporary novelist, Willa Cather. Especially through *O Pioneers!* (1913) and *My Antonia* (1918), Cather had not only placed rural Nebraska on the map of American literature but also refocused the gaze of frontier writing to the experience of immigrant women, to that civilizing energy her earth mothers draw from their almost mystical sense of being at one with the land.

Cather's Nebraska is a territory victimized by a ruthless American materialism and capitalism, a place that breaks those settlers equipped for intellectual life rather than pioneering.[27] Cannon admired the psychological depth of Cather's work as well as the eugenic message she conveyed via her celebration of the earth mother; these Nebraska novels served as her guide to writing rural Minnesota. The attempt suffered, however, from what Allan Nevins, reviewing *Red Rust* for the *Saturday Review of Literature,* identified as "lack of expert technical mastery."[28] In a review for the *Atlantic Bookshelf,* M. E. Chase complained: "Mrs. Cannon is too much mistress of the situation. One wishes she would not hold her characters by such tight reins, nor drive them with such curbed bits."[29]

Like *The Clan Betrays,* the novel has one defining theme and unifying objective: the defense of racially restrictive immigration. In her immigration articles for the *Atlantic Monthly* and the *North American Review,* Cannon had worked the panic strategy of dysgenics; in *Red Rust* she chose to concentrate exclusively on the beneficial impact of immigration, and she did so by focusing on immigrants whom most Euro-Americans, and especially the eugenicists, regarded as a culturally backward but "closely allied racial" group (SC, 330): Swedish Americans. In fact, a year after *Red Rust* was published the Eugenics Research Association (ERA), in an attempt to popularize the eugenic agenda, sponsored an essay contest on "comparison of both the crude birthrate . . . and the 'vital index' . . . of the Nordic peoples and non-Nordic peoples in the Americas"; the following year the organization would ask for contributions on "peoples of Nordic, or chiefly Nordic origin in all parts of the world."[30]

Once again Cannon was right on target. *Red Rust* is a novel about the rejuvenation and reinvigoration of the glorious old Anglo-Saxon stock by racially desirable and consanguine white Nordic immigrants. Whether she was portraying a farm boy who reinvents himself as a scientist, crude farmers who scratch a living out of inhospitable soil, pioneer women who transform the prairie into their garden, or a frontier drudge who is liberated to become a homemaker and helpmate, Cannon worked with discourses deeply rooted in American myth and experience, associating her newcomers with the defining features of the American Dream. *Red Rust* was conceived as a counterdiscourse to an undifferentiated nativist phobia that aimed at closing the nation's doors to all foreign supplicants. Her narrative was the eugenicist's apology for continued immigration under the heading of a radically restrictive racialized policy.

The *New York Times,* in its review of 26 February 1928, went to the core of the matter when pointing out "the intentional analogy of the superior hybrid wheat to the American hybrid nation" which the text establishes. The context the *Times* evokes locates the novel firmly in the history of the American eugenics movement, which started with the American Breeder Association in 1904, designed to spread information on the laws of heredity among "animal and plant breeders."[31] Its *American Breeder's Magazine* published articles on crop cultivation next to those on scientific racism or immigration policy. In its use of "hybrid," however, the *Times* ignored—or rather took for granted—that the hybridity Cannon extols is not merely defined as white; it reinvigorates the Anglo-Saxon component by adding the light-skinned Nordic while implicitly excluding the darker southern and eastern European racial component. Using the caterpillar motif, Cannon mainstreamed Swedish Americans by depicting them as racially competent to reinvent themselves as Americans. *Red Rust* is first and foremost a discourse on immigration as invigoration, purification, and renewal. Racialized Americanization is the master theme of this novel, to which all others are subservient.

Cannon based *Red Rust* on personal experience and extensive research. Since her childhood days she had been familiar with Swedish immigration and its impact on society in Minnesota: Swedish maids ran her mother's kitchen; her father, Henry James, employed Swedes as gardeners and stablemen, and on his duck hunting expeditions he hired Swedish guides. In the Minnesota of her youth,[32] Swedish settlers had begun to play an important political role, and by the time she wrote her novel, there were those who claimed "that Minnesota did not care about the governor's origins, as long as he was a Scandinavian."[33] Cannon tapped Harvard's libraries, studying Ephraim S. Seymour's *Travels in Minnesota in 1849* (1850), Michael A. Mikkelsen's *Bishop Hill Colony* (1892), and Kendric Charles Babcock's *Scandinavian Element in the United States* (1893, 1897) as well as several articles on the religious aspects of Swedish emigration. She devoured "travelers' accounts of [Sweden], fairy tales, books about the Lutheran religion, memoirs, and autobiographies."[34] Dr. Cannon's colleague of Swedish descent, Dr. Otto Folin, met a volley of questions on Minnesota farm life; Cornelia bombarded the Department of Agriculture with requests for information on wheat;[35] her parents provided material from the Swedish Historical Society in St. Paul; and in the Widener Library she discovered letters Swedish immigrants had written home. *Red Rust* was the most carefully researched novel she ever wrote.

Cannon knew that the Swedish American immigrant community of Minnesota was heterogeneous,[36] that a considerable percentage settled in the cities. Still, in her novel she chose to subscribe to the "rural myth" of the stereotypical farmer who moved to America to escape the poverty of rural Sweden—migration as a rags-to-riches plot. She took this reductive approach not to denigrate Swedish culture but to glorify Americanness, to celebrate the process of Americanization as one of material, intellectual, and emotional liberation and growth from which both the immigrants and the natives profit. Her Swedes are part of the mass migration that occurred during the last two decades of the nineteenth century. Half a million Swedes, often entire villages, left their native land for the New World. Cannon adhered closely to actual historical records in showing that a large segment settled in Minnesota, partly because the land resembled their European home, partly because railroad companies with charters in this state promoted migration to the area.[37] There they formed closely knit, ethnically homogeneous, and culturally contained settlements which enabled them to maintain social norms they had brought with them from the Old Country.[38]

Like Willa Cather's Nebraska prairie, Cannon's Swedish American frontier is a social space, anti-intellectual, materialistic, provincial. Like the regionalists of the American 1880s and 1890s, Cannon betrays her antimodernist nostalgia for rural life, for that mystical sense of being at one with the land of the past. And yet, adhering to Cather's model, she abstained from re-pastoralizing this rural realm as Nature. Her protagonist Minnesota emerges as a landscape already contained midway between "wilderness" and "culture." Cannon's first-generation settlers are a stubborn, heavy people, unemotional to the point of inner paralysis. Industrious as they may be, they are slow to adopt new ways and skeptical of new technologies. She acknowledged that nineteenth-century Sweden had Europe's highest literacy rate, but at the same time, most of her modestly literate settlers consider reading a waste of time and energy.[39] They submit to what Cannon calls "the stupidity of hard labor" (*RR*, 9), and even though she reports material progress, she depicts their cultural life as one of deprivation. Only on Sundays, at church and other communal occasions such as barn raisings, do they awaken from their stupor and become social beings. Cannon's delineation of the cultural deprivation of first-generation Swedish American rural life reiterates images of suffering, tragedy, cultural aridity, and even ultimate personal obliteration that Willa Cather had first introduced to the immigration novel through *My Antonia,* but without balancing the all-pervasive deprivation topos with the creative resilience, the "artistry and female identification"[40] that took *O Pioneers!* and *My Antonia* beyond a portrait of victimization. In that, Cannon anticipated the tenor of disillusionment that was to characterize one of the most popular self-representations of this community, Vilhelm Moberg's book *The Unknown Swedes* (1950).[41]

Red Rust refuses to sentimentalize rural poverty and cultural deprivation, but it also avoids the despondency of naturalism, which Cannon rejected as "bleak and unpleasant," making "life hardly seem worth the effort."[42] At the center of her narrative is hope and promise as personified by the second generation, and thus the evolutionary paradigm: the sons embrace technology, and the girls, maids in native American households, visit their families dressed up in "nice" American clothes, praise American cooking, and carry America into New Sweden. As in *The Clan Betrays,* progress means Americanization, the assimilation of the culturally inferior but racially compatible immigrant into the American mainstream—with the important difference that there is no need for Cannon to extricate the desirable genius from the undesirable mass; all Nordics are compatible. Consequently the themes of alienation and traumatic conflict over the immigrants' loss of identity, which were central to Willa Cather and the divided-heart motif of Swedish American self-representation,[43] are absent from *Red Rust,* as are conflicts between first- and second-generation Swedish Americans. Her first-generation immigrants arrive determined to become Americans; maintaining Swedish customs, they silently admire those children who learn "these nice American ways" (*RR*, 220), and Cannon leaves no doubt that, without any racial boundaries existing, cultural assimilation is only a matter of time. The deprivation encountered by the first generation consequently is neither that of a cultural uprooting nor that of racial deficiency but one of hard labor and poverty, and it is transitional.

The second-generation Swedes can be embraced by her readers because they in turn are firmly on their way to embracing Americanness. The profit is theirs—and it is the nation's, too, for these new Americans of a "closely allied racial" stock will revitalize the exhausted master race and strengthen that endangered plant, Anglo-American civilization, which, according to Cannon, "dies easily at the top" (WI, 808). Furthermore they contribute to the nation's social stability by laboring for a booming economy assailed by "the recalcitrancy of [American] labor" (COC, 634). The immigration discourse in *Red Rust* explicitly supports the country's restrictive immigration legislation by embracing Swedish Americans as people with "nationality-based identities that were presumed to be transformable" and with "a racial identity based on whiteness that was presumed to be unchangeable."[44] In the novel this process of Americanization is personified in Matts Swenson: five years old when his family emigrated to the United States, he affirms Americanness without qualification, and is thus representative of the second-generation settlers in his community.

Cannon invented Matts to embody the model immigrant, but she also created him to develop a discourse that was of almost equal importance to her and sustained the immigration theme: a celebration of the American genius and his helpmate. Matts has to be both a personification of the promises of racially compatible immigration and thus a representative white man, and the scientist-hero and thus the exceptional individual—a duality that causes structural and ideological ruptures within the narrative. Model immigrant, model scientist: Ruth Suckow, reviewing *Red Rust* for the *New York Herald Tribune* of 28 March 1928, called Matts a "hero . . . of the washed-out variety" with a life "of unrelieved noble sweetness." A genius, Matts is an outsider whose intellectual curiosity is interpreted as laziness, his experiments as abnormal. "Swenson's got hard luck," says a neighbor, pitying Matts's father. "Only one boy, and him cracked" (*RR,* 95). Cannon later claimed that a friend from Minnesota had told her about a Swedish farmer "whose inner life and interests lay apart from those about him, and who lived in a world of ideas uninteresting and incomprehensible to his neighbors."[45] She fused this information with her experience as the wife of a scientist devoted to his research, thus creating a protagonist who combines in himself the characteristics of the American Adam and a twentieth-century scientific spirit, a scientist-hero forever removed from the crowd.

Matts's self-generation as scientist is both a discourse on evolution and a lecture on the failure of American public education. American democracy, Cannon held with Dewey, could prosper only if it provided its citizens with the best education possible; it must be available to the talented of any background, and it is of special importance for those who have to make the transition from one culture to another. Matts is a heroic figure whose superior intelligence conquers his deficient education, the community's skepticism, and the nation's failure to identify and promote talent. Step by step he acquires the skills that enable him to do his work, but years are wasted because there is nothing to assist him: it is only by chance that he comes across Darwin's articles in the *American Farmer's Journal;* then he is lucky enough to meet a businessman who sends him *The Origin of Species*. What a waste of genius, Cannon exclaims, as she uses an agent from the Agriculture Department as her spokesman: "I'll never be satisfied with my country for all its boasters until we take time to pick out the really great ones in our midst and give them a chance" (*RR*, 261). Matts's is an intellectual Horatio Alger narrative in which the American educational system plays a most unheroic role. He succeeds in making his contribution to American science not as a result of his encounter with a supportive democratic environment but in the face of America's blindness. The fact that he makes it against all odds, however, qualifies him as an American hero in the best Benjamin Franklin tradition.

Cannon used Matts's transformation into an all-American hero to establish a link between her eugenic ideas on immigration, on public education, and on intellectual elitism, but she also invented him to present her readers with an alternative model of the American scientist that challenged basic assumptions of the male scientific establishment of the day. It was a precarious balancing act. Married to a researcher deeply involved in the politics of science, she was aware of the competitiveness and personal bickering that scarred academic life. Consequently she was fascinated by articles Paul de Kruif, a staff member at the Rockefeller Institute in New York, published in the *Century Magazine* early in 1922 as well as by the fictionalized representation of de Kruif's experience in Sinclair Lewis's novel *Arrowsmith* (1925).[46] She too was eager to write a novel affirming integrity as a precondition to scientific excellence, but Walter B. Cannon was too prominent in the scientific establishment for her to attack institutionalized science directly.

Matts, the Swedish American farm boy turned scientist, was the solution to her problem: an immigrant from the lower strata, unencumbered by institutional ties, he enabled her not only to celebrate the scientist as America's twentieth-century hero but also to link this discussion to the eugenic agenda of purification and reinvigoration in order to express her reservations about the solution to corrupt institutionalized science offered in Lewis's novel: Arrowsmith escapes to a scientists' community in Vermont and separates from his wife and child. This severance of family ties challenged Cannon's most fundamental notions of white middle-class morality as well as her belief in the intellectual's obligation to the perpetuation of "the race." Cannon employs the Carlylean concept of greatness by maintaining that loneliness is the ultimate condition of the great man—both a precondition and a result of his achievement. Yet she also subverts it, thus providing the novel with a touch that is both autobiographical and eugenic, for Matts's work acquires a superior quality, and he experiences a sense of fulfillment, only after he has surrounded himself with a family. Once he can share his dream with loved ones, his thoughts become "radiant with eager hope and happiness" (RR, 156). The immigrant partnership-marriage offers an invigorating and purifying alternative to the almost antisocial hermit model of the American male scientist as it reconfirms Cannon's dogma of duty to the race.

The same argument applies to the emotional realm Cannon evokes. She prided herself on having opened new emotional space to a husband suffering from his Calvinist upbringing; equally, her Lena is a woman able to satisfy Matts's craving for the companionship of an exceptional wife. Lena "had something rich and fine to offer him, some glimpse of an inner life unknown to his experience." A woman of naturally refined taste, Lena is a civilizer in an environment where the fierce struggle for survival threatens to obliterate individuality, "a current of fresh air to a man smothering in a sealed chamber" (RR, 76). She creates the atmosphere Matts needs for his genius to unfold. Her love finds expression in her unconditional support of Matts's ambition—but the price she pays is self-denial, a submergence of her innermost needs to his. Cannon has her heroine define her identity as self-in-other, in terms, that is, in which Cannon loved to portray herself in her epistolary representations—the brilliant scientist's perfect helpmate; the woman who adds warmth, love, vitality, laughter, and community to the life of the lonely genius. The immigrant Lena proves her eligibility for genuine Americanness and can be accepted into that proud circle of enlightened American womanhood because she, too, affirms the separate spheres model to which Cannon and the readers she addressed subscribed, because her devotion empowers the genius to make his contribution to America.

Cannon further enhances Lena's essential Americanness by endowing her with that inner resilience required of the scientist-hero's mate to cope with the tragic aspects of this sacrificial role. Matts's sole passion is research, and Lena, the sensuous, womanly woman, learns early that theirs is a "companionship of doing" (RR, 150). For a novelist as firmly rooted in literary conventions as Cannon, it is revealing as well as amazing, also from a eugenic point of view, that this perfect couple remains childless. Realizing that her yearning "for a more complete fulfillment" will meet with no response, Lena transforms her eroticized self "in tender humility" (RR, 147) into the helpmate: "Her love was increasingly satisfied to give" (RR, 174). Cannon leaves no doubt that the woman pays a heavy price for her husband's progress; she must suppress a definer of her womanhood—her sexuality. Her compensation is the glory of sacrifice as the purest expression of love: "To the man who lives in pursuit of an idea, internal conflict is death. . . . Any passion which threatens to create a divided mind must be denied, or it will in the end destroy what is more precious even than itself" (RR, 223). Being a helpmate at its core spells the sacrifice of the woman's precious self to the man's needs. By means of the immigrant theme, the novel essentializes this role, transforming it into a racial marker and qualifier: by endowing an immigrant woman with the resilience Cannon associated only with enlightened white American womanhood, she proves Lena's adaptability to the American norm.

In "The Genesis of Red Rust" Cannon treats Lena almost like an intruder who forced herself upon the plot: "My hero's marriage was a surprise to me."[47] She was using the literary convention of the story writing itself, but there was a kernel of truth in what she claimed: Lena, the woman designed as a minor character, made her way to the center of the narrative; the theme of the frontier woman competes with the novel's other themes to claim a defining role in Cannon's Americanization narrative. For her children Cannon made the frontier experience heroic in the formulaic mode of conventional American historiography, but in Red Rust there is little room for nostalgia. As in Willa Cather's novels, pioneer life is a struggle for survival, incessant labor that stifles the mind as it exhausts the body. If the frontier man's life is one of brutalizing labor, that of the woman is even worse. Not only must she shoulder the responsibility of creating a home in the wilderness and participate in the man's backbreaking toil, but also she carries the burden of childbearing.

Still, this is not a victimization narrative but a narrative of Americanization and racial reinvigoration. Of the three stereotypes of frontier women that Beverly Stoeltje identifies in "A Helpmate for Man Indeed: The Image of Frontier Woman"[48]—the refined lady, the helpmate, and the bad woman—the novel's Americanization discourse tolerates only the helpmate. Like the pioneer women of the American master narrative, the first-generation women of New Sweden transform the wasteland into a garden.[49] Their contributions are silently acknowledged by their men, defining their status within the domestic realm as in the community. Like Cather, Cannon pays tribute to these women's cultural work, to their negotiations of continuity and innovation, to their share in building a perfect America, to their contribution as earth mothers to a eugenically desirable new generation of vigorous Americans. This representation expresses Cannon's pride in white American womanhood and her determination to allot a place to these immigrant women within this realm of white Americanness. The evolutionary paradigm allows her to make this move: this becomes clear through the roles the novel's second-generation Swedish American young women, working as maids for American families, imagine for themselves.[50] Like Lena's daughter Christina, they dream of a conventional middle-class marriage, of a domesticity in which they will raise children while their husbands will provide the family income. Cannon affirms these women's gendered American Dream in the image of Christina returning to New Sweden after her American apprenticeship: she is now "the slender young lady with the flower-trimmed hat and the neat shoes" (RR, 220)—Americanization and mainstreaming via the woman's body in transformation, the true woman as civilizer.

The only female immigrant character in Red Rust bearing traits of the literary stereotype of the frontier drudge is Lena Jensen. This drudge role allows Cannon to shed light on yet another defining feature of the novel's eugenic Americanization discourse: racial regeneration. When the reader first encounters her, Lena, an exhausted mother of five, is married to the abusive alcoholic Olaf Jensen. Cannon's representation of her plight takes the reader beyond the national myth of the invincible pioneer woman: Lena is beaten, starved, overworked, raped. This episode acknowledges violence as part of the pioneer woman's experience. Yet at the same time the novel's Americanization discourse, to which Cannon subordinates all narrative strands, does not allow her to penetrate the surface of the events she evokes. To appropriate Lena for her salvation-through-Americanization strategy, she must portray Lena's victimization by an abusive man as exceptional, and Lena must be saved. The familiar strategies of the domestic novel and melodrama serve as Cannon's safety valve. Her stance that her heroine's lot is an extreme one from which only a good man can rescue her provides the plot with a curious fairy-tale quality. Feminist liberation rhetoric and anti-emancipatory discourse intersect in the writer's eagerness to reinvent the Swedish American frontier drudge as an American heroine so that she can claim her place in America's liberation and racial regeneration myths.

In the decade after *Red Rust* at least four other frontier novels written by women confronted the subject of women's tribulations, and it is revealing that of those four narratives, only two ever found publishers: Agnes Smedley's *Daughters of Earth* (1929), Tillie Olsen's *Yonnodio* (written between 1932 and 1937 and published in 1973), Mari Sandow's *Old Jules* (1935), and Meridel LeSoeur's *The Girl* (written in 1939 and published in 1978). Each of these texts rejects traditional representations of the abused frontier woman as individual pathology by linking it to what Melody Graulich calls "patriarchal definitions of gender and marriage"; they all depict violence against women as systemic: "Abuse of women appears as socially acceptable, rather than aberrant, behavior. . . . [The] causes for their brutality are embedded in their society's attitude about women and marriage and in its sanctioning of male power and authority."[51]

Cannon had no feminist objective in writing *Red Rust,* nor was she opting for systemic change. She created Lena to celebrate the metamorphosis of a brutalized immigrant woman into a happy American wife and mother. She made her point by reporting events from neither the female victim's nor the male victimizer's perspective but from that of male innocence, that is, through Matts's eyes. Since she had gone to great lengths to portray her protagonist as a man of supreme sensitivity, his response acquires unchallenged textual authority. Matts is the only male in New Sweden who senses "that it was pretty hard on the women—this business of opening a new country" (*RR*, 30), and his awareness of Lena's despair makes him wonder "if other women—if his own mother—had dark hours of hopelessness" (*RR*, 33). Yet even this model man of feeling is taken by surprise when forced to observe Jensen's brutality. Matts, Cannon insists, "had always lived among people who expected women to work to the limit of their strength. The men about him were often rough in their speech to the women of their families, but he had never seen a woman struck" (*RR*, 42). He is torn between "astonishment, bewilderment, an agony of effort to understand, [and] above all by an overwhelming pity" (*RR*, 47). His inability to understand is expressed in the futile attempts he makes to lighten Lena's burden, only to realize that these efforts arouse Jensen's jealousy and culminate in new violence.

Withdrawal, a closing of eyes and ears, is the sole response open to a man whose experience excludes the reality he is forced to witness. The unease that Cannon's approach evokes in the critical reader is deepened by her reluctance to get at the roots of Jensen's behavior. From letters to her parents we know that she drew the character of Jensen from "Jens, our morose coachman,"[52] whom her father had repeatedly threatened to fire for abusive drunkenness. Like the other men in New Sweden, Jensen is "a tremendous worker, who drove others as hard as he drove himself" (RR, 8), and his mind is dulled by "the stupidity of hard labor" (RR, 9). Cannon, however, renders his condition pathological by linking it to alcohol: Jensen drinks secretly and to excess, and the more he drinks, the less able he is to keep his aggressiveness under control. But why does he turn to alcohol in the first place?[53] Cannon never raises this question, and so she creates the static figure of a brute who drinks because he is evil and/or is evil because he drinks. Her representation was based on flawed hermeneutics—the hermeneutics of evasion that originated in the writer's obsession with affirming Americanization as liberation and progress.

The novel fails to delineate the systemic causes of violence, but it offers a compelling picture of its consequences both for the woman as victim and for her children. The scars they bear are physical, psychological, and—of utmost importance from a eugenic position—dangerous for "the race." The Lena whom Matts first encounters is a miserable, broken creature who enters the "windowless cabin" her husband has built "without a change of expression. She was thin and white, with dark circles under her eyes, and held the little boy wearily as if his weight were too much of a burden for her" (RR, 28). Jensen's manic struggle against the land and his brutality have transformed her into a drudge. "I have been that man's slave and dog, to kick and abuse, for fifteen years," she admits. "I shall be his slave and dog till I die" (RR, 46). The most eloquent expression of her deathlike stupor is her silence. Cannon offers two key scenes depicting the mutually enforcing roots of this voicelessness: the husband's silencing of his wife, and the silencing effect of the victim's sense of shame. Remnants of Lena's vitality surface when she defies her husband's priorities, coaxing Matts into cutting a window into the wall of her cabin. Jensen, interpreting her action for what it is, an act of rebellion, "[strikes] at her with his clenched fist" (RR, 37), rendering her temporarily mute. Yet it is only the next day, when Matts visits her, that he realizes how effective Jensen's strategy actually is. For if Lena is deprived of a voice by this blow, she is even more so by her sense of shame. "There are so many things to knock against when you live in one room," (RR, 44) she tells him. Fear, shame, and pride combine in aggravating her isolation and thus her vulnerability. With Lena, her children too grow mute. The little boys' laughter is stifled, their voices lost as soon as their father enters the cabin, and fourteen-year-old Christina has been prematurely aged by the horrors she is forced to witness. The victims of Jensen's violence are caught in a vicious circle: the silence Jensen imposes is empowered by their shame, and with not a single voice to cry out for help, the community can pretend that the evil blooming in their midst does not exist.

Matts is unable to understand how Lena can "consent with such a man" (*RR*, 34), but the novel leaves no doubt about Lena's social entrapment. She is a woman living in a social void, and with five children to feed, she is totally dependent on the one man who supports them: Jensen. It dawns on Matts that her love for her children—the most sacred relationship in a woman's life according to the gendered discourse to which Cannon subscribed—forges her most substantial fetters: "A woman with children must have been, always and everywhere, a prisoner to the man who could support her" (*RR*, 43). Cannon thus transfigures Lena's submission to Jensen's brutality into a heroic act of survival for the sake of her children. The novel imposes an essentializing naturalization paradigm on this evocation of Lena's sacrificial strength that, similar to the self-abnegation she will perform as Matts's helpmate, confirms her racial qualification as mother within the standards of white American womanhood.

The novel represents Jensen's behavior not as a social phenomenon with which society has to deal but rather as the problem of an individual family, of individual pathology. Consequently Cannon also seeks a solution on an individual level: the rapist and wife beater, for whom there is no place in Cannon's American scenario, is killed in a harvesting accident caused by his drunkenness. It is not simply a deus ex machina solution that frees Lena for her American future with Matts; it is also a eugenic requirement. In eugenic terms Jensen's brutality and his alcoholism are expressions of individual or family degeneration, with a terrifying impact on the next generation and the body politic.

The novel dramatizes this cross-generational contamination when the drunken Jensen rapes Lena; their child inevitably grows up feebleminded and violent, and in his programmed imbecility he will in the end kill the American genius Matts. Jensen's death thus is a eugenic necessity, for it transforms Lena from a breeder of contaminated offspring into a paragon of white American womanhood—or almost so: after giving birth to the "idiot child," Lena no longer qualifies for American motherhood. This also solves the riddle of why Cannon denies the novel's idealized couple, a rejuvenated Lena and the American genius Matts, children, in violation of literary convention. It is a narrative choice that must be positioned in the context of a nationwide debate over compulsory sterilization and its implementation in a large number of states. It intersects with Cannon's class biases: five children borne by a lower-class woman is all her eugenic agenda can tolerate. Lena and Matts's childlessness thus becomes a signifier of their social and racial responsibility; it represents them as the deserving poor and thus further enhances their racial desirability and qualification as mainstream Americans.

Red Rust became a best-seller, and Cornelia Cannon enjoyed her lionization. Proud to be Mrs. Walter B. Cannon, wife of the famed scientist, she now chuckled when Dr. Canon was labeled "the husband of the famous novelist." As Ralph Barton Perry joked in a tribute to Walter:

> Cornelia does not need your pity,
> These are her words to end my ditty:
> "Don't think to lay me on the shelf,
> I've got a little Fame myself."[54]

Yet her triumph was dampened by deep sorrow, for she could not share it with the one person she longed to impress most of all: during the summer *Red Rust* went into print, Frances H. James died. "You can never know what it means to me to feel when anything happens to me, pleasant or unpleasant, that there is a dear mother who is supremely interested in it," Cornelia had admitted to her mother on 15 February 1923. Now this source of strength was gone. Motherlessness came to a mature Cornelia, yet it caught her unprepared and left her orphaned.

In June 1928, feeling rich on royalties, the Cannons departed for the Southwest. If the children had hoped for luxury, they were disappointed, for their frugal provider insisted on a routine of meals in diners and a room or two, at a maximum of a dollar each, at local farms: roughing it indeed, in what Helen called "camp spirit."[55] The itinerary promised Nebraska, Colorado, Mesa Verde, Arizona, and the Grand Canyon, the splendors of Utah and Yellowstone. They were determined to enjoy this time together because all realized that it would probably be the last trip they would take as a complete family group. Three of the children, Bradford, Wilma, and Linda, were attending college, and Marian was in high school; life beyond family was beginning to claim the youngsters, and they were eager to soar. They did not know, as they returned to Cambridge, that they were in for yet another special treat before the family dispersed: a six-month European sojourn.

In spring 1929 Dr. Cannon received an invitation from the École de Médicine at the University of Paris to join the faculty as a visiting professor. He sent off his polite refusal without consulting his family, seeing "no reason to uproot himself from his work," but he had not reckoned with Cornelia's travel bug. "My mother, not one to take such a decision lying down, especially one that involved travel," Marian Schlesinger recalled, "announced in turn to my father that he should . . . immediately withdraw his refusal."[56] He did and prepared for his professional life in Paris; Cornelia prepared for adventure. After all, she had made a good income from *Red Rust,* and happily rich, she was determined to use it her way: a three-month tour of Italy for herself, her daughters, and her artist sister Margaret. Her first investment was a Cadillac.

They arrived in Genoa aboard the *S.S. Roma* in September 1929, where they began an automobile journey that took them from Venice all the way down to Sicily and then, via glorious Florence and Tuscany, to the Alps. It was a car full of women, paint boxes, collapsible stools, and sketchbooks, following Cannon's *Baedeker* itinerary, yet taking detours, stopping, loitering, sketching "onion domed churches in the Dolomites, villas in Tuscany, Roman ruins in Pompeii, peasant huts in Calabria, and the Greek theater in Taormina with Mount Etna in the distance in mild eruption."[57] Italy was heaven, and they delighted in the minor carnival which the appearance of a Cadillac with a party of women in it caused. The travelogue "Art Awheel in Italy," which Cannon wrote upon her return to Cambridge, would be a celebration of women soaring. Shortly before Christmas, while the United States was still stunned by the blows dealt to its economy on Black Tuesday and Black Thursday, they joined Dr. Cannon in Paris, where they took up lodging at the Hôtel de l'Université, a hostelry frequented by Americans. Cornelia Cannon's correspondence with Bradford and her Minnesota kin focused exclusively on life in France, while the Great Depression seemed nonexistent.

In Italy "Mother" had been in control; in Paris the girls tried free flight as fledgling artists. Cornelia's letters, however, reveal her sense of disorientation, intensified by memories of those glorious months of Italian freedom. Her spontaneity clashed with the formality of French academic life; her fierce Americanism was incompatible with the expatriate spirit that permeated the atmosphere of the American colony in Paris. A visit she paid to her Radcliffe classmate Gertrude Stein thus could only end in frustration: in one corner of the Stein salon we find a belligerent Cannon admonishing Stein that "no expatriated American can understand America truly," and in the opposite corner Stein replying, "as though squashing a bothersome insect, 'I have it all within me!'"[58] Cannon's attitude toward her stay in Paris was best summed up in a remark she made as the family departed for a trip through southern France and into Spain, then on to Switzerland and Germany, with Dr. Cannon in charge of the itinerary, the schedule, and the Cadillac: "Those glad days of limping through Italy with a car held together with strings and surgeon's plaster, singing as it went, are gone forever."[59] In June they met Bradford in Rotterdam, but their travel plans were cut short when Dr. Cannon suffered an attack of hematuria. After consulting specialists in London, who determined that he needed surgery, the Cannons decided to return to Boston immediately for the operation.[60]

In June 1930 the family left a Europe that had enchanted them with its museums and operas, its food and wine, its artists and sublime landscapes, its ancient cities and villages that seemed beyond history. It was a Europe struggling to forget the devastation caused by the Great War—and in battling both forgetting and forgiving, it was giving birth to new hatred, a fierce nationalism, and ultimately fascism. Beautiful, mysterious, enchanting Europe was only between wars.[61]

CHAPTER 8

"The Melting Pot in Action!"

HEIRS

T HE CANNONS RETURNED TO CAMBRIDGE IN JULY 1930, TO
a household that had been moved across the street, and to a country
reeling under the impact of the Great Depression.[1] The stock market crash
of October 1929—according to John Kenneth Galbraith the result of a
fundamentally unsound economy, wild speculation, deficitarian banking
and corporate structures, gross imbalances in incomes, unbalanced distribution in foreign trade, and a lack of analytical tools[2]—led to a panic and
set off a terrifying downward spiral. Within months, thousands of banks
had collapsed; businesses unable to get credit laid off hundreds of thousands of workers or closed; farmers lost their land, employees lost their
jobs, and families lost their homes or faced eviction. Soup kitchens and
"Hoovervilles," named after a feckless administration, went up all over
the country. By 1933 industrial production, foreign trade, and the gross
national product had fallen by 50 percent, and approximately 15 million
Americans, 25 percent of the workforce, were out of work.[3] The American
way of life was on the point of collapse.

In 1932 President Hoover, with his halfhearted interventions and lack of
sensitivity to people's needs, lost his bid for reelection. The new president,
Franklin D. Roosevelt, represented the depression as an infection and the
suffering country as a diseased body; he prescribed "the killing of the bac-
teria in the system rather than . . . the treatment of external symptoms."[4]
Together with his "Brain Trust," he fired off a volley of interventionist
measures—the first New Deal of 1933 and the second of 1935—designed
to stabilize the economy and to calm the rebellious spirit and labor unrest

that were spreading. Social engineering was the tool the administration employed to improve the economy and social conditions through carefully measured government interventions, among them the Emergency Banking Act and the Agricultural Adjustment Act, then later the National Labor Relations Act and the Social Security Act. A number of government agencies were created to push the reform efforts: the National Recovery Administration, the Federal Emergency Relief Administration, the Public Works Administration, the Civilian Conservation Corps, and, of utmost importance for the arts, the Federal Writers' Project. Despite these massive measures, 9 million Americans were still out of work by 1939. Despair and anger were pervasive.

The New Deal and its interventionist program were fiercely contested from the start for violating the balance of powers, for regulating the relation between employers and employees, for strengthening the labor unions. Especially the welfare measures accompanying the Social Security Act of 1935, which guaranteed support to dependent children, the disabled, and other "deserving" poor through its categorical assistance program, aroused protest. In March 1933, in the face of skyrocketing unemployment rates, Henry Ford blamed the jobless for their misery, pleading that there was "plenty of work to do if people would do it."[5] Reviving social Darwinist arguments against "irresponsible philanthropy" that had already been virulent in nineteenth-century social reform and the early-twentieth-century progressive debates, critics of the New Deal contended that these assistance programs not only undermined self-support and self-respect but also led to transgenerational dependence on charity.

For advocates of eugenics, however, more than personal responsibility and taxpayers' money were at stake: public relief, they feared, would threaten America's already precarious racial and class balance by increasing the birthrate among the nation's most undesirable. Margaret Sanger warned the Roosevelt administration, "As long as the procreative instinct is allowed to run reckless riot through our social structures[,] ... grandiose schemes for security may eventually turn into subsidies for the perpetuation of the irresponsible classes of society."[6] "Relief babies" became the eugenic scarecrow of the depression years, not only among the New Deal's opponents, and calls for a "biological new deal"[7] as well as sterilization of what H. L. Mencken identified as "polluters of the race"[8] were heard across the board, from the most conservative elements to leftists, in unholy but powerfully pervasive alliances transcending the incompatible agendas and objectives of their specific eugenic leanings. Not just Mencken but Aldous

Huxley, Erskine Caldwell, Margaret Sanger, Tillie Olsen, and John Stein-beck, as well as popular films and magazines, supported and lauded the President's Research Committee on Social Trends for the eugenic measures it prescribed in 1933.[9] Under the shock of the depression, the eugenics movement was transformed, becoming more diversified and, through that, more powerful than ever before—all-pervasive. Conservatives, liberals, re-formers, and radicals spoke as with one voice when it came to designing preventive measures against what Earnest Hooton decried as "a progres-sive deterioration of mankind as a result of the reckless and copious breed-ing of protected inferiors," on the one hand, and, on the other, to redefining welfare with Howard Odum to mean "the functioning of society so as to produce in each succeeding generation more and more of the 'strong,' the 'normal' and 'good' and less of the 'week,' 'abnormal' and 'bad.'"[10]

The Cannons, who had departed on their jubilant European tour in September 1929, never dreaming that the crash was only weeks ahead, returned to a country devastated by the impact of crisis, to a nation that would have to renegotiate its most fundamental beliefs as the depression came to define the thirties, transforming them into the "Red Decade." They, too, were fearful of the unemployment, the poverty, the labor disputes, and the despair that would permeate the country in the years ahead; they wor-ried about social unrest, the eruption of violence, but especially the loss of American spirit that seemed to accompany the collapse of the economy.[11] In a letter to her children of 27 December 1934 Cornelia James Cannon complained about "the disastrous effects of federal relief on the self re-liance of communities. . . . The thing must be modified or [we] will be a spineless people, living on air in vacuo." The Cannons thus joined the anti–New Dealers in their outspoken opposition to the drastic economic and social measures the Roosevelt administration prescribed, but they fully embraced and subscribed to the powerful eugenic subtext of its redefini-tion of welfare in the service of a reinvigorated race, the alliance it forged between hereditarian theory, environmentalism, and social reform.[12]

Their personal suffering during the depression was negligible. Cornelia Cannon could find no publisher for "Art Awheel in Italy" in a country par-alyzed by despair. She lost those royalties from Red Rust they had invested in the stock market[13]—but her income from the Pueblo novels was safe, and the money from Red Rust had taken the Cannons to the Southwest and to Europe. That was what counted. At one point Harvard opted for salary cuts,[14] but what remained was plentiful and secure. More important than the political earthquakes of the 1930s seemed to be the changes they faced within their "self-contained" family circle during the Red Decade, and in this their response paralleled that of the early war years. For the Cannons, the twenties had been defined by a house full of children, friends, and kin. By the mid-thirties Cornelia, Walter, and the Cannon sisters had the house to themselves; in 1938 even Ida and Bernice were living in a place of their own, and in 1939 Cornelia and Walter moved into an apartment at 12 Prescott Street.[15] In June 1933 Cannon remarked to her "Dearest children" that she now had "three children to whom to write." And, she added, "when Bradford departs to St. Louis I shall have four! Such is the reward for bringing up a large and flourishing family."[16]

First the children went off to college, then they graduated into careers and families of their own. Wilma, the artist, was the first, leaving for China in May 1932 to marry the sinologist John K. Fairbank. Linda, sent off to Constantinople, returned to marry Charles Harry Burgess, a geologist from Wyoming, and moved west. The family's youngest, Helen, married the psychiatrist Douglas D. Bond in 1937. Bradford launched his career as a surgeon in St. Louis; he married Ellen DeNormandie in 1938. Marian was the last to tie the knot: in 1940 she married Arthur M. Schlesinger Jr., Harvard professor of history. Class mattered when it came to the Cannons' inner circle, as a 1925 exchange with Bradford, who had defended a classmate's romantic interest in a waitress, reveals. His mother lectured him and, through him, all her potentially endangered children. "I explained that there were no permanent classes," she informed her mother about this correspondence, but nevertheless "there were groups whose experience and background is too different for happy social relations."[17] She had implanted in them a firm sense of class and obligation to "the race." Now, as they chose partners the Cannons could accept as socially and racially desirable, Cornelia's letters celebrated each son-in-law as a genius added to a family of geniuses, and Ellen as Woman Perfect. Small wonder that her correspondence of the 1930s contained almost exclusively family news.

Part of this family news was Dr. Cannon's deteriorating health. In the early thirties he, a victim of his x-ray experiments, was diagnosed with Hodgkin's disease and lymphomatous infiltration of the skin, or mycosis fungoides.[18] His colleagues at the Harvard Medical School estimated that his life expectancy was approximately five years. He had to submit to surgeries that deprived him of his strength, while the periods in between operations were marred by rashes, indigestion, and sleep disorders. In the mid-1930s Cornelia Cannon found herself with her wings clipped, gradually drifting into the role of nurse. Death was making a home with the

Cannons, but both decided equally to accept and ignore this unwelcome companion. They continued to lead an active life, a life of commitment, of work, of enjoyment whenever possible; they traveled around the world together and embraced the exciting role of grandparents, cajoling fourteen productive years out of Death.

But none of these dramatic changes seemed on the horizon when the Cannons returned to Cambridge in June 1930. On the contrary, happily saturated with adventure, they embraced home, were eager for the familiar, longed-for continuity. And Cornelia Cannon returned as a writer who now had two novels on the market.

After the commercial success of *Red Rust,* and with letters of congratulation, laudatory reviews, and invitations arriving daily, in 1928 Cannon had immediately begun work on a novel set in small-town New Hampshire—*Heirs.*[19] It would be her most autobiographical and deeply felt work of fiction. Her son paid tribute to this personal link in a letter: "Every description brought memories to me. I feel that I know every place that you describe, the auction in Salisbury where we got the couch and the dealers were about, the old road up behind Sanbornton Mtn., the big pipe carrying water at Franklin, the family over at the end of the road, old Mrs. Stevens, perhaps, the Polanders down the hill. . . . [T]he reality and tragedy of it all made me weep from beginning to end."[20] Bradford's analysis went right to the point, for in contextualizing her plot, his mother had liberally used her beloved Franklin setting, her familiarity with the New Hampshire landscape, her fascination with the local folk, her concern over rural poverty, her fear of "racial decay,"[21] as well as her eugenic interest in recently arrived Polish "pioneers." Every page bespeaks a writer who is thoroughly at home in the land she evokes. The personal rootedness that sustains this novel is reminiscent of the lovingly nostalgic atmosphere of Harriet Beecher Stowe's New England novels and Sarah Orne Jewett's local color tributes to rural Maine. In its sincere commitment to New Hampshire life, its customs, its landscape, and above all else its people, *Heirs* takes Cannon beyond the Victorian social problem novel and associates her with this New England regional tradition, a tradition defined by white middle-class women writers like herself.

As the novel was written before the family's departure for Europe and before the Great Crash, it contains no reference to the depression. The rural poverty and the restructuring of New Hampshire's agrarian sector which she delineates refer to a process that had been transforming rural New England since the late nineteenth century. Yet Cannon had no eye for the economic context; her argument is a monocausally biologistic one, illustrating how firmly situated she now was at the center of American eugenics. As in *Red Rust,* the unifying theme of *Heirs* is racially restrictive immigration and the racial makeup of a future America. Cannon worked with two complementary narratives to elaborate on the issue at stake—a narrative that traces the biological exhaustion of the old Anglo-Saxon New England, and a narrative of reinvigoration and renewal through racially desirable immigration. There are neither detours nor excursions.

In the novel the twenty-eight-year-old Anglo-American teacher Marilla Lamprey marries the mill owner Seth Walton, but their marriage suffers from infertility. During a tour of Italy, Marilla finally realizes that there is a life beyond motherhood when a cablegram recalls her: Seth is suffering from poliomyelitis, and she returns in the multiple roles of nurse, lover, and business partner. The Waltons' afflictions are embedded in the blight that, according to Cornelia Cannon, has befallen the region's Anglo-Americans—biological exhaustion and, as a consequence, economic failure. It was essential for Cannon that she categorize this blight as regional, for she saw her own family, with its roots in the Midwest, as exempt from this fate; five healthy children were her proof that the essential racial gift the Cannons made to American was that of vigor.[22] New England, however, has become an area in decline, and Cannon uses metaphors of autumn and death to sustain the atmosphere of decay and doom that, for her, has come to define the region and its people.

Still, *Heirs* is a novel of hope, for while its New Hampshire protagonists succumb to "strange blights which fall upon races, and breeds within races, which suddenly reduce their fertility" (*H,* 190), Cannon refuses to join forces with those among her contemporaries who identify this loss of vigor with the end of the American Dream. Instead her firm belief in American exceptionalism and the efficacy of biological engineering techniques empowered her to challenge her readers to embrace the promise for renewal personified by a new generation and "race" of settlers: Polish immigrants. Vigorous, industrious, thrifty, honest, and—of utmost importance—closely allied in racial terms,[23] these heirs to an exhausted New England are racially equipped to cope with the hardships of New Hampshire life. On the eve of Black Thursday, at a time when the modernism of a Lost Generation proclaimed the nightmarish quality of the American Dream, Cannon confronted her audience with a narrative that is painfully naïve in the stubbornness with which it celebrates, as well as frightening in the reductive eugenic reading to which it submits this dream. Alienation, fragmentation, all the definers of modernist despair are absent from a text that tackles social and individual issues with the confidence of a nineteenth-century *roman-à-these* that problems are there to be solved. Eugenic didacticism straight up!

Cannon tackled the issue of racial decline by drawing heavily on very personal experience, and this autobiographical narrative of despair and self-liberation is intertwined with the optimistic eugenic message of the text. Bradford, as did all of Cannon's acquaintances, promptly identified the Franklin "originals" of the novel's Lovell protagonists, but only Cannon's most intimate relatives were aware that the novel's autobiographical connections went beyond the Franklin setting to her childlessness during the first years of her marriage. Autobiographical readings of literary texts tread on dangerous ground, yet a careful perusal of the Cannon-James family letters and Dr. Cannon's diaries justifies this approach to the infertility episodes in *Heirs*. As in *The Clan Betrays* and *Red Rust*, the mask of fiction enabled Cannon to articulate personal insecurities that were incompatible with the public persona she performed.

As we have seen, Cornelia James had not been a passionately enamored bride, only confident that there was a way of balancing the emotional deficits she anticipated: children. Yet her body betrayed her for almost six years. Though she did not discuss her inner turmoil in her letters, we can get a glimpse of the other, private Cornelia James Cannon and her most intimate response by turning to *Heirs*. Cannon depicts her main protagonist, Marilla, as a woman defined by her longing for motherhood. When her hopes are disappointed, she is devastated, overcome by a stupor of racialized guilt and personal pain. Still, Marilla's tribulation is a fate that transcends the personal, and it does not come as a surprise. The structure of the narrative as well as its imagery prepare the reader for this deprivation. From the very start Cannon embeds Marilla's experience within a closed system of signs that characterize her as the representative of an exhausted race: the individual woman's inability to give life stands for the end of Anglo-American New England.

Cannon's discourse on infertility among native-born New Englanders confirmed eugenic warnings, but it also sounded a battle cry against a male misogyny that blamed women, and especially the New Woman's desire for education and personal autonomy, for what they dreaded as white America's racial emaciation. Marilla's impassioned longing for motherhood and her extreme suffering over the sterility of her marriage must be read as Cannon's aggressive refutation of both the medical profession's warning that education would shrink the uterus and Theodore Roosevelt's charge that America's "racially desirable" women—that is, middle- and upper-class women of Anglo-American descent—were responsible for the nation's racial decline because they refused "to breed freely."[24] In her defense of white American womanhood Cannon acquitted women of her class of this bluntly sexist charge by representing them as victims of a biological process and a cultural conditioning that transcended gender and were beyond their control.

She made her point by inventing a heroine who impresses through her skills as a teacher, her motherly qualities, and her active, challenging mind, but she is also drawn as an anachronism, as a woman whose physical appearance links her to the past and ultimately to death. She wears her hair "braided and coiled round her head in the manner of a bygone time"; her regular beauty with its "shadow" of melancholy reminds Cannon of "some old daguerreotype," and "the slender physique of the typical New England woman" evokes images of death: it is not the contributions the region's pioneer women made in the process of conquering the wilderness that are conjured up but their gravestones, "designating them as the first, second, or third wife of some stalwart pioneer husband" (H, 3). Years of living with a depressive father have "filched the first bloom of youth from her face" (H, 4). Her beauty is that of the richness and maturity of the New England foliage and thus associated with the end of fertility, with nature longing for rest—with, from the eugenic perspective, a premonition of racial doom.

Marilla's relation to the land confirms this imagery of movement that is exclusively directed toward the end of things. Her ancestors had struggled to subdue the wilderness, and they prospered, but with each generation their strength declined. By the time we reach Marilla's parents, only fragility and melancholy remain. Since her parents' untimely death, Marilla has depended entirely on the "assistance of hired men who came and went in an endless procession of feeble mentality and incompetence," and she has allowed the land to return "to the more primitive state from which it had been wrested by the labor of generations" (H, 12). Nature reclaims what generations had wrested from her, but Cannon refuses to sentimentalize or aestheticize this process. She describes the end of a cycle of civilization—the return of wilderness rather than renaturalization, degeneration rather than regeneration, the physical and mental exhaustion of woman and man after centuries of ceaseless toil; finally, ruin and decay. Marilla acknowledges that her "race" has reached the end of its history when burning her father's diaries: people without a future have no need of a past. This destruction thus can have no liberating quality for the woman as she sets out to begin a new life in a new town; it is another sign of defeat.

Just as Marilla is beyond youth, the man with whom she hopes to build a future is associated with a calmness that borders on paralysis. Seth Walton is approximately thirty-five, and she is attracted to his "keen face and alert expression characteristic of the best type of the New Englander" (*H,* 37). Yet despite the engaging physiognomy of the successful business-man, his neighbors brand him as the last of a once powerful New England genealogy, "a real old bachelor," a man so afraid of women and the vitality they represent that he prefers to live with his sister. Similar to Heming-way's soldier-hero, he is a man whose war experience has deprived him of his vitality and voice; the always quiet man withdraws into himself "and doesn't talk much about anything" (*H,* 58). Marilla and Seth are attracted to each other, and yet the metaphors Cannon employs signify that what they offer is the companionship of the lonely. It will not bring forth new life, for they are people in whose faces "all superfluous flesh" seems to have been "refined away" (*H,* 67).

The relationship is encoded with images of decay: they meet on a farm so neglected that even an experienced auctioneer fails to stir the crowd into bidding, and they take their first excursion together on a beautiful late October afternoon. Enchanting as "the brilliant color of the leaves" is, so many leaves have already fallen "that it was possible to see deep into the forest" (*H,* 104). The people they meet on a trip foreshadowing eugenic apocalypse are of a contaminated, doomed "race": they visit an impover-ished farm inhabited by an embittered couple, their frustrated daughter, her shiftless husband and retarded child. On their way to see these people without a future, Marilla and Seth pass the local hermit—a descendant of the first settler who signed the original charter founding Lovell, and, as Seth informs Marilla, "the last of the line" (*H,* 102). Living apart from society, refusing to nurture a family, he renounces his responsibilities toward his race and its future. His sole relationship to another human being spells doom: a sexual liaison with the feebleminded Ruby Fox. The encounter during which Marilla and Seth decide to start a life together takes place on a cold, overcast December day. Seth almost collapses after a walk through deep snow. It is an exhausted, emaciated man who proposes to Marilla, not a vigorous lover, an invalid needing a woman's nurturing care, not the potential father of a new generation. The relationship has the potential for a happy mutuality, but it is without transgenerational perspective.

Cannon characterizes Marilla as the physically stronger partner in this relationship, but she also suggests that, despite her longing for children, her heroine lacks an essential prerequisite for that role: sexual vitality. Marilla is unaware that anything might be amiss until her Polish pupil Ewa calls her an old maid. Examining her reflection in the mirror, Marilla knows that, according to her culture's standards, she is more attractive than the Polish teenager, yet she also realizes with a shock that "something was lacking! . . . Could that ever justify a New England woman in exchanging the austerity and the self-control of her world for the self-revealing abandon of a more primitive creature?" (H, 93).

The confrontation between the sexually assertive Polish adolescent and the asexual New England woman has a paradigmatic quality for Marilla's individual experience and for the relationship between the old and new pioneers which this scene represents. Marilla is unable to embrace Seth as a lover. She enjoys his company, but whenever their conversation acquires a touch of the erotic, she withdraws. From Cannon's eugenic perspective, this legitimate defense of the female self against the intruding male Other becomes tragic, a form of deprivation when it is based less on a woman's healthy pride than on the absence of sexual vitality. "Was hers a woman's nature, made for tragedy, which yearns for motherhood yet ever shrinks from the love of man?" she has Marilla ask. "Had the crown of virginity . . . been already pressed upon her brow, marking her forever apart from the mothers of the race?" (H, 112). Marilla's inner conflict culminates in the scene in which Seth professes his love: "She hesitated and half withdrew, when, softer than the snow that was falling about her, she seemed to feel the clinging of tiny hands and to hear . . . the sweetness of children's voices. Her heart expanded with rapture. The passion of her inner life forced its way to the surface as she clung to him" (H, 153). Seth's role is that of the provider of sperm; as a lover he is conspicuously lacking. The passion expressed in this awkward episode is understood, in a reductive sense, as instrumental for the achievement of a goal Marilla defines in nonsexual terms: motherhood.

The asexual quality of Marilla's love is further emphasized by the fact that she can embrace Seth's love only when he is physically weakened: "The man from whom she had shrunk when he was vigorous and well had power in his weakness to draw her unresisting to him. His dependence on her woman's care roused in her slumbering passions" (H, 151–52). Her love is nurturing and healing, a genuine mixture of the mother's doting on the dependent child and the nurse's sympathy for the sick, but it defines Marilla exclusively in terms of motherhood while it emasculates and ultimately infantilizes Seth. Like Charlotte Brontë's Jane Eyre, Cannon's heroine can give herself only to a man who has been partly unsexed; but what Brontë affirmed as woman's empowerment, Cannon's eugenic discourse deplores as womanhood in decline and, with that, as a threat to the future of "the race." The union achieved in *Heirs* cannot be procreative because it is one between people without, as Marilla later understands, "primitive ardor" (*H,* 288).

Marilla reaches the end of hope when a Boston specialist, in an honest but brutal "lecture on eugenics," suggests in a biologistic reading of the theory of the rise and fall of nations that the Waltons might be representative of the blight befalling old New England families, "a mysterious sterility that occurs in a certain percentage of every human group and that seems to be exaggerated in some old New England strains." He warns her, "Yours is a late marriage of descendants of families of gradually diminishing fertility, and you might possibly be the last of your line" (*H,* 191). The woman who has defined herself exclusively in terms of motherhood cannot help despising her body when it fails to fulfill her dream and her racial obligation, and she withdraws from a man whom her instrumentalizing love had reduced to a sperm donor. She succumbs to self-hatred: "She was like an unstrung harp whose strings no longer vibrate when they are struck" (*H,* 283). The marriage deteriorates, and eventually Marilla leaves Seth for an extended Italian tour and a self-reinvention as an artist.

Her Italian reawakening, with its subtle feminist undertone, is undermined in the novel's final chapters. Marilla is recalled by a cable informing her that Seth has been diagnosed with polio. The emotions that sweep through her are identical with those she experienced during their courtship; the woman who cannot embrace the virile man longs passionately for the invalid. Cannon reinstates the childless Marilla as mother by emasculating Seth. "You'll be my child and lover, too," she promises, and although he would rather "have been loved for his man's self, for the power of his will and the force of his character" (*H,* 304), he submits. The novel's parting image of Marilla and Seth is that of husband and wife reconciled to the knowledge that their family history will come to an end with them, yet finding happiness in each other. Night engulfs the racialized image of the white mansion without a future; night, the end of movement, the absence of sound signify the peace Cannon's protagonists achieve for themselves.

"Through the hours while the darkness held there was no stir or sound in the white house on the hill" (*H,* 309). Stagnation and voicelessness are the definers of New England's master race.

This is the readers' final glimpse of the Waltons; it is not, however, the final statement, the ultimate message of *Heirs.* Through the Waltons, Cannon grappled with what she perceived as the tragic racial blight afflicting New England—the end of a once vigorous superior race. Her novel, however, moves beyond fatalism and thus defies the sense of closure implied in this scene. The novel's final paragraphs invite readers to turn their eyes toward a dingy apartment downhill, where they encounter the very opposite of what the house upon the hill prophesies—movement, light, life: "Below in the village the lamp burned till dawn in the crowded sleeping quarters over the store where the Lewenopskis made their home. There . . . were smothered groans and Polish cries for help. When the light in the east began to brighten, Ewa Lewenopski, with sharp pain and scant sympathy, brought her fourth child into the world . . . having blindly obeyed the ancient injunction to multiply and replenish the earth" (*H,* 309). At first sight this paragraph seems to mobilize all the biases fanned by nativist and eugenic discourse: while the representatives of the (for Cannon) highest level of civilization, her beautiful, sophisticated Anglo-Americans, are resigned to face the end of their history, a new race of vigorous and fecund semi-barbarians is taking over. While the refined New England wife is denied a child, the Polish peasant woman Ewa, more brood mare than woman in her blind submission to her sexuality, produces a whole litter of sturdy offspring. Groans and animal-like cries in a foreign tongue drown out sophisticated English speech and Anglo-American voicelessness. The white mansion on the hill is threatened by the dark, overcrowded immigrant breeding quarters in the netherworld.

In the novel Polish peasants have replaced American laborers in the Lovell Woolen Mills, and Polish settlers purchase dilapidated New Hampshire farms, while Anglo-American children constitute a minority in the local schools. In the decade before World War I, 1.4 million Polish immigrants were admitted to the United States,[25] most settling in Pennsylvania or the Midwest. Some, however, chose rural New Hampshire, attracted by its wool industry as well as by the promise of cheap farmland. In 1922 Cannon reported from Franklin: "Two more Poles have bought places near us. We expect to be a Polish settlement finally. They make quiet hard-working neighbors, though we are told they will bring all their relatives."[26] Their numbers were small—a total of 8,217 between 1899 and

1915[27]—and even at the peak, Poles never made up more than 10 percent of workers on the payrolls of the Manchester cotton mills.[28] Still,
Cannon's representation in *Heirs*, as in her correspondence, creates the
impression that foreigners have begun to outnumber native-born white
Americans: almost all scenes featuring Poles portray them in large family
groups or crowds, and every episode describing the selling off of a New
England farm is succeeded by one in which Poles acquire property and
force profits from the exhausted soil. Has the United States reached the
zenith of its development? Is it facing that painful period of decline which
the course of empire doctrine, from Polybios through Giovanni Battista
Vico and Edward Gibbon to Oswald Spengler, invoked as the irreversible
fate of nations? Was not Theodore Roosevelt right when he warned Anglo-
Americans against a sophistication that rendered them unwilling as well as
unable to reproduce, empowering immigrants of non-Anglo-Saxon origin
to outnumber the superior "race"? The xenophobia that Cannon's minor
New England characters express at the ceaseless energy and sheer number
of Polish newcomers, their distrust of Catholicism, their ridicule of the
Polish language, and their denigration of foreign customs all seem to support this impression. And yet *Heirs* is an aggressively eugenic counterdiscourse to Daniel Brewer's bellicose screed *The Conquest of New England
by the Immigrant* (1926), which railed against the "Karolczaks, Olszewskis
and Szunskis" and "Anglo-Saxon decadence."[29] The novel's selectively integrationist message also deconstructs the narrow nativist stance of the
memorial album published on the occasion of the Boston Tercentenary celebration, which denounced Polish immigrants, along with those from Italy
and Portugal, as "invaders."[30] *Heirs* affirmed what Cannon had predicted
in a letter of 1922 to her mother: "What a chance for Americanization!"[31]

Despite conflicts evolving between the old settlers and the new, despite
the cultural gaps she delineated, Cannon challenged her readers to overcome their fear of the Polish Other and to embrace them as a promise for
continuation in New England. The Poles in *Heirs* represent progress and
movement, a renewal of vital forces; that is, they are guarantors of the
survival of her white American Dream. The novel can thus be seen as a
twentieth-century affirmation, from a eugenic point of view, of President
Lincoln's fourth State of the Union Address of 1864: "I regard our immigrants as one of the principal replenishing streams which are appointed
by Providence to repair the ravages of internal war and its waste of national strength and health."[32] (Lincoln extended this invitation to European settlers, while he was hoping to settle the emancipated slaves and free

African Americans to territories outside the United States, a nineteenth-century version of selectivity.) As a progressive Cannon agreed with the call for "Americanization" that Woodrow Wilson had expressed in his famous speech "What It Means to Be an American." These ideas, enhanced by the call for racially informed selection, served as her ideological basis when she decided to rewrite the course of nations doctrine from an American eugenicist's perspective in *Heirs*. The great empires of old rose and fell as if in submission to Nature's cycle of birth, maturation, aging, and death, she conceded, but the United States will defy this tragic cycle as long as it keeps alive what renders it different from and—in Cannon's eyes—superior to any other nation: that it is a dynamic and selectively open nation. The American objective of subduing a wilderness and building a nation may have resulted in the exhaustion of the New England pioneers, but this need not be the end of "the race," she pleaded, if only we continue to rejuvenate and reinvigorate white America by integrating those who are eager and racially equipped to reinvent themselves as Americans. Cannon's argumentative strategy was thus based on those progressive eugenic assumptions that had earlier determined her approach to the Swedish pioneers in *Red Rust:* her belief that the nation needed racially qualified immigration, and her unshakable trust in the superiority of Anglo-American civilization to which newcomers "of closely allied racial groups" (SC, 330) could not help aspiring. This racialized Americanism enabled her to welcome the eugenically desirable Poles as "Other-as-malleable," as generic Americans. Cannon challenged her readers to discard their nativist we/they dichotomy and expand the borderlines of how "we" could be racially defined. Cannon's spokeswoman for this argument is Marilla. When the superintendent of the Lovell schools informs her that her pupils will be Polish, Marilla expects children who are "dark with black hair and eyes" (*H,* 32). When she meets the first Polish children, she does not even recognize them as such: "A little boy stood in front of the house, holding a younger child in his arms. His square face was deeply tanned and his blue eyes looked startlingly light by contrast. His fair hair . . . hung in straight strings over his forehead . . . [and] the plump baby in his arms was smiling and clean" (*H,* 32). Everything about these obviously poor children suggests familiarity; images of light coloring and cleanliness evoke a sense of belonging. Only this sameness that she perceives in the Polish, only the racial mainstreaming to which she subjects them, enables her to embrace them wholeheartedly: "If this was what a Pole looked like, she was glad to have Polish children to teach. . . . These attractive little children, except for the broad faces and short stature, seemed to her like any other healthy young Americans" (*H*, 32). The representative American, as defined by Cannon through her heroine, is white-skinned, blond-haired, blue-eyed, and so is her future American.

To make her point the author wasted no words on the confusing issue of ethnic diversity, citizenship, and nationality—Russian, German, Austro-Hungarian—in her definition of "Polish," just as there was no room within this construction of racial sameness for the Polish Jew. By portraying her newcomers exclusively in terms of the reductive normative standards she herself affirmed, by aggressively mainstreaming them, Cannon selectively transcended her own and her readers' widespread fear of immigrants from eastern Europe. The novel's metaphors of light defy as well as affirm, in her insistence on whiteness, the metaphors of darkness of the anti-Polish nativist discourse. Cannon's inventions of sameness and generic white Americanness are further enhanced by the values her immigrants are made to represent. Her Polish protagonists are of peasant stock, with a European past of excruciating poverty, and they are characterized by an almost proverbial thriftiness and industry,[33] characteristics that studies of Polish Americans confirm.[34] Their extreme living conditions in the past enable them to "live on what the ordinary American throws away" (*H*, 21), and this frugality allows them to acquire property. They "work in the mill all day and run the farm for rest and recreation" (*H*, 21). Like the pioneers of old, these are people willing to conquer the wilderness, and in their struggle to establish their autonomy by acquiring land, by aspiring to the status of the independent farmer, they are twentieth-century reincarnations of the American farmer whom Crèvecoeur and Jefferson celebrated as the essence and guarantor of American democracy. These are not invaders, bent on destroying what generations of Americans have built.[35] Like Marilla's and Seth's ancestors, they are pioneers of compatible racial stock eager to profit from the country's resources by contributing their skill and vitality. As Cannon exclaims through *Heirs,* embrace these strangers as the future of America, as deserving heirs.

Of equal importance to Cannon's strategy of racial mainstreaming and the evolutionary paradigm she evokes is the attitude toward the United States which her Polish protagonists display. In the first generation theirs is a bicultural, compound identity, a two-part cultural identification that adds the new, the American, without parting substantially with the old, the Polish. In the private realm they practice what Michael Kammen describes as typical of immigrant populations: "They simply *added* historical

Americanism to their identities."[36] The new settlers in Puritan New England are Catholics, and Cannon's narrative acknowledges the persistence of subcultural norms and residuals;[37] but these are not barriers to acculturation, for the ultimate goal of these immigrants, independent of generation, is the glorious metamorphosis into Americans, and they are racially designed to perform this transformational act. In Cannon's hierarchical concept of racially related cultures of a consanguine whiteness, the progressive lower culture begs for admission to the higher. "You show me how to make American home?" Ewa asks Marilla (H, 199). Ewa's husband, Stanislaw, a foreman who attends night school, expresses the immigrants' need for guidance toward the privileges of Americanness: "No one born in New Hampshire could know how much a Polish boy had to learn and unlearn before he could begin to be a real American" (H, 220–21). It is a scene evoking the Carlylean exclamation "Guide me, govern me! I am mad and miserable, and cannot guide myself!"[38]—a passage on the class hierarchy and responsibility that permeate British social problem novels. *Heirs* insists that it is the duty of the culturally superior Anglo-Americans "to give," as Marilla reflects, "this child of ancient peasant background the findings of modern civilization!" (H, 34).

More than that, teaching the immigrant becomes a strategy of survival for the exhausted "race." The class hierarchy distinguishing the Anglo-American teacher from the Polish supplicant remains uncontested, but education is the key to acculturation of the racially desirable, and so Cannon has all the Polish children attend American public schools.[39] Her enlightened New England protagonists feel free to advise Polish parents how to bring up children; they hang American pictures on the walls of Polish homes. Still, this is a hierarchy seen in dynamic terms. Education and acculturation over generations will eventually erase difference. The novel was Cannon's invitation to open the doors of the white House upon the Hill to those who are essentially "like us." Introduce them to the blessings of America, and they in turn will reempower the nation to dream the white American Dream by giving of their vitality.

Cannon's belief in the saving quality of a union between the sophistication of the old with the vitality of the racially compatible new is illustrated in the marriage between two of Marilla's favorite pupils—Esther Hilton, of New England stock, and Thaddeus Borek, son of Polish immigrants. Marilla vigorously defends this match against class, ethnic, and religious biases in both communities: "'Thaddeus is one of the finest boys I know, good to his mother, works hard at the mill all day, and helps his father every night on the farm. He's bright, too, and goes to night school . . . probably Esther's back of that!' 'No good'll come of it,' said Mrs. Rogers. . . . 'Him a Catholic and her a Protestant.' 'I guess they can manage that . . . [,]' said Marilla. 'Why, Esther's the melting pot in action!'" (*H*, 272). As in *The Clan Betrays*, the vigor and ambition of the new, personified in the blond Polish man, is refined and raised to a higher level by the love of the model white American woman, he representing the gift of life, she the gift of civilization.[40] Together they spell hope for a future America.

Heirs delineates the economic decline of rural New Hampshire that accelerated after World War I, but the causes of decline Cannon identified were exclusively of a biologistic nature: at the center of her discourse is the tragic fate of a once powerful "race" reaching the end of its history through biological exhaustion. Still, it is an optimistic text, with its hope firmly rooted in Cannon's belief in the manifest destiny of the white American nation, in the central axioms of the American Dream, and in the possibility of eugenic rejuvenation and reinvigoration. But Cannon's optimism, which drew its strength from the integrationist policy she propagated, was conditional and based on exclusivist presumptions. The mainstreaming to which she submitted her Polish protagonists not only reveals her eugenic biases but also illustrates that "requirements for whiteness"[41] are constantly renegotiated in shifting contexts.

CHAPTER 9

"Starved Kittens"

BIRTH CONTROL, RELIEF BABIES,
AND *DENIAL*

I N THE MIDST OF THE PROSPEROUS 1920S, WITH THE AMERICAN
economy booming, Margaret Sanger used her welcoming remarks at the
Sixth International Neo-Malthusian Conference in New York to inform
those in attendance about the mind-boggling costs of social support programs. She contended that the "American public is taxed—and heavily
taxed—to maintain an increasing race of morons which threatens the
very foundations of our civilization." Not only would birth control, and
especially sterilization programs for the physically "unfit," prevent "undesirable" segments of the population from reproducing, she promised,
but also these measures would lighten considerably "the economic and
social burden now hindering the progress of the fit" and become "the first
sensible step towards the solution of one of the most menacing problems of
the American democracy."[1] As the nation faced the collapse of its economy,
mass unemployment, and impoverishment in the 1930s, and as state and
federal governments were forced to spend steadily increasing percentages
of their income on relief programs,[2] anti- as well as pro–New Deal voices
took recourse to a similar combination of eugenic, reformist, and financial
arguments to legitimize both an antireformist scare rhetoric and a reconceptualization of welfare as a tool for the improvement of the nation's
genetic makeup.

Especially after the implementation of the second New Deal in 1935,
the nation's most influential dailies and journals allied themselves with the

eugenic camp's cry of alarm, cautioning that tax money, by supporting the poor, was actually inducing them to produce "more of them."[3] Extensive relief measures as written into the Social Security Act would inevitably result in financial catastrophe and the eugenic apocalypse unless balanced by well-designed family planning programs, they claimed. The Cannons were competent and devoted vocalists in this newly empowered eugenic choir. Cornelia Cannon, too, complained of "the disastrous effect of federal relief on the self-reliance of communities,"[4] and Walter Cannon became "untrustful of the too-smooth FDR and his too-certain New Dealers."[5] Their progressivism as well as their belief in the nation's need for positive and negative eugenic measures found confirmation in the all-pervasiveness of the eugenic paradigm which Susan Currell evokes for the depression era: from "a separate 'scientific' discourse propagated by a few adherents," eugenics developed into "a central underlying feature of the newly leisured modern state."[6]

This was the context in which Cornelia James Cannon finally decided to transform herself from a quiet supporter of birth control into an activist. She joined the movement when it had reformatted itself by allying with the medical profession and the eugenic movement, and after shifting focus from women's rights to family planning. The ultimate incentive for Cannon, however, came with the movement's participation in the relief baby discussion of the depression years, and especially its almost exclusive "concentration on a doctors-only bill"[7] that would allow physicians to provide contraceptive advice. As a doctor's wife she felt personally offended that in Massachusetts physicians giving advice on sex hygiene and contraceptive devices were prosecuted under the obscenity statutes. This problem acquired acute topicality when Dr. Antoinette Konikow was arrested in February 1928 for breaking this law. The Birth Control League of Massachusetts under its president Blanche Ames Ames took up her defense.

During the thirties, the League focused almost exclusively on passing the doctors-only bill—a long and frustrating struggle in a state in which the influence of the Catholic Church in alliance with the Irish American political machine was stronger than in any other. Time and again the bill was defeated by a legislature intimidated by Cardinal O'Connell's claim that the law would encourage unchastity among both married and unmarried people, and by charges that birth control was a communist ruse designed to destroy the nation by provoking a dysgenic catastrophe. The bill was, its opponents contended, "the essence and odor that comes from that putrid and diseased river that has its headquarters in Russia."[8] As late as 1937 courts in Massachusetts "declared a physician guilty of a criminal offence in providing contraceptive care to a married woman whose life might be endangered by pregnancy."[9] With each defeat in the State House, the League narrowed down the definition of what birth control should and could accomplish. The women's rights issue had been discarded long since; now even a doctor's rights were subject to drastic limitations. Though the League insisted that contraceptive advice should be available to married couples only, even that definition proved too broad in the face of Catholic opposition. Birth control ceased to be an issue of prevention and became one of spacing between births, and not for every married woman but for mothers only.

Finally the League agreed to the compromise that advice should be given exclusively to sick mothers, to mothers suffering from heart conditions or tuberculosis, to mentally impaired women, and to women from families with criminal records. In 1935 the president of the BCLM issued a statement that contraceptive advice would be confined "to married woman whose physical or mental condition is such that it is believed that immediate pregnancy would be dangerous."[10] The movement had reached its nadir: birth control became "family planning," an instrument to restructure the nation according to eugenic prescription. The establishment in the 1930s of a special branch within the League, the Mothers Health Council (MHC), paid tribute to a reorientation that was a denial of everything the original movement had stood for. With birth control no longer a woman's right but a doctor's privilege, more than 1,200 physicians in Massachusetts alone endorsed the bill. Even Walter B. Cannon decided in his final decade that his authority might be useful, and for a while he served as chairman of the National Committee for Medical Rights in Massachusetts—a move applauded by and liberating his spouse.

The more restrictive the movement's aims and the more pronounced its eugenic objectives, the more active, visible, and audible Cornelia Cannon became. Her support of this transformation was expressive of her basically eugenic reformism, but of equal importance was her outrage at the state's disrespect for the medical profession, at the influence of the Catholic Church, at raids against birth control clinics, at a public discourse that denounced as immoral what her enlightened progressivism perceived as the reasonable path. In the 1930s Cannon's name began to appear on the League's letterheads, first as secretary and treasurer, then, in the mid-thirties, as vice president, and in 1939–40 she served as president pro tem of the Massachusetts chapter. She worked tirelessly for the cause, lecturing all over Massachusetts, drafting press releases, organizing rallies, posting circular letters, giving interviews, and appearing on radio programs. In 1935, at the height of the depression, she asked Sanger to speak at her home in Cambridge. In her reminiscences of this memorable day, which she recorded in 1965, she still chuckled at the consternation this move caused among her acquaintances, Cambridge ladies who could not well afford to decline Mrs. Walter B. Cannon's invitation: "I invited my friends, who came reluctantly to my house as though to a funeral parlor, entering without greeting as though amazed to find themselves in such a place. I think they expected to see someone with horns and a tail and their surprise at modest, feminine Mrs. Sanger, speaking with conviction about the dangerous subject, was chiefly a reaction of astonishment. I asked for questions after the speech, but none were asked. The audience departed as quietly as possible, untainted by the experience."[11]

All these activities bespeak Cannon's identification with the League's policy during this period, and they document her anger at the social ostracism its disciples suffered, but they were also expressive of the freedom she enjoyed in the 1930s. Her children were grown and starting families of their own. Her husband's career could no longer be impaired by her work, for the medical profession had changed its attitude toward birth control. The League made good use of this woman, who brought to its ranks everything that could possibly be expected of the ideal representative: a writer's popularity; authority as the wife of one of the country's most respected physiologists; the experience of an organizer; the skills of an orator and writer; an enormous amount of energy and enthusiasm, if not zeal. And who could counter more effectively the old but still valid outcry against "race suicide" than a mother of five and proud grandmother of a steadily growing flock of eugenic model children? In the 1930s Cannon became one of the Massachusetts League's most devoted activists.

It was in the midst of the depression, in response to the concerns that New Deal measures aroused among the eugenic camp, and at the height of the controversy over the doctors-only bill that Cannon once again decided to use her reputation as a novelist to further a eugenic cause. In between lecture tours and birth control campaigns she wrote her last novel, *Denial*,[12] a propaganda text with the exclusive aim of denouncing her state's anti–birth control policy and of supporting the BCLM's battle for the doctors-only legislation. At the novel's center are Mary and Fred Holton, a respectable white working-class couple from western Massachusetts. The novel opens on their wedding day, and it accompanies them through their short married life. The happiness of these industrious New Englanders is destroyed by a rapid succession of pregnancies and self-inflicted abortions that damage Mary's health and drive the family into financial ruin. Although Mary is warned to avoid additional pregnancies, the doctors she consults are legally forbidden to offer contraceptive advice. Fred finally leaves her with a cruel "I thought I was marrying a woman, not a rabbit!" (D, 169). Mary commits suicide, taking her sickly children with her. As a model for her plot Cannon used the notorious Sadie Sachs episode popularized by Margaret Sanger in her *Autobiography:* Sanger claimed she met Sachs, a working-class woman who had contracted an infection through self-induced abortion, when working in New York and nursed her back to health. When Sachs later asked her doctor for contraceptive advice, his reply was "Tell Jake to sleep on the roof."[13] Sachs died after yet another abortion. The story was never authenticated, but Sanger used it success-fully on her lecture tours, and Cannon made only slight changes when she adapted it for her novel.

Cannon found no publisher for her manuscript, and she did not archive the rejection slips. Birth control, and especially abortion, were touchy issues, and most publishing houses avoided controversies of that kind, but it would be short-sighted to blame only publishers' cowardice for the rejections. The novel was written in a terrible hurry, in bits and pieces and between numer-ous birth control activities; Cannon produced a text that had the aura of a neglected child, and more than that of an unwanted child. For in truth she was disgusted that she had to waste her talent and time on a novel she did not want to write, as she admitted in family letters, and her anxiety was enhanced by her husband's response to her endeavors—embarrassment, even loathing. To understand Cannon's attitude toward her writing project, we need only recall that all her other novels had a eugenic agenda; none explicitly mentioned birth control

In the depression decade, the decade when Cannon, too, once again took up her pen, the America novel with a cause was experiencing a power-ful revival. The collapse of the economy and the mass suffering that en-sued also resulted in a reorientation of the majority of American writers from modernist experimentation toward a documentation of the sense of despair they witnessed everywhere in the country. Literary historians spoke of an antimodernist turn, but novels like James T. Farrell's Studs Lonigan trilogy (1929–35), John Dos Passos's *USA* (1938), and later John Steinbeck's *Grapes of Wrath* (1939) and Richard Wright's *Uncle Tom's Children* (1938–1940) and *Native Son* (1940), show the modernist and documentary discourses of the period in dialogue, their authors united in their urge to comment as writers and intellectuals on the fundamental challenges to the American Dream they observed and experienced.[14] When Cornelia James Cannon adopted a documentary style of writing for her birth control novel, she thus was in respectable, even majority company; yet it was company whose political positioning as leftist modernists she shunned and whose experimental core she rejected. In her novel the American Dream remains unchallenged, and where Lillian Hellman, Dos Passos, Farrell, Wright, and others began to negotiate more radical alternatives to American capitalism, Cannon's was a monocausal eugenic reading of the depression. Adopting defining features of Erskine Caldwell's southern eugenic gothic novel *Tobacco Road*[15] to a New England setting, she prescribed eugenic measures as the cure for the social and economic upheavals her beloved America was facing.

Denial was an unwanted, unloved book in which Cannon invested a minimum of effort, relying simply on the well-established patterns of fiction with a cause. In narrative structure and technique the text combines the characteristics of the Victorian social problem novel, the expositional strategies of the muckraking narratives, and, despite Cannon's explicit rejection of naturalistic writing style and philosophy, the relentless determinism of naturalism as well as eugenic scare tactics that characterized key naturalistic novels such as Stephen Crane's *Maggie*, Edith Wharton's *Ethan Frome*, and Frank Norris's *McTeague*:[16] plot, character construction, imagery, and dialogue in *Denial* all submit slavishly to the author's propagandistic intent. The novel depicts protagonists on a one-way road to destruction, lives without a spark of hope. As in the nineteenth-century narratives that served as her models, Cannon's heroine and hero are innocent, ignorant young people, too good to be true, prototypical victims of forces outside their control. *Denial* is a tale of unrelieved dreariness, with an inevitability of death that becomes stifling. Cannon dutifully approached publishers, but when she met with rejection, her response was an uncharacteristic one of quiet resignation. The manuscript was buried in a box, and she never made the slightest attempt to follow up suggestions for improvement, accepting the publishers' "no" with relief.

By the time Cannon decided to tackle birth control in a novel, the birth control movement had become "a rich women's" cause, organizing its local activities "through upper-class women's clubs, even high-society charity groups,"[17] and this was also the audience Cannon targeted. In order to cater to these readers' sympathy, she submitted slavishly to the tyranny of their expectations, modeling her heroine on the innocent victim protagonists who play such a prominent role in the popular nineteenth-century sentimental and social problem novels. Mary Holton brings to her marriage all the qualities Cannon's middle- and upper-class readership regarded as essential for successful relationships: devotion to the idea of home and family, beauty, industry, thrift, and prudence. Mary and Fred postponed their marriage until they had saved enough to purchase their household goods, and as a frugal housewife Mary turns the cottage into a home to which Fred returns with pleasure. Theirs, Cannon suggests, will be a perfect place in which to raise children.

Mary's enthusiasm during her first pregnancy is sincere, as is her determination to become a good mother. Yet from the very beginning Cannon insists that a working-class woman's ability to live up to middle-class conventions of motherhood is limited by both her financial and her intellectual means, and it follows logically for her that contraceptive practices should be encouraged among these women as a measure against dysgenic population trends. It is quite clear from the argumentative structure of the text that the issue for Cannon was not birth control as a woman's right; it was family planning as part of a restructuring of society along eugenic guidelines and in accordance with the depression's eugenic reformulation of welfare in the service of national reinvigoration: large families for those white Americans physically, intellectually, and financially equipped to support them, small families for the poor, and none for the eugenically undesirable.[18] The novel takes a clear stand on all these issues. Mary's model is Mrs. Comeau, the mill manager's wife and the novel's personification of positive eugenics. A mother of eight, she is admired because, as one of the laborers states, she "makes no fuss over having a big family. Keeps herself young besides." Cannon shares her protagonist's reverence for this "smart little mother" (D, 12), but she also leaves no doubt about the vast distance between the idolized rich woman with her class privileges and her humble admirers. Mrs. Comeau is a persistent presence in Mary's life, yet she is a heroine in absentia; she and Mary never meet.

Mary must find a model of her own class. The representative women in her all-white working-class setting share a different fate from Mrs. Comeau's, and Cannon asserts that she had better adopt the vastly different attitude toward childbearing and child rearing which they have developed as their survival strategy. They form a chorus of warning voices that permeate even the novel's carefree opening chapters. Mary's maternal friend, Mrs. Forte, informs Mary on her wedding day that for her part "there aren't going to be any more babies to mess things up. Four's a big enough family for poor people like us" (*D*, 22). Through the formula "enough . . . for poor people" Cannon turns Mrs. Forte into a model of social and eugenic responsibility, a spokeswoman for Emma Goldman's proletarian eugenic prescriptions.[19] Mrs. Ryan, Mary's neighbor, describes her marriage as a constant struggle against pregnancy; it has left her in a state of emotional paralysis. And even Mary's mother expresses her gratitude that, as she puts it, "God was good to me and sent me only three children before your father died" (*D*, 68); her husband's untimely death was a blessing in disguise, delivering her from biological bondage.

Cannon's naïvely happy heroine is surrounded by tragic voices that articulate what Goldman described as the working woman's "dread of conception."[20] Their inability to exert control over their reproductive functions has transformed motherhood from what Cannon affirmed as a woman's true destiny into biological slavery. The result is deteriorating marriages, hopeless, ugly poverty, social decline, and too many children considered genetically "unfit" for life in a competitive society. The working-class women in *Denial* contribute to the dysgenic development against which the eugenicists of the day cried out, but although Cannon sustained the movement's anxiety as well as its strategies of positive and negative eugenics, she differed from its most conservative spokespersons in one important aspect: as in Goldman's writing on birth control, the respectable poor women in her novel—and they are a majority—have large families not because they are irresponsible or sexually unrestrained. On the contrary: Massachusetts law, by denying contraceptive advice, forces them to reproduce beyond what they consider reasonable. None of these women submits to her fate, and some go to terrible extremes to limit the number of their children, thus proving their willingness to practice eugenically responsible motherhood. It is state law that perverts them from healthy mothers into the "excessive breeders" of miserable children the eugenicists abhor. Massachusetts prevents the "biological New Deal" the nation desperately needs, and which responsible individuals of all classes and all political orientations demand, Cannon claims.

In the opening chapters Mary is too naïve to understand the vicious circle in which these women are caught. Then her daughter is born, and Mary, warned by her doctor that she must avoid additional pregnancies, is thrown into the chorus of suffering women, for no matter where she seeks professional help, the response is denial. Although she is enlightened enough to ask her doctor for contraceptives, he only puts her off with a humiliating "Get Fred to sleep upstairs" (*D*, 66). Sexual abstinence after only one year of married life is the answer from a man who must be confronted with this anxious question almost on a daily basis. What Mary does not know, however, is that her kindly doctor uses this brusque pose in self-protection, for he is well aware that in providing contraceptive advice, he would violate Massachusetts law.

The only help Mary receives comes from the sisterhood of poor women, but although Cannon invites her readers to acknowledge this solidarity, she is also anxious for them to understand the women's limitations. All they can do is ease Mary's burden; they cannot solve the problem. Mary's mother manages the household before and after the birth of Mary's children. Mrs. Forte talks to Mary about the contraceptive practices of working-class women—methods that fail.[21] Mrs. Ryan, who has undergone self-induced abortions, shares her secret with Mary,[22] and Mary's friend Anna sends her to a Boston clinic. Even the grimy Mrs. Smith tries to help out in her careless way. Local churchwomen support Mary's impoverished family. Yet what Mary craves is neither charity nor whispered pseudo-wisdom, Cannon lectures; it is professional advice. With that, she could easily reclaim control over her destiny and live the kind of decent working-class life to which she and her husband—deserving poor of the Mayhew paradigm—aspire from the very start. This advice, however, is denied to her by a legal system that is as blind to the needs of individual women as it is ignorant of the dysgenic catastrophe threatening the nation.

The novel's true culprit is Massachusetts's birth control legislation. Its limitation of doctors' rights is blamed for all the other problems the writer relates, in a kind of dysgenic chain reaction, to the original act of denial: sexual frustration; families on relief; eugenic decline. In their desperate but vain search for knowledge, Mary and the novel's other working-class mothers are twentieth-century female ghosts of the Carlylean Chartist, whose cry for help—"Guide me, govern me!"[23]—echoed leitmotif-like through the Victorian social problem novel. Their characterization shows how deeply Cannon agreed with Carlyle about the stewardship the privileged owe to those socially beneath them. It illustrates that she either was oblivious to or chose to ignore the manifold and very effective self-help activities developed among the American working classes and American labor organizations, especially during the depression. Hers was a classist paternalism strengthened by her friend Robert M. Yerkes, who argued in 1919 "that the average man can manage his affairs with only a moderate degree of prudence, can earn only a very modest living, and is vastly better off when following directions than when trying to plan for himself."[24]

At no point in *Denial* is the issue simply birth control; it is always and exclusively family planning and eugenics. All the working-class heroines suffer from too many pregnancies, and they desperately seek help, yet none uses feminist arguments, and none rejects motherhood as such; in this they personify middle-class domesticity. All they desire is the right to space their children so they can live up to these ideals, and there is no sign that Cannon felt uncomfortable with this position. The only statement containing a hint of feminism is Mrs. Forte's "I don't see what harm it can do us women to know everything there is to be known about ourselves, everything the doctors or anyone else have found out. After all, I say to myself, it's my life and I've got a right to make it, not just take it" (D, 69), but then she, just like the birth control activist Cornelia Cannon, is already a mother and has made her contribution to "the future race."

In order to avoid the controversial women's rights aspects of birth control as well as the race suicide theme, Cannon focuses her readers' attention exclusively on one issue, the inability of doctors to provide contraceptive advice to women "unfit" to bear children. She plays it safe by making her heroine a very sick woman: as a child, Mary suffered from rheumatic fever, and her weakened body is not up to the challenge of pregnancy. She also suffers from excessive nausea, pulmonary problems, and depression, and after months of incessant sickness she almost dies in childbirth. It takes Mary weeks to get up from the sickbed and months before she is strong enough to enjoy the role she had anticipated—motherhood. A period of respite follows, too brief, however, to stay the process of decline. Slowly her interest in her appearance revives, she manages her household, is a loving wife, so happy that she forgets her tribulations. Consequently she is duly horrified when Mrs. Ryan confesses that she has practiced abortion. "I nearly killed myself doing it," she admits, but she is proud of her decision, for it guarantees a better life for her family: "I did it for the sake of the children we already had. We could give them enough to eat and nice clothes to wear and the three of them had all the schooling they wanted" (D, 71).

Less than four months after the birth of her daughter Judith, Mary is pregnant again, and the dreary routine of suffering escalates; she is still weak and in shock at being caught again, and her physical and emotional condition is desolate. When her time comes she is so exhausted that the doctor—a luxury for working-class women in the first place—has to "take her child with instruments" (*D*, 101). This time recovery is even slower; still, Mary refuses to "settle down into ugliness and the habits of slovenliness" (*D*, 129). Cannon eagerly depicts her protagonist's Herculean attempts to get a hold on her life so as to make her point that this is a woman who, with proper advice, would fulfill all the requirements of working-class motherhood. This guidance, however, is denied, and as a consequence Mary is forced to travel a road that can only lead to catastrophe. Pregnant with her third child, she seeks help in a Boston clinic. The gynecologist's diagnosis is mitral stenosis—a weak heart—and an extreme case of edema. He tells her in the plainest words that she "ought never to have another child" (*D*, 182), but he cannot tell her how: "The law of this State forbids it" (*D*, 183). After the birth of another sickly daughter, and pregnant again, Mary induces an abortion, only to find herself pregnant once more a few weeks after. At the age of twenty-three, after four years of marriage, she is in a state of fatigue from which there is no escape but suicide. The message is clear: a desperately sick woman, whose demand for contraceptive advice is based on the most basic of all natural rights, the right to life, is sentenced to death by laws that claim to protect morality, marriage, and the family. Doctors are denied the ability to fulfill their most sacred professional obligation: to protect life. The Massachusetts legislation on birth control becomes a killer of women.

Although her primary concern in *Denial* was to promote the doctors-only bill, Cannon fused this debate with the eugenic discourse of the depression era. The approach she took, however, was typical of her eclecticism and that of her time—using eugenic discourse wherever it could be made to support her line of arguments, and creating a fusion with environmentalism and social reformism wherever the eugenic argument alone threatened to undermine her propagandistic intent. In that, not only does her writing reflect the political and ideological transformations and adaptations to which the cause of eugenic improvement was subjected under the impact of the depression, but also she succeeded in appropriating for her strategic ends those aspects of the New Deal's welfare discourse and praxis that she found compatible with her eugenic objectives. At first sight the Holton children seem to personify the hereditary "unfitness" argument which eugenicists imposed on the nation's poor: sickly, whimpering babes, undernourished and with skin rashes, prematurely old infants painful to look at, "starved kittens" (*D*, 244), children so feeble that they will never be anything but burdens to the nation. In a process of continuous decline, each baby girl Mary brings into the world is weaker than the one before, children, so says Cannon, for whom it would be a blessing to be released from their suffering, children who should never have been born. Mary's suicide, and the (mercy) killing of her "unfit" children, becomes a tragically heroic act—the white working-class mother's refusal to be reduced to a breeder, the eugenically responsible woman's decision not to burden America with a littler of charity babies.

And yet Cannon's delineation differs from contemporary eugenic discourse in one decisive aspect: she avoids hereditarian and essentialist arguments in connection with the Holton family. On the contrary, the opening chapters are designed to characterize Mary and Fred as an ideal white couple physically and morally equipped for working-class parenthood. Their first daughter is a healthy, sturdy child. The increasing frailty of the babies that follow is thus traced not to hereditary defects but to the fact that a sick, exhausted woman is refused the right to recover physically before deciding to have another child. Cannon's use of eugenic arguments here is an adaptation of the feminist and working-class eugenics Goldman propagated in her autobiography of 1931 when she wrote: "Woman no longer wants to be a party to the production of a race of sickly, feeble, decrepit, wretched human beings. Instead she desires fewer and better children."[25]

Mary and Fred are absolved from the eugenic label "unfit," as are their neighbors the Fortes and the Ryans. Cannon did so because it was her intention to propagate changes in the legal system as a panacea for social problems that she reduced to biological and legal issues, and in this she implicitly rejected the analytical approach and social criticism of a James T. Farrell, a Clifford Odets, a Lillian Hellman, and other depression-era writers. Consequently it was essential for her to document that a large percentage of the lower classes are eager to act eugenically and with a sense of social responsibility. Her white working-class parents are victims, not perpetrators. Nevertheless, in her eagerness to cater to her white middle-class readers' support for eugenic measures, she also employed the eugenicists' scare tactics. *Denial* addresses both her readers' reliance on common sense and their fear of the brutes in their midst, their panic lest their civilization be "repeopled with stone-age individuals," a warning Cannon had articulated as early as 1922 and now reiterated in the frightening context of the Great Depression. "Excessive" fertility among the "unfit," she argued, threatened the genetic balance of American society. The narrative strategy she developed to make her point was to impose on her American working-class protagonists a division she adopted from Victorian social problem discourse, that is, the stark contrast and hierarchy Karl Marx and Friedrich

Engels saw between the proletariat and lumpenproletariat,[26] and Henry
Mayhew's differentiation between the "deserving" and the "undeserving"
poor, redefined in eugenic terms as, respectively, racially and eugenically
desirable and undesirable. This eugenic turn enabled her to play the harp
of hope and blow the trumpet of doom at the same time.

The novel's "deserving"/desirable poor are the Holtons, the Fortes,
and the Ryans; the "undeserving"/undesirable poor are personified by the
Smith family. Mrs. Smith, a "large, shapeless, dirty" woman with "untidy"
clothes and hair looking "as if it had not been combed for days" (D, 140),
is the mother of seventeen babies, twelve of whom have survived. A Catholic (of course), she legitimizes her huge family through church doctrine, but
Cannon's narrative exposes the woman's self-justification as a religious
pose. Such women are not pious parents who embrace children as God's
gift but rather careless creatures that breed a litter of brutes who roam the
streets, live off garbage, and will never be responsible citizens. Mrs. Smith's
description of her offspring combines images of shiftlessness with those of
social menace: "I don't bother about them much. . . . In winter the big ones
go to school when they aren't playing hockey. I got a girl, Susie, working
out for a lady. . . . I guess she'll be leaving there pretty soon. My oldest
boy run away a while back and I don't know where he is. . . . My second
boy's in jail. . . . I don't worry about him" (D, 140–41). The Smiths' unfitness is further emphasized by their reliance on relief, redefined by Cannon
as charity, which they take for granted. Cannon depicts them as both a
burden and, as the boys' criminal record shows, a menace to society, as
contaminated contaminators.

The Smiths must be understood as Cannon's New England version of
the Jukes and Kallikak families in the influential and immensely popular family studies that scientists such as Richard Dugdale and Henry H.
Goddard had conducted since the 1870s—chronologies of vice, mental
defectiveness, and social deterioration that ultimately called for the elimination of these "unfit" and "dangerous" elements through sterilization.[27]
Even more important for the Smith episode, however, is Erskine Caldwell's
Tobacco Road of 1932, a novel set in rural Georgia that appropriates for
itself the success of the family studies and Caldwell's father's research on
"the Bunglers" and combines it with the depression era's reinvigorated
eugenic discourse. By its transgenerational and progressive evocation of
vice and fecundity, poverty and crime, feeblemindedness and promiscuity,
idleness and degeneracy in the poor white southern Lester family, Caldwell
offered an easily accessible fictionalized comment on the welfare and ster-

ilization controversies of the day.[28] Cannon obviously modeled her Smith family on this narrative, but with a twist that revealed her strategic intent as well as her regional biases: whereas she could somehow relegate Caldwell's Lesters to the uncurable "southern condition," the Smiths were an avoidable source of contamination, created by Massachusetts's eugenic mismanagement, in a New England setting that could and should be the nation's eugenic model and pioneer.

Reports in American journals about "race hygiene" and coercive sterilization practiced in Nazi Germany began to render the propagation of coercive birth control programs, and especially sterilization, politically precarious in the United States by the mid-thirties, despite the pervasiveness of the eugenic discourse. The eugenics movement as such, however, displayed none of these reservations. In 1934 Davenport's most devoted ally at Cold Spring Harbor, Harry H. Laughlin,[29] argued that "Hitler should be made an honorary member" of the Eugenics Research Association,[30] and he and his fellow travelers boasted that American sterilization legislation had served as a model for the German Hereditary Health Law. The admiration was mutual, for in 1936 Laughlin received an honorary degree from the Ruprecht Karls University of Heidelberg.[31] American eugenicists, encouraged rather than deterred by developments in the Third Reich, continued to call for extensive implementation of sterilization—calls that intensified as welfare costs exploded with the exploding unemployment rates.

In the notorious *Buck v. Bell* decision of 1927 the Supreme Court had affirmed the constitutionality of coercive sterilization, and many states passed sterilization legislation in the twenties, thirties, and forties; recent scholarship reveals that at least seventy thousand individuals were sterilized before the end of the Second World War.[32] During the prosperous twenties the focus of the debate had been on eugenic considerations; that is, sterilization was propagated as "improvement" of the national body or as a preventive measure against the fecund "unfit"—the physically impaired, "idiots," criminals. Now financial considerations were added to the arguments: public welfare not only drained the nation's precarious financial resources but also encouraged the "undesirables" to "breed excessively," eugenicists charged, clamoring for drastic extension of the sterilization programs. Like Erskine Caldwell's *Tobacco Road*, Cannon's novel participated in this debate through a powerful subtext focusing on the "excessive" fertility of the mentally impaired. At the Boston clinic Mary meets a woman who has "five idiot children" (*D,* 175) and is pregnant with a sixth. Cannon abstains from direct comment, but it is clear that the solution here is no longer the spacing of children. And the mother of this tragic brood knows this: she asks for a therapeutic abortion. Just as Cannon had naturalized the displacement of the Pueblo Indians by having her Indian protagonist celebrate the white man's essential superiority, she now uses a woman who would be a target, consenting or not, of the sterilization policy implemented in many states to legitimize the practice.

It is, however, a cry for help that, from Cannon's perspective, does not touch the basic problem in that it only aborts what should never have been conceived. The woman seeking help therefore has to be read as a strategic device. By evoking the woman's eager consent to abortion, Cannon was able to soften the controversial issue that was, indeed, much closer to her heart, coercive sterilization, which had to be negotiated with utmost circumspection in the context of her novel's immediate objective: the doctors-only bill. As her letters of the period reveal, Cannon's immersion in eugenic and economic debates had already brought her to the point where she had lost her original qualms at justifying coercive sterilization of individuals she considered unable to practice birth control—the hereditary "unfit," which for her translated into criminals as well as the physically and mentally impaired, and finally the socially irresponsible like the novel's Smith clan. As early as 1933 she wrote in a letter to Wilma and John Fairbank: "I have become almost fanatical for sterilization. People who dump their children on the rest of us to support and flit off with other ladies and gentlemen should be deprived of the power to do such wrongs to the children and the world."[33] Yet she was too experienced a social reformer not to realize that any aggressive advocacy of these ideas might endanger her present political agenda. For the time being she did not sidestep the coercion issue, but coercion was reconceptualized as the answer to a desperate mother's prayer for help.

Of utmost importance to the novel's message within the context of the depression and the New Deal controversy over the Social Security Act and its categorical assistance programs is the link that Cannon established between "excessive" fertility and economic decline. The Holtons marry in the "Golden Twenties," the decade of economic prosperity, and they are exposed to the suffering caused by the Great Depression—to wage cuts, shortened workweeks, workforce reductions, and finally unemployment and social displacement. Still, this working-class family is not victimized by economic crisis. Cannon's focus on birth control was so one-dimensional, the propagandistic intention of her novel so narrowly defined, that the nation's economic collapse became a negligible entity, a sideshow of minor importance. Her reductively biologistic reading of the depression context renders her a model of contemporary eugenics discourse, with its avoidance of socioeconomic analysis and its determination to preserve the nation's social and racial stratification. With Sanger, Cannon defines birth control as the ultimate "palliative to poverty," a strategy Nancy Ordover identifies as a "technofix" central to the eugenic agenda of the Red Decade. "'Fix' is operative here," Ordover maintains, "referring both to the liberal *fix* ation on technology (in this instance reproductive technology) as a quick and allegedly painless alternative to deeper, more efficacious structural changes, and the belief that such measures will *fix* the lives of the poor."[34]

In the face of unparalleled social misery among the lower classes, of starvation, Hoovervilles, eviction, and soup lines, Cannon's monocausal technofix approach acquires a cynical quality. Mary and Fred have to move into a miserable shack; they must accept relief not because Fred's wages are down and he loses his job but because they are denied the right to plan the size of their family, Mary reflects: "They had indeed asked for help, not for humiliating orders from the welfare agencies, but for the knowledge which was certainly the right of every husband and wife. It had been denied them, cruelly denied them. . . . If Judith . . . had been walking and independent before another child came, how different everything might have been. Their little would have gone further" (D, 238–39). Forced to bear more children than they can properly care for, the couple descend from the decency of what Cannon normalized as working-class poverty—"their little"—to hapless pauperism and the humiliation of accepting charity.

Relief, defined in the Social Security Act as the citizen's right, is thus reconceptualized as a measure imposed on the "deserving poor" against their will, corrupting them in the act. Mary's spine is broken not because Fred makes less money during the depression; she is defeated because the hungry mouths she was forced to bring into the world compel her to accept relief: "She flushed painfully. . . . A year before she would have carried the food back herself or thrown it in the river but that time had passed. Her need was now too great" (D, 205–6). From an agent of her own history she has metamorphosed into an object of charity, and this has happened only because she was denied release from her biological bondage. Worse, her children are no longer hers; they are relief babies, a social and eugenic burden. Cannon differed from neo-Malthusian experts, who blamed the nation's poor for their deplorable state,[35] when she rendered her respectable working-class protagonists victims of Massachusetts's birth control laws. Still, her narrative establishes a link between family income and the socially acceptable size of families and thus explicitly supports the contemporary populist rallying cries against relief babies which were escalating in 1935. Cannon's eugenic position acquired an almost vindictive touch that eventually caused even some of her allies to distance themselves. The Great Depression, however, is a protagonist that is absent from her narrative of social decline.

Denial could have been a courageous, perhaps even a powerful novel. It is neither. Cannon never accepted it as her brainchild but treated it as a burden she had taken upon herself. She worked hard to represent lower-class women as victims rather than perpetrators and thus developed a counterdiscourse to the neo-Malthusian specter of the pauper breeder-woman. Still, the novel's focus on the doctors-only issue undermined the right of women to acquire control over their bodies and their reproductive functions. In introducing the relief baby, the idiot child, and the criminal son, Cannon moreover took a first decisive step beyond birth control as the right of parents to space their children toward birth control as coercion. The novel raised Cannon's progressivism and pragmatism, her birth control commitment, and her eugenic convictions to a precarious, openly classist and racist extreme. And it is possible that Cannon sensed this when she reread what she had written. Perhaps this is the true reason why she was so ready to bury the manuscript in a box and forget it like an aborted child, though more likely this is only the biographer's wishful thinking.

Her efforts as a birth control activist invite a more realistic reading of her motivation. The Cornelia James Cannon of the depression decade was not just a devoted eugenicist; she was also too much of a pragmatist not to realize that many of her contemporaries, insensible to the argument of poor mothers' alarming death rates, were more likely to leap into action when hit in their pocketbooks.[36] She used this insight to rouse the public when, on 5 January 1935, she, as first vice president of the BCLM and head of the Publications Committee, published the following notice in the *Boston Evening Transcript*:

The Birth Control League of Massachusetts
Taxpayers!
Nearly a quarter of a million children were born last year to
families entirely supported by you through public relief. Our
organization exists to help those parents have only as many
children as they can support.
Will you help us to do this PREVENTIVE WORK?

Contributions may be sent to our office,
3 Joy Street, Boston
Mrs. OAKES AMES, Pres.
Mrs. CORNELIA JAMES CANNON, First Vice-Pres.[37]

Blanche Ames Ames, the BCLM's president, was enraged. In a letter to Cannon of 6 January she protested against this unauthorized use of her name and reminded her that such a program "would be cruel and unfair to these families who are on relief through no fault of their own. We stand for something more than saving money for the taxpayers' pockets."[38] After bitter controversies Cannon resigned from the Publications Committee but defended her position in a statement to the *Boston Herald*: "My understanding of the purpose of the league is that the economic aspects are absolutely fundamental, as well as the health aspects. . . . The Massachusetts organization has been handicapped by its failure to state its aims clearly and boldly. I regard the movement as virtually stalled here as a consequence."[39]

The novel *Denial* reveals that Ames's protest against this neo-Malthusianism had no effect on Cannon. The problem of relief babies can be solved only by birth control, she continued to argue throughout the depression, just as the effects of the economic malaise could be softened if only the nation reduced the birthrate of the poor. The idea that pauperism might be systemic, caused by flaws in the American socioeconomic system, was unacceptable to Cannon. All the nation needed was birth control, a well-designed program of positive and negative eugenics. This neo-Malthusian position was even boosted when she began to travel the world. She became a pioneer advocate of the family planning, marriage counseling, and sterilization programs that Planned Parenthood would advocate for the Third World in the 1950s and 1960s.[40]

CHAPTER 10

"In the Face of What We See"

Journeys and Homecomings

T HE CONTROVERSY BETWEEN CORNELIA JAMES CANNON AND
Blanche Ames Ames and her allies within the BCLM over the issue
of relief babies was bitter and ugly, and it dragged on for months. It was
embarrassing, for it was fought in public and exposed the combatants to
public ridicule; it was painful on a very personal level, for after all, these
were women who had been united by their birth control mission for years,
who had faced social ostracism, outright slander, and the male power structure of state, church, and medical profession together. The feud continued
even after Cannon resigned as vice president, for she repeated her attacks
against Ames in interviews to which the League could not help responding,
accusations and counteraccusations flying back and forth like explosive
Ping-Pong balls. The brushfire was prevented from erupting into a blaze
only because, in February 1935, Cannon escaped on a trip west, combining family visits, birth control lectures, and readings. In early March she
met her husband and their youngest daughter, Helen, in San Francisco,
eager for even greater adventure: a tour around the world, with Hawaii,
China, Korea, Japan, the Soviet Union, Scandinavia, and Great Britain on
the itinerary.

They departed from the United States in the year when the unemployment caused by the Great Depression reached terrifying dimensions and
the Dust Bowl catastrophe made 350,000 "Oakies" homeless. That year
the New York Group Theatre responded to the national despair by producing several agitprop plays by Clifford Odets, including *Awake and Sing*
and *Waiting for Lefty,* prototypes of American proletarian drama and a

call for action that tried to go beyond reformist closure. The Cannons traveled from a crisis-torn nation to a region that, as the Japanese occupation of Manchuria of 1931 foreshadowed, spelled war; they were guests of a Soviet Union in the grips of Stalinism; and they traversed a Europe where Hitler was steadily expanding his terrorist power. They traveled a world on the brink of yet another violent eruption, and they anxiously recorded these developments and were eager to experience the world out there while wrapping their exclusive Americanness around them like a protective shawl.

In September 1934 Dr. Cannon had received two invitations: the Rockefeller Board asked him to participate in a research project at the Peking Union Medical College (PUMC) during the spring and summer of 1935,[1] and his Russian colleague Ivan Pavlov[2] wanted him to deliver the opening address at the International Physiological Congress in Leningrad in August. Even though he hated the very idea of leaving his laboratory, and his physical condition made travel uncomfortable, even hazardous, this time around his wife did not need to cajole him into accepting. The offer was too tempting: not only would he be able to meet with his friend Pavlov, and not only would the Cannons travel as privileged guests of the Soviet government,[3] but also, en route to the Soviet Union, during his research period in China, they would be reunited with their children, Wilma and John Fairbank and Marian, who were making a temporary home in Peking in the mid-thirties.

Cornelia Cannon supported these plans with all the enthusiasm and managerial skills she could muster, but she would not travel as spouse only. While Walter drew up research plans, she developed a schedule that, though tailored to his invitations, would enable her to travel as partner with a mission of equal significance. Wisely using the connections the Fairbanks had made in Japan and China, talking her husband into asking for his colleagues' support, writing letters to businesspeople, diplomats, missionaries, educational institutions, and hospitals, she succeeded in appropriating Dr. Cannon's tour as Cornelia James Cannon's first birth control trip around the world. Whether they stopped in Honolulu, Kobe, or Peking, in Ta-t'ung, Seoul, or Tokyo, in Gorky, Moscow, or Leningrad, in Scandinavia or Great Britain, while Dr. Cannon convened with colleagues, she met with local activists, lectured, visited birth control institutions, posed as vice president of BCLM whenever convenient,[4] and collected any piece of information useful for her cause. During their long sea passages and train rides she would hammer away on her Corona, typing reports on birth control in the countries through which they passed. The pile of manuscripts that accumulated justifies the assumption that she planned to write a book on birth control around the world; it is equally legitimate to suggest that she designed those meetings with local and national leaders of the movement to reconfirm her position in the BCLM and to get back, via international experience and well-documented lionization, at her rival, Blanche Ames Ames. She collected information, and she preached the gospel of birth control. When asked for a few remarks at a reception in Dr. Cannon's honor, she would advertise the cause; when invited to read from *Red Rust* to college girls in Peking, she would slip in family planning advice; hardly a guest in the Fairbank home, no travel companion, no missionary in a remote orphanage stood a chance of not hearing the term. Away from the political sensibilities of American peers she need not curb her speech, and so she lectured extensively on relief babies and the blessings of "sterilization of the unfit."[5]

During her trip her role as Cornelia James Cannon, traveling American writer, was subordinate to that of Cornelia James Cannon, birth control advocate. Still, she wrote continuously—family letters, articles on admirable women she met in China and Japan, a report on her encounter with the Soviet secret police and detention in Sverdlovsk, an open letter to Stalin, even the first draft of a piece eventually titled "Why So Panicky about Communism?" None ever made it into print. Perhaps what was new and exciting to Cannon could no longer excite the readers of the *Atlantic Monthly* or the *North American Review;* perhaps her rather positive evaluation of life in the Soviet Union and especially of abortion practices were regarded as unprintable; perhaps her tirades against relief babies, her aggressive propagation of coercive sterilization, and—ultimately—her condoning of mercy killing on the eve of World War II, the Holocaust, and the Third Reich's "racial hygiene" atrocities shocked even the willfully blind among her former allies for birth control and eugenics into a realization of what Cornelia Cannon, consciously or unconsciously, had come to stand for. Among her liberal children, her improvisational narration, her hasty generalization, and her sarcasm in overdrive tended to be dismissed, tongue in cheek, as "just Mother," but for the reading public her position, and especially her strategies of presentation, became increasingly unacceptable. Cannon traveled around the world writing incessantly, yet the trip took her ever closer to the end of her career as a published author. "I took great pains to put myself down on each form as a 'housewife,'" she commented dryly on her unpleasant encounters with spy-obsessed Japanese officials in Korea on 10 June 1935, "for I am not going to be watched as a 'writer.'" It was a prophetic statement. Her public writing career was over. Birth control and eugenics, however, would continue to be among her most cherished companions.

The Cannons arrived in Peking on 14 April, thoroughly rested from their sea voyage to China, and enchanted with the country after a delightful car ride from Shanghai via Hangchow and Nanking. In Peking they resided with the Fairbanks. Dr. Cannon was immediately and happily absorbed by his professional duties. "Father might as well be in Cambridge, for, except for his rickshaw ride to the PUMC every day and the week ends in the country he sees only rheostats and smoked drums and the inside of cats," his wife marveled.[6] She, however, set out to see as much of Peking and of China as she could, often with "her" rickshaw man Ding, who "miraculously and silently" appeared whenever she decided to launch yet another excursion.[7] She was greedy, even voracious for new sights: trips to the temple of Wofussu, to the Ming tombs, to the mission at Tung Chow, to the Chinese Wall and Ta-t'ung; the Cannons even climbed China's sacred mountain Miao Feng Shan—or, better, were carried up, "the most unsportsmanlike way, and the nicest."[8] Cannon was enchanted with the marvel of China's historic sites; she praised "with what human pleasantness these people negotiate their way through the crowded streets";[9] she enjoyed the apparent eagerness of servants to please her; she was full of esteem for the upper-class Chinese women she met; and she basked in the buzzing Peking street life as well as in the calm beauty of her children's courtyard. Together with Helen she even took Chinese lessons, eager to communicate without the interference of translators.

There was a genuine willingness to appreciate what China offered, a sincere desire to praise and understand. Yet she also traveled as Cornelia James Cannon, white progressive and pragmatist, with the American reformer's gaze. She eloquently and always loudly pitied every Chinese woman with bound feet, and nobody could stop her from upbraiding mothers for mutilating their daughters; only her family's "No, in thunder" deterred her from organizing Boy Scouts to weed the grass on the temple roofs in the Forbidden City; she "nearly wore out [her] abdominal muscles helping to push the rickshaws."[10]

She praised generously anything she could associate either with genuine Chinese tradition or with her American definition of progress. One example must suffice. She had always harbored deep skepticism about missionary activities, but now her American reformer's zeal and the pauperism she observed taught her to admire missionaries for teaching orphaned children, for the medical service they offered, for their "civilizing" endeavors. "Though they come to evangelize they remain to civilize and to open some of the good things the west has to offer to the poorest and the most suffering of this overcrowded land," she wrote to her kin on 22 May. That she was unaware of the condescension in her American reformer's gaze can be seen in her sincere outrage at the arrogance that fellow American travelers displayed toward the Chinese. When she observed a delegation of the American economic mission led by Cameron Forbes, she denounced them as "a lot of the crudest type of business men who freely tell the Chinese how inferior they are, what slow trains, poor monetary systems, inferior utensils for eating, etc. how they knuckle under to the Japanese when they ought to fight them,"[11] never dreaming that the difference between their stance and hers was one of quantity rather than quality. Wherever she went, she preached the gospel of improvement, which to her was identical with adopting "nice" American ways of cleanliness, gender relations, garbage removal, sanitation. And yet she also adjusted "to the life of leisure and service to which her daughters had accustomed themselves with such ease."[12] There came a point when she actually enjoyed the rickshaw. She learned to ignore the disabled beggars crowding the path to Miao Feng Shan, opting for the eugenic solution of giving "to the well to keep them well."[13] She felt she had arrived when, on a trip to Ta-t'ung, she censured mothers for binding their girls' feet, and "they pointed to my feet and said how big and ugly they were, and I had no more to say."[14]

China taught her to close the American reformer's eye, at least every once in a while, but she was unable to discard the eugenicist's gaze. No matter how deeply she sentimentalized the gentle ways in which the people dealt with their crowded everyday life, the word "overpopulation" with its frightening implications tainted everything she saw. The longer she traveled about China, the more her initial pity for paupers, for orphans, for beggars was replaced by a sense of helplessness, which rapidly expanded into anger, frustration, even nausea. She learned to steel her heart by taking refuge in those self-protective racial Othering, even distancing,[15] moves we find in the response of many Western travelers to poverty-stricken, densely populated regions outside the Western Hemisphere. Yet it was more than that, for as Cornelia Cannon pushed through crowded streets, visited orphanages and infirmaries, and stumbled over beggars, she began to see masses of dark people, waves and waves of a strange humanity rather than individual women, men, and children. And as her racial consternation became panic, she ultimately ceased to see human beings at all. "They were not really *human*," she wrote about the destitute whose wailing accompanied her on her way up the country's sacred mountain. "They had an animal-like clinging to life."[16] During a tour of Peking's pauper quarters under the guidance of a Chinese social worker, Cannon dismissed destitute women of her own age as "awful old hags," and she was unable to understand why her companion refused to assent when Cannon suggested that she tell one "wretched creature to commit suicide."[17] She was up in arms over bound feet, but infanticide as a form of misogynic population control, practiced by despairing mothers against baby girls, she learned to shrug off, deploring the alternative—a foundling hospital for girls—as "sentimental foolishness." She wrote to her Radcliffe classmate and fellow birth control activist Mary Howland on 25 April: "For the present I am inclined to think the older method more practical and probably more humane." Her manic fear of what she perceived as overpopulation even extended to the solution she proposed to Japanese occupation. "I feel it would be better for [the Chinese] to fight," she commented on 10 June. "They could spare a million or two and never notice it."

A letter of 22 May documents that Cannon was aware of the transformational processes to which she was succumbing, yet she was beyond battling these impulses. "The callousness about human life is horrifying at first sight," she admitted, "but before long you find yourself taking the same attitude." Her response on a visit to a Peking hospital for opium addicts reveals the lengths to which she was now ready to go. It was the hospital's policy to offer three weeks of treatment to addicts and to brand them with a cross before releasing them; recidivists faced instant execution. Imposing on the Chinese situation the Victorian differentiation between the deserving and undeserving poor and its American racialized appropriation, which she also used in her American welfare discourse, Cannon saw only biologically programmed misfits without hope, in numbers that stunned her, and she longed to blot out those she could not bear to tolerate in her world. "As I looked at them and heard their histories, most of them prostitutes, afflicted with gonorrhea and syphilis, with a low mental age, tattered and wan, I thought in my heart the true mercy would be to line them all up against the wall and end it all."

Although she wrote extensively about the suffering of Chinese women under male despotism, her sisterly sympathy was limited to those of the higher strata. In the addicts she did not see suffering women, nor could she pity their benumbed toddlers; they became "retards" and carriers of disease, contaminated contaminators, a menace to the human race. Was she aware that she was crossing that dangerous line from social Darwinism to mercy killing, even murder? Would she have cared if she did know? The half-joking conclusion she drew from this experience in a letter of 29 May to Mary Howland is revealing. "They are going to work at the problem of opium addict control vigorously, even to the extent of shooting any who revert . . . , and I am hoping that they will see that birth control is even more fundamental socially. Then we shall see the shooting of women who have more than four children!" she, a mother of five, remarked. "Or perhaps the shooting of the fathers." She was joking, and yet she was dead serious. It was a statement she could make only because her distancing from the oriental Other had reached the point of absolute perfection: for her there was no link between these fallen Chinese women and the Chinese she embraced, between these addicts and herself; they were of a different species. Anything to reduce these awful numbers. Anything.

If Cannon's attitude toward China and the Chinese was ambivalent, her view of Japan was, if possible, even more so. The Cannons' journey through occupied China and Korea had roused their ire against the Japanese invaders. "Father is really so anti-Japanese that he surprises me,"[18] Cannon reported shortly before their departure from Peking, but although she, too, protested at war atrocities, she could not help lauding the "progress" that she associated with the Japanese occupation. Her observations were affected by the racial hierarchy she established between the Chinese and the Japanese, which attributed to the latter a place at the top. She congratulated the Japanese for performing coercive abortions on Chinese women, and she nodded approval of the "improvements" effected by Japanese ingenuity in Chinese transportation and administration. "You cannot have both freedom and the amenities of the sanitary life in the orient,"[19] she joked, justifying her callousness by permanently Othering as well as homogenizing the combatants as "Orientals."

It was an oscillation between admiration and aversion that was to characterize her entire response to Japan. She celebrated the luxuriant beauty of the land, the gentle hospitality of the Japanese people, especially in rural areas, the cleanliness of the country, the quality of Japanese research institutions, the infrastructure, the work ethic, the splendor of historic sites. Above all her letters constructed a sisterhood with Japanese women, a gesture of bonding that nevertheless assumed white American womanhood as normative. On the one hand, her heart reached out to that majority of twentieth-century Madame Butterflies, those "perfect dears" who, she assumed, submitted silently and gracefully to male tyranny, but on the other, she was eager to communicate with that small elite who had taken up the good fight for women's rights. "One cannot help loving them," she wrote about Japanese women in a condescending letter of 17 June, and at the same time she could not wait "to meet the suffragists tomorrow and take the taste of these male tyrants out of my mouth."

This discourse of female bonding clashed sharply with images of a nation bowing to military might, of men reducing their wives and daughters to breeders, of xenophobia and spy mania, of aggressive imperialism. The Japan of Cannon's letters fell into two gendered segments: a feminized nation of gently suffering women and pacifist feminists versus a male realm of imperialism, power, and violence. "I should be wretchedly unhappy about Japan if it were not for some of the noble women I have met, who have told me frankly that they are bitterly opposed to the Manchurian adventure, that they think Japan is doing wrong in North China, that the militarism under which they live does not represent the heart of the people,"[20] she contended. It was a gendered dichotomy that enabled Cannon to embrace the Japan she defined as woman while she distanced herself from a nation she depicted as male oppression. "The *people* of Japan are delightful, courteous beyond anything we rude westerners are capable of," she sighed in a letter of 17 June, "but their international manners are atrocious." Feminist, cultural, and nationalist discourses intersected, strategies of racial and classist Othering and identification overlapped in Cannon's attempt at boundary management in a cultural setting where her hermeneutics failed her.[21]

"Now for Russia and birth control and abortions galore," she announced to Mary Howland on 4 July. The Cannons' was a long and strenuous trip before the tourist industry had effected the kind of standardization that would guarantee at least a minimum of comfort. They boarded the Trans-Siberian Railway in Vladivostok on 10 July, and after an eight-day trip they arrived in Sverdlovsk, grimy beyond recognition but lionized by an "avalanche of commissioners" and "an orgy of welcoming speeches."[22] Cornelia James Cannon delved deeper into Soviet reality than she would have anticipated in her wildest dreams when she was arrested by the secret military police (GPU) for trespassing on the grounds where Tsar Nicholas and his family had been murdered, but her status as privileged guest protected her against more substantial tribulations; there was even an official apology. From Sverdlovsk the Cannons flew over the Urals to Kazan and then traveled up the Volga to Gorky and Moscow, where they were joined by Bradford. Their final stop was Leningrad and the Fifteenth International Physiological Congress.

Cannon's eagerness to delve into the Soviet experiment, which she expressed in her letter to Mary Howland, went far beyond birth control. Most of all she was jubilant at once again moving among people "of her own kind," she admitting with a sigh of relief, "I saw with a distinct start of pleasure fair European faces, after having for so long seen nothing but the swarthy Asiatic."[23] Also there was the reformer's curiosity about the Soviet experiment: on the one hand, she was fed up with an anticommunism in the United States that reviled the Soviet Union as an empire of darkness; on the other hand, her indignation was aroused by reports about Stalin's mass incarcerations of critical minds and the sufferings to which the old Russian intelligentsia were exposed. There was only one way of negotiating these conflicting sets of information: to go and see for herself. Cannon felt privileged indeed that life offered her this splendid opportunity to move beyond images and judgments that depended entirely on the authority of others. Her letters to her family, though written with the awareness that they would be censored, illustrate her determination to embrace the new as promise.

From beginning to end her representation of what she observed was encoded in caterpillar imagery that empowered her to appreciate transformation, improvement, and dynamism where a focus on the status quo could only have decried deficiency and deprivation. In many ways she approached the Soviet experiment with the same transformational expectations and Americanized gaze that had enabled her to embrace Swedish Americans in *Red Rust* and Polish Americans in *Heirs,* and Dr. Cannon shared her views. As the Trans-Siberian crossed the Russian steppe on its way from Vladivostok to Sverdlovsk, as the Cannons gazed at isolated farmhouses, miserable villages, ugly factories, and dreary housing projects which the new government had built in the Siberian wilderness, as they observed the rugged crowds herded into dilapidated railroad stations, the images they conjured up were not the distancing symbols of a nation in chaos and decline; rather they used the familiarizing metaphors of their American history and its mythologization, that is, images inviting identification: the westward movement, pioneers subduing the wilderness, a country that looked "like wild parts of Minnesota," a "lovely land" that "cries out for settlers," a region that spelled hope and promise.

They were frustrated at the lack of comfort, and appalled by the filth and unsanitary conditions aboard their famous train, but they ascribed these, in essentialist terms, to Russian "nature" rather than blaming the system—"simply Russian, not communist."[24] True to their reformist leanings, however, they started "making notes on these matters to present to the proper authorities as an evidence of our appreciation of their generous hospitality to us."[25] As guests of the Soviet government the Cannons were guided to those carefully selected model institutions that had sprung up all over Siberia. Cornelia found much to admire: factories in the wilderness, model prison camps, orphanages, summer camps for working-class children, public schools and parks, palaces transformed into museums or veterans' hospitals, and above all, well-staffed abortion clinics. The Soviet Union, a caterpillar nation on the road to greatness, was already a birth control heaven. As the result of this nationwide implementation of birth control, Cannon, like many scientists of the day, predicted a eugenic utopia: there was the healthy enthusiasm that made the faces of kindergarten children glow, and she lauded the pioneer spirit she detected in young intellectuals and workers alike. "How I wish we were not too superior to learn from these people," she exclaimed after a tour of "the Children's City" near Moscow.[26]

Socialism to the privileged American tourist Cornelia James Cannon, who saw the Soviet world as "a huge laboratory in which various methods of living together are being continually tried out,"[27] meant well-equipped public schools and day care centers, birth control wherever she turned, an invigorating pioneer spirit among the general population. It was also a socialism grotesquely Americanized by the progressive's appropriating and transvaluing gaze, and as such she could embrace it. By the time the Cannons reached Leningrad, Dr. Cannon, despite the many discomforts they had experienced, and despite the suffering and brutality they had witnessed during their sojourn, was not just polite when he spoke of a glorious future for the Soviet Union and its people. Stressing the "similarities in the experience and conditions of the American and the Russian people" and praising a political system that exploits the nation's "inexhaustible natural wealth" not for private gain but for "the benefit of all the people," he prophesied: "The success of that ideal should in time make the people of the Soviet Union the most comfortable and the most prosperous in the world."[28]

And yet it was an enthusiasm they could not sustain; the reversal in attitude that had characterized Cornelia Cannon's Chinese experience repeated itself, as did her racialized reading. Perhaps they were simply exhausted by travel; perhaps it was the high degree of hope they invested in the Soviet experiment; perhaps it was the Americanizing gaze to which they had submitted socialism; or perhaps it was their pragmatism. But the longer the Cannons traveled the country, the more people they met in a more intimate manner, the more Cornelia allowed a discourse of pain and disillusionment, even of absurdity, to permeate and overlap that of affirmation. During the first days of travel we come across brief references to gulags seen from a great distance; there is that momentary glimpse of a prisoner train heading east, and the abortive encounter with a man "dressed in a gray peasant smock but clean and with a face of unmistakable quality," to whom she longed to speak, "recognizing each other as kin through all the differences of race"[29]—images of potential tragedy, but kept at a distance. Yet these encounters grew on the observer, and once Cannon had to associate them with individual fate, and especially with the fate of individuals of her own class—a well-educated woman and mother facing her husband's deportation and the disintegration of family and home; Mrs. Pavlov's longing for the beauty of a religious service and her keen sense of religious deprivation—they came alive and transformed Cannon's mode of seeing. Her class consciousness opened her eyes. "In the end, if the plan for a better society works out successfully, will we say that these tragedies are negligible?" she wondered, pondering the Chamberlainian nexus between means and ends. "As a matter of fact the most humanitarian ideal of society yet conceived is being forced on a huge nation, with a ruthlessness and cruelty that has caused millions to suffer and die. What a strange paradox!" she marveled.[30]

Questions piled up in her mind for which she had no ready answers. "To be sure there are cruelties and inequalities in every society," she admitted, remembering the Sacco and Vanzetti case and lynchings back home. "The only question is in which is there the chance of having the least. And how does one or the other protect the individual most successfully? Are personal liberty and initiative worth saving and what society best preserves them? And what is their value to the whole? One cannot be dogmatic in the face of what we see."[31] One solution to the dilemma she decided upon was an open letter to Stalin, in which she condemned the administration's persecution of the old bourgeoisie as "methods of medievalism" and charged: "The supreme tragedy to my mind is that you are continuing the old brutalities in the name of a social ideal whose luminous beauty is besmirched by such association."[32] Her trip eventually taught her that no amount of reform and "progress" in one realm could justify the inhumanity this transformational process entailed wherever she went. "Here I am, convinced that this country has discovered and is trying to put into practice a great type of society, so noble and humanitarian that the rest of the world must . . . perhaps in the long run adopt it," she wrote, evoking her emotional turmoil for her family on 10 August, "and yet revolted by its bigotry and cruelty which could mar an even greater effort for social justice." Dr. Cannon got to a point where he became unable to bear the horror of the contradictions. All he could think of was "to get out" as quickly as possible.[33] "We are half way round the world and Father is in a glow of joy because he is now on his way home,"[34] she reported. Both Cannons felt as if a heavy load had been taken off their backs when their train finally crossed a bridge into Finland. "What it is to be in a free country!"[35] Cornelia exclaimed with her usual enthusiasm.

The dilemma she faced was how to deal with the humanitarian catastrophe she had witnessed in the Soviet Union without at the same time discrediting her thoroughly Americanized socialist dream. As always in confronting social issues beyond her comprehension, Cannon took recourse to race as all-purpose explanation: socialism as she understood it was not responsible for the perversion she had observed; it was simply that the Russian people as a "race" were not equipped to perform and effect the kind of transformation she envisioned. "I can hardly keep my reforming hands off,"[36] she exclaimed. But these people ignored her advice about how to improve sanitary conditions on the Trans-Siberian Railway; they would not listen when she talked about the fate of dissidents; and they just could not get excited over buildings that were never completed or crumbled almost as soon as they went up. In the end, tyranny and brutalization were not aberrations but the typical, though tragic, results of an essentialized and static "Russianness," of "*real*" inferiority."[37] The Russians were, she concluded, "a barbarian people"[38] after all.

Her racialized reading of the Soviet Union under Stalin reiterated an analysis that Frederick Adams Woods, a biologist at MIT, had published in the *Journal of Heredity* in 1919. "The racial elements in the make-up of Russia are mainly Slavic," he contended in "Is Anglo-Saxon Temper by Nature Averse to Bolshevism?" The Russians "have indulged in much anarchy in the past. Historical evidence strongly suggests that there is something inherent in the temperament of the Slav causing him to yield much more easily than his Nordic neighbor to the temperament of mob violence."[39] Identifying communism with violence and chaos, and establishing a racial link between "the Slav" and Bolshevism, Woods saw the Russian Revolution inextricably tied to the racially inferior Russian realm. Whereas

Woods proclaimed the Anglo-Saxon racially averse to Bolshevism, however, Cannon designed a different mission for Anglo-Saxonism: if socialism were to succeed, it could do so only under the guidance of a superior race. "Much as I criticize and find fault I do think [the Russians] have the form of society to which the rest of us must come in time," she insisted in a letter of 15 August and offered a racialized solution that she lifted almost undiluted from Hippolyte Taine and the Victorians' Anglo-Saxon school of historiography: "If only England or France or ourselves could do it, with the efficiency possible to us, no one in the world could resist the example." As always in the progress of civilization, as interpreted by Cornelia James Cannon, Anglo-Saxons, with the help, perhaps, of the best of the Romance world, would have to take on their reformist responsibility as the superior race; only Anglo-Saxons were capable of producing that perfect society where the essentially inferior Russians must fail.

A few weeks later Cannon extended her definition of the savior race to include the "Nordic" element. It was a step that came easily for her. After all, American racial discourse included these nationalities in its construction of a consanguine white race,[40] and she herself had celebrated the transformation of Swedish immigrants into American pioneers in Red Rust. Traveling through Scandinavia, and especially Sweden, she had—"strangely enough"—encountered people who seemed both determined and racially equipped to translate her Americanized socialist dream into reality: "They have no slums, an unemployment situation that is not too great nor beyond hope, an extension of birth control technique which is giving them a stationary population, and socialistic and cooperative activities that will in time bring socialism to a people trained and tried in the ways of organizing and managing such a state. They will do what Russia is doing, without the brutality and suffering of her poor people, in a manner consonant with their racial habits and with a preservation at all stages of that precious freedom which is coming more and more to seem to me the only worth in life."[41] The racialized eugenic paradigm structured her approach to the past, her reading of the present, and her hopes and anxieties for the future.

On 13 September 1935 the Cannons boarded the SS Scythia in Liverpool to sail back to the United States. "I am hoping that when I come home with freshly opened eyes, I will see our imperfections freshly and work for change," she wrote to her children that night. Although she would not and could not cease subjecting the world to her Americanizing gaze and transvaluation, Cornelia Cannon had indeed had her eyes opened through encounters with cultural realities and social issues that challenged her perceptive capacities. Her life after this trip around the world testifies to both the genuine efforts she made to keep those eyes wide open and the limitations that lay in the all-pervasiveness of race as the lens through which to see that world. The Cannons were horrified at reports of Stalin's crimes and the Moscow show trials, and they knew about the conflict-laden alliance between the Loyalists, communists, and socialists during the Spanish civil war, yet they joined, in 1937, the Friends of Spanish Democracy; Dr. Cannon served as chairman of the Medical Committee for Spanish Democracy,[42] and they continued to provide financial support for the refugees after the defeat of the Spanish Republic.[43] During World War II Dr. Cannon organized medical relief for China, and he became president of the American-Soviet Medical Society.[44] The American press and conservative colleagues charged him "with being a Bolshevik, a supporter of communism, an enemy of the Roman Catholic church, and in general a Red, with all the dark insinuations then implied in that term."[45] It was a reputation that he, according to Arthur Schlesinger Jr., "endured stoically."[46] His wife stood by him. Because she saw the Soviet experiment as tainted by totalitarianism, Cornelia Cannon decided to put up stiff opposition against anticommunist persecution in the United States, which she identified as expressions of totalitarian leanings, and as early as 1937 she protested in writing against anticommunist investigative committees appointed by various state legislatures. "The danger in the present hysteria is not to communism but to ourselves," she warned. "As soon as we resort to the methods of the enemies of freedom we are no longer free. Those who are fearful of the spread of communism themselves lack faith in democracy."[47] In the 1950s she spoke up against McCarthyism and the activities of HUAC, and in 1958 she traveled to the Soviet Union to express her displeasure with cold war America. She was indeed seeing with new eyes, and she had the courage to act accordingly.

Cannon's effort to see anew also awakened in her an awareness that she had better move beyond the narrow boundaries which her clinging to race as "the ultimate trope of difference"[48] imposed on the way she perceived the world around her, but here she was less successful. She seemed forever suspended between sympathy for individual victims of racism and economic exploitation, especially when they were of her own class and well educated, and her eugenic phobia, which proved resistant to experience. In many ways the conflict between intellect and emotion that tore Cannon on an individual level confirms Dan O'Meara's finding that "racial policy is open to a sequence of somersaults, deviations, and permutations which endlessly confuse those who regard it as the product of a monolithic racial ideology."[49] African Americans never ceased to be the white race's burden for her, yet she gave generously to the NAACP and protested Klan violence. Equally, she continued to fear Jewish immigration as a racial threat to her America, and she would forever dread educated Jews as competitors in the professional realm, where they "would constitute the entire medical profession of the country if they were not restrained,"[50] but with her husband she supported Jewish refugees from Nazi Germany.[51]

Her utter confusion surfaced in a family letter of 5 March 1934. She reported on a dinner conversation that, inspired by terrifying news from Hitler's Germany, focused on the treatment of Jews in the United States. Transcending convenient we/they dichotomies, she wondered "what we must do to fortify ourselves against the horrors of that prejudice and injustice." In her answer race and class, a refusal to acknowledge systemic causes, empathy for the victim, and racialized rationalization formed a painful chorus: "I think myself we have got to get over the habit of thinking of *race* and think of the *individual*. As [Dr. Cannon's colleague] Dr. Cohn says, there is no obligation to like a disagreeable Jew any more than there is to like a disagreeable Frenchman, but neither is there any justice in cataloguing the fine ones with the others in a lump." And then, in another somersault four years later, when Nazi Germany was preparing for the "Final Solution" and anti-Semitism in the United States was reaching frightening dimensions,[52] Cannon wrote in her (unpublished) essay "Can the Jews Save Themselves?": "The racial prejudice from which they suffer cannot be wholly without foundation. There must be some inborn characteristic of the Jewish people which inspires the suspicion and dislike they meet everywhere."[53] Clearly Cannon was blissfully unaware—as was that acquiescing Euro-American majority who thought and felt as she spoke and wrote—that her celebration of racial exclusiveness, her amalgophobia, her propagation of sterilization of the "unfit" were intimately linked to what was happening in Germany and in the Deep South.

Cannon returned to Cambridge invigorated by the belief that change was necessary and possible in the realm she defined as home, and she was even more convinced that birth control was the solution to most of the problems humankind faced in the 1930s and 1940s. The Great Depression, relief programs, racial strife, social unrest, political radicalism, another world war: after her trip around the world, her expedition through the crowded streets of Peking into the netherworld of Chinese opium asylums and beggar lanes, her tours through Russian abortoriums and the revelation she had experienced as a guest in the birth-controlled Scandinavian Elysium, she was more confident than ever that her nation's and, with that, the world's problems boiled down to overpopulation, and she devoted her life to preaching the solution—birth control. On the one hand, she had left the United States an activist whose reputation as a progressive reformer had been slightly tainted by the neo-Malthusianism she had displayed in her campaign against relief babies. On the other hand, she had worked hard to reinvent the trip as a sojourn among birth control experts all over the globe, and when she returned to New England, she saw to it that the expertise and authority thus acquired were acknowledged by her now partly alienated peers.

Birth control in the Soviet Union, in China, in Scotland, in Sweden: Cannon now traveled the United States as a lecturer-expert of international experience and reputation. There were radio interviews and newspaper reports. The BCLM reembraced its successful and highly visible ally, for the League needed her voice in the doctors-only controversy more than ever. When Ames resigned as president, Cannon even succeeded her as president pro tem in 1939.[54] She gave generously of her time, her energy, and her enthusiasm. She would have liked to give even more, but her novel *Denial* found no publisher, her book on birth control around the world never materialized, and she even failed to see in print individual articles she drafted on birth control practices in various Asian and European countries. As rejection slips continued to pile up on her desk, she had to acknowledge that being a writer had become a burden. She might have made a career as a family planning activist had her husband's deteriorating condition in the late thirties and during World War II not forced her to rechannel her energy.

Diagnosed in 1932 with mycosis fungoides and lymphatic leukemia,[55] Walter Cannon survived beyond everyone's wildest expectations. But in the late thirties he developed bouts of facial paralysis, severe skin itches, bilateral deafness, ulcerated lesions, and skin cancer and had to submit to several operations. Still, he embraced the life of an active scientist almost to the last. Although Harvard failed to provide him with laboratory space after he retired in August 1942,[56] he focused on shock research during the war; accepted an exchange professorship at New York University in 1944; participated in projects and visited laboratories run by former students and colleagues in Argentina, Brazil, Canada, Chile, and the Philippine Islands;[57] joined Dr. Arturo Rosenblueth's team in New Mexico in the spring of 1945;[58] and wrote, with Cornelia as secretary, his autobiography,

The Way of an Investigator. He also participated vigorously in the political realm, devoting time to the China Relief Legion, the American Bureau for Medical Aid to China, the American-Soviet Medical Society, the Medical Committee for Spanish Democracy, and even to the birth control movement. The Cannons still traveled whenever his condition permitted, treating themselves to hibernation in Florida, an extended tour of Guatemala, and an enchanting stay in New Mexico, but fear of yet another infection was their most faithful travel companion, and only an emergency flight brought Dr. Cannon back alive from Mexico City to Boston in the summer of 1945.

Like the protagonist of her novel *Heirs,* Cannon all of a sudden found herself in the role of wife transformed into nurse. Her family letters document that she chafed at having her wings clipped and struggled to find satisfaction in a new kind of usefulness and the shift in the distribution of power that the situation entailed. In precious periods of relative calm in between her husband's bouts of sickness, Cornelia Cannon even resumed her writing. This time she hoped to build on her success as an author of children's books by drawing on her Chinese adventure. "I decided to create a book while [daughter-in-law Ellen Cannon] was creating a grandchild [Sarah], and I am already deep in it, finding my old zest for writing coming back after several years of indifference and positive distaste," she announced on 17 June 1943. "It is to be a child's story of the expedition of Abbe Huc, illustrated by Marian." A year later she was in the midst of yet another revision, her enthusiasm considerably "cooled off."[59] Vanguard Press had agreed to publish the book,[60] but for reasons that remain undocumented, Cornelia James Cannon's last children's novel, *To the Roof of the World,* never made it into print.

She also dealt with her limited mobility by adding a new title to her name during the decade between her trip around the world and her husband's death in 1945: that of grandmother. A veritable deluge of grandchildren descended on the Cannons. By 1945 one girl and four boys had been born to Ellen and Bradford; Linda had four children, Helen and Marian two each; only the Fairbanks remained childless.[61] By 1953 Cornelia boasted twenty grandchildren, her personal firewall against "race suicide." During the summer months the Cannon farm took on the appearance of a children's paradise. Walter Cannon, suffering from sleeplessness, attacks of itching, and extreme fatigue, bore this invasion of diapers with a remarkable sense of humor; his wife was jubilant whenever the house was packed. Grandmother was the private role in which she gloried, but it was more than that: the grandchildren were a proud confirmation of success in the struggle for that pure and healthy, vigorous America to which she had devoted her skills as a writer and as a birth control activist. Cornelia knew that her children—including the partners they had chosen, and the offspring they produced—represented the best, from a eugenicist's point of view, that white America had to offer, and consequently she celebrated each grandchild as a guarantor of a great American "race" and future. Twenty Cannon grandchildren versus worldwide overpopulation? No ideological dilemma for Cornelia James Cannon, for there can never be too much of a good thing.

And then there was another war. Cannon had long since given up on the Old World. "Cut ourselves loose from Europe, let the Turk over run [sic] it, and let them all die in an orgy of mutual slaughter," she had written to her mother on 18 January 1923. It follows that World War II became a bitter reality for her only after Pearl Harbor, and with the changes this attack on her America wrought in her family. During World War I, two lines of activities had competed: Walter Cannon's research in France and Cornelia James Cannon's work with the Radio boys on the home front. This time around everything was different; the entire family was involved, while Grandma Cannon looked on in wonder and patriotic pride. Dr. Walter Cannon served as chairman of the committee on shock and transfusions established by the National Research Council; Lieutenant Dr. Bradford Cannon performed plastic surgery on soldiers in an army hospital in Pennsylvania; Wilma Cannon Fairbank advised the State Department on cultural relations with China, while her husband was with the Office of Strategic Services in China; Marian's husband, Arthur Schlesinger Jr., was with the Office of Strategic Services in Washington and later in Europe; Lieutenant Dr. Douglas Bond, Helen's spouse, had joined the U.S. Army Medical Corps at Randolph Field, Texas, while Linda's husband worked for the improvement of bar aluminum under Donald Nelson in Washington.[62] As always, Cannon reported on the activities of the various family members and was generous in her praise, but the war was remarkably absent from her letters.

On 1 October 1945, at the age of seventy-four, Walter B. Cannon died on their Franklin farm. The autopsy report read: "Mycosis fungoides involving the skin, lungs, myocardium, liver, spleen, intestine, bone marrow, and lymph nodes. An active febrile illness with broncho-pneumonia terminated life."[63] During his long illness Cornelia had stood by him, drastically reducing her activities, with the exception of family letters. Following her husband's death, she gave in to depressive spells and periods of self-reproach in which everything that had been precious for her—her devotion to family, her mobility, her success as a writer and political activist, her independence—seemed blurred and tainted by a coat of guilt. Neglect of marital responsibilities, insufficient love, blindness to her husband's merits: all the expectations for true womanhood that she had challenged and affirmed in her eclectic ways suddenly surfaced with a vengeance. "I think she momentarily lost her nerve after he died, for under her high-spirited exterior she was a deeply emotional person, and the security of his affection was the wellspring of her life," Marian Cannon Schlesinger remembers. "For a brief moment, one caught a glimpse of those private dreads and thoughts that were usually rigorously controlled out of her strong sense of pride and self-discipline."[64] Extreme physical and emotional exhaustion combined, after fourteen years of living with death, and for once she lacked the stamina to fight off emotions she had always kept at bay.

Once again she tried writing as an act of survival. The family papers contain fragments of a Walter B. Cannon biography, to be called *Life with Father*.[65] The title signifies on the title of his autobiography, with its exclusive focus on his public persona as a scholar. She soon gave up on this manuscript without a word of explanation. She then spent months on a more modest project, a book on their Russian sojourn, *Feasting with the Bear*, dedicated to Walter's "beloved memory."[66] She failed to find a publisher, and the manuscript was deposited in that growing pile of "unpublishables." Perhaps she finally realized that her concept of biography, thoroughly rooted in the Victorian celebration of greatness pure and untainted, was incompatible with the expectations of modern readers and the demands of the postwar literary marketplace; perhaps she came to acknowledge that her husband's had been a life and personality beyond the reach of her skills and intent as a writer. Perhaps the need to succeed in a public career, to move in the light of public acclaim, evaporated once the person with whom she had joyfully and lovingly competed for that acclaim was gone. Perhaps she ultimately learned to embrace the fulfillment and satisfaction that lay in being Cornelia James Cannon.

Until she was well into her nineties she continued to travel extensively, embracing the title "Globetrotting Grandmother" with which her friends in Cambridge honored her.[67] At the age of eighty-nine, preparing for a trip to Guatemala amidst rumors of revolution, she warned her children not to waste money on ransom should she be kidnapped: "'Old lady with fresh dental plates, useless knees and incurable disease of old age and approaching senility.' Not worth $30 so refuse to pay!"[68] Usually traveling by herself, with only a miniature suitcase to her name, and always on an individual ticket and itinerary, she toured the globe and saw India and the Philippines, Guatemala and Israel, Italy and France, Yugoslavia and Egypt, and she wrote about her adventures in family letters that fill volumes. In 1958 she even took another trip to the Soviet Union. Wherever she traveled, she went as a missionary of Planned Parenthood, equipped with hundreds of condoms, which she distributed among bus drivers in Yugoslavia, waiters in Rome, tourist guides in Israel, barmen in Bombay, hotel porters in Guatemala, farmers in the Philippines.[69] In the postwar decades the American eugenic movement, determined to continue its struggle for the genetic improvement of "the race," yet forced to redefine its rhetoric in response to the atrocities the Third Reich had committed in the name of eugenics, shifted focus from compulsory sterilization advocacy to family planning and marriage counseling. Cannon, too, submitted so the work could be continued under a more acceptable and legitimate label.[70] She always traveled as a woman with a revised eugenic mission, a veritable "birth control zealot," and the woman whom Arthur Schlesinger Jr. recalled as "an incurable meddler"[71] absolutely refused to feel defeated when her suggestions met with rejection. "I shall simply have a dozen more suggestions to take its place," she answered to her daughter Wilma's criticism. "The acceptance of my wild ideas never worries me. All I ask is to retain my freedom to *make* them."[72]

Cornelia James Cannon was in her early nineties when she finally moved into a retirement home in Franklin—always hoping that one of her children would provide a home for her, yet understanding that this could not be.[73] All her daughters and sons had made a career as a physician, artist, politician, scientist, teacher, diplomat, art historian, or with an adoption NGO; each boasted a large and demanding family. There were divorces, deaths, families coming apart. Intellectually curious to the last, Cannon tried to participate—and make suggestions—even when it came to where she ought to die and when. And how she would be remembered. She died in Franklin on 11 December 1969 at the age of ninety-three, honored by the *Boston Herald* as "Birth Control Proponent,"[74] a final triumph. They forgot to add "writer," a final defeat. Defeat? "Well, it is a lovely dream, anyway!"[75]

NOTES

INTRODUCTION

1. Marian Cannon Schlesinger, *Snatched from Oblivion: A Cambridge Memoir* (Cambridge, Mass.: Gale Hill Books, 1979), 123.
2. Constance Russell, "New Boston Road: Here and There since 1907" (1979), unpublished manuscript, CJCP, 37.
3. Schlesinger, *Snatched,* 124.
4. Cited ibid.
5. See CJC to FHJ, 11 September 1923, CJCP.
6. Morris Dickstein, "Introduction: Pragmatism Then and Now," in *The Revival of Pragmatism: New Essays on Social Thought, Law, and Culture,* ed. Dickstein (Durham: Duke University Press, 1998), 7.
7. Charlene Haddock Seigfried, *Pragmatism and Feminism: Reweaving the Social Fabric* (Chicago: University of Chicago Press, 1996), 263.
8. Or, as an alternative, an actress—a dream discouraged by her kin and consequently discarded. See chapter 3.
9. The Cornelia James Cannon Papers consist of four clearly defined segments. Material documenting her birth control activities is in the Sophia Smith Collection at Smith College, Northampton, Mass. A large segment of her public records, and especially those documenting her relationship of more than seventy years with Radcliffe College, are in the Cannon Family Papers, Schlesinger Library, Radcliffe Institute for Advanced Study, Harvard University, as are most of her private records, including family letters, diaries, and unpublished manuscripts (CJCP). Her correspondence with her husband is in the Walter B. Cannon Papers (WBCP), held by the Harvard Medical Library in the Francis A. Countway Library of Medicine. Some personal material, especially manuscripts of unpublished texts, scrapbooks, and photos, are in the possession of Marian Cannon Schlesinger (CJCP/MCS). All otherwise uncited quotations are from these sources.
10. This was the formula Walter B. Cannon, according to his daughter Marian, used to describe his spouse's approach to life.
11. CJC, "The New Leisure," *NAR* (September–November 1926): 504.
12. Arthur M. Schlesinger Jr., *A Life in the Twentieth Century: Innocent Beginnings, 1917–1950* (Boston: Houghton Mifflin, 2000), 184.
13. Linda Cannon Burgess, "Observations of Cornelia and Walter Cannon" (1940), unpublished manuscript, CJCP/MCS, unpaginated.

14. Schlesinger, *A Life,* 184.

15. Marian Cannon Schlesinger to author, 9 October 2001.

16. See Donald J. Childs, *Modernism and Eugenics: Woolf, Eliot, Yeats, and the Culture of Degeneration* (Cambridge: Cambridge University Press, 2001); Lois A. Cuddy and Claire M. Roche, eds., *Evolution and Eugenics in American Literature and Culture, 1880–1940: Essays on Ideological Conflict and Complicity* (Lewisburg, Pa.: Bucknell University Press, 2003); Daylanne K. English, *Unnatural Selections: Eugenics in American Modernism and the Harlem Renaissance* (Chapel Hill: University of North Carolina Press, 2004).

17. See Lawrence Buell, *New England Literary Culture: From Revolution through Renaissance* (Cambridge: Cambridge University Press, 1986), 294–303; Merrill Jensen, ed., *Regionalism in America* (Madison: University of Wisconsin Press, 1951); Sylvia Mayer, *Naturethik und Neuengland-Regionalliteratur* (Heidelberg: Universitätsverlag Winter, 2004); Eric Sundquist, "Realism and Regionalism," in *Columbia Literary History of the United States,* ed. Emory Elliott (New York: Columbia University Press, 1988), 501–24; Perry D. Westbrook, *Acres of Flint: Writers of Rural New England, 1870–1900* (Washington, D.C.: Scarecrow Press, 1951).

18. See Deborah O'Keefe, *Good Girl Messages: How Young Women Were Misled by Their Favorite Books* (New York: Continuum, 2000).

19. Schlesinger, *A Life,* 181.

20. See, for example, WBC to CJC, 5 January 1918, WBCP, S IX B 165, bound volume of World War I letters, 323.

21. Angelique Richardson, *Love and Eugenics in the Late Nineteenth Century: Rational Reproduction and the New Woman* (Oxford: Oxford University Press, 2003), 24.

22. Francis Galton, *Inquiries into Human Faculty and Its Development* (London: Macmillan, 1883), 25.

23. For this use of "race," see Henry Louis Gates Jr., "Introduction: Writing 'Race' and the Difference It Makes," in *"Race," Writing, and Difference,* ed. Gates (Chicago: University of Chicago Press, 1985), 16; Abdul R. JanMohamed, "The Economy of Manichean Allegory: The Function of Racial Difference in Colonialist Literature," ibid., 80; Robert J. Norrell, *The House I Live In: Race in the American Century* (New York: Oxford University Press, 2006).

24. Jürgen Heideking and Christof Mauch, *Geschichte der USA* (Tübingen: Narr Francke, 2006), 208–9; Barbara M. Solomon, *Ancestors and Immigrants: A Changing New England Tradition,* rev. ed. (Cambridge: Harvard University Press, 1959).

25. CJC to FHJ, 14 February 1923, CJCP.

26. See Hazel Carby, *Reconstructing Womanhood: The Emergence of the Afro-American Novelist* (New York: Oxford University Press, 1987); Jean Fagan Yellin, *Women and Sisters: The Antislavery Feminists in American Culture* (New Haven: Yale University Press, 1989).

27. Cited in Maria I. Diedrich, *Love across Color Lines: Ottilie Assing and Frederick Douglass* (New York: Farrar, Straus and Giroux, 1999), 289.

28. See Angela Franks, *Margaret Sanger's Eugenic Legacy: The Control of Female Fertility* (Jefferson, N.C.: McFarland Press, 2005).

29. Written with Ben L. Reitman, 1916. See Diane Paul, "Eugenics and the Left," *Journal of the History of Ideas* 45, no. 4 (1984): 567-90.

30. See Nancy Ordover, *American Eugenics: Race, Queer Anatomy, and the Science of Nationalism* (Minneapolis: University of Minnesota Press, 2003), 15.

31. Theodore Roosevelt cited in Donald K. Pickens, *Eugenics and the Progressives* (Nashville: Vanderbilt University Press, 1968), 121, 79.

32. Ruth Frankenberg, "The Mirage of an Unmarked Whiteness," in *The Making and Unmaking of Whiteness,* ed. Birgit B. Rasmussen et al. (Durham: Duke University Press, 2001), 81.

33. Charles W. Mills, *The Racial Contract* (Ithaca: Cornell University Press, 1998), 12, 13–14.

34. See Paul Spickard, *Almost All Aliens: Immigration, Race, and Colonialism in American History and Identity* (New York: Routledge, 2007).

35. English, *Unnatural Selections,* 24; see also chaps. 1 and 4. See John Nickel, "Eugenics and the Fiction of Pauline Hopkins," in Cuddy and Roche, *Evolution and Eugenics,* 133–47; Jamie Hart, "Who Should Have the Children? Discussions of Birth Control among African American Intellectuals, 1920–1937," *Journal of Negro History* 79, no. 1 (1994): 71–84.

36. English, *Unnatural Selections,* 2.

37. See Elizabeth Fox-Genovese, "Placing Women's History in History," *New Left Review* 133 (1982): 5–29.

38. Gayatri Chakravorty Spivak, "Three Women's Texts and a Critique of Imperialism," in Gates, *"Race," Writing, and Difference,* 263.

39. Andrew Schlesinger to author, 4 October 2001.

40. See CJC, "The Class of 1899," *RQ* (April 1924): 23–25.

41. Cited in Sarah Deutsch, *Women and the City: Gender, Power, and Space in Boston, 1870–1940* (New York: Oxford University Press, 2000), 15.

42. CJC, "What Ideals Do We Wish to Preserve?" *NAR* (December 1922): 808.

43. See Cheryl Greenberg, "Twentieth-Century Liberalism: Transformations of an Ideology," in *Perspectives on Modern America: Making Sense of the Twentieth Century,* ed. Harvard Sitkoff (New York: Oxford University Press, 2001), 56–57.

44. CJC, "Selecting Citizens," *NAR* (September 1923): 331.

45. CJC, "The Reaction of a Radical," *AM* (November 1919): 715.

46. Jean Strouse, "Conversation: The Secret Life of Biographers," *New York Times Book Review,* 17 October 1999, 11.

47. Schlesinger, dedication to *Snatched.*

48. Schlesinger, *A Life,* 184.

49. W. H. Auden cited in Robert Skidelsky, "Only Connect: Biography and Truth," in *The Troubled Face of Biography,* ed. Eric Homberger and John Charmley (London: Macmillan, 1988), 1.

50. Eric Homberger and John Charmley, introduction, ibid., xi.

51. Marian Cannon Schlesinger to author, 9 October 2001.

52. Strouse, "Conversation," 11.

53. See Mary A. Favret, *Romantic Correspondence: Women, Politics, and the Fiction of Letters* (Cambridge: Cambridge University Press, 1993); Janet G. Altman, *Epistolarity: Approaches to Form* (Columbus: Ohio State University Press, 1982); see also *Correspondence: A Special Issue on Letters; Prose Studies* 19, no. 2 (1997).

54. See Schlesinger, *A Life,* xiv.
55. Peter Gay, *Education of the Senses* (New York: Oxford University Press, 1984), 415.
56. Diedrich, *Love across Color Lines,* xxi.

1. "PERSONIFIED MISCHIEF"

1. Schlesinger, *A Life,* 183–84.
2. CJC and Helen Sommers, *Life at Newport* (1939), unpublished manuscript, CJCP/MCS, unpaginated; hereafter cited as *LAN.* All quotations in chapters 2 and 3 whose source is not otherwise identified are from *LAN.* Additional information is based on Schlesinger's Cambridge memoir *Snatched from Oblivion,* esp. chap. 2.
3. CJC, "My Ancestors," *AM* (October 1925): 570.
4. CJC, WI, 808.
5. See S. J. Kleinberg, *Votes for Women: Women in the United States, 1830–1945* (Houndmills: Macmillan, 1999), 58–79 and 152–75.
6. See Lois W. Banner, *Women in Modern America: A Brief History* (San Diego: Harcourt Brace Jovanovich, 1984), 4–5.
7. HWH to HNJ, 14 January 1887, CJCP.
8. On the role of friendship among women, see Carol Smith-Rosenberg, *Disorderly Conduct: Visions of Gender in Victorian America* (New York: Oxford University Press, 1985), 60ff.
9. Schlesinger, *Snatched,* 31.
10. Richardson, *Love and Eugenics,* 35.
11. See Maureen A. Flanagan, *America Reformed: Progressives and Progressivism, 1890s–1920s* (New York: Oxford University Press, 2006); John Buenker et al., *Progressivism* (Cambridge: Harvard University Press, 1977); Robert M. Crunden, *Ministers of Reform: The Progressives' Achievement in American Civilization, 1889–1920* (New York: Basic Books, 1982).
12. See Edward J. Pfeifer, "United States," in *The Comparative Reception of Darwinism,* ed. Thomas F. Glick (Chicago: University of Chicago Press, 1974), 168–206; Barbara MacKinnon, ed., *American Philosophy: A Historical Anthology* (Albany: State University of New York Press, 1985), chap. 4.
13. See Kenneth L. Kusmer, ed., *From Reconstruction to the Great Migration, 1877–1917,* vol. 4 of *Black Communities and Urban Development in America, 1720–1990* (New York: Garland, 1991).
14. See Spickard, *Almost All Aliens;* Howard Zinn, *A People's History of the United States, 1492–Present* (New York: Harper Perennial, 2003), 264–70; Christopher M. Sterba, ed., *Good Americans: Italian and Jewish Immigrants during the First World War* (Oxford: Oxford University Press, 2003); Roger Daniels, *Coming to America: A History of Immigration and Ethnicity in American Life* (New York: HarperCollins, 1990).
15. Galton, *Inquiries into Human Faculty,* 25.
16. Richardson, *Love and Eugenics,* 3. Richardson focuses on eugenics in England, but her conclusions can also be applied to the United States. It is important, however, to keep in mind that whereas class was central to the British context, race moved center stage in the United States.

17. See David W. Blight, *Race and Reunion: The Civil War in American Memory* (Cambridge: Harvard University Press, 2001).
18. See William L. O'Neill, *The Woman Movement: Feminism in the United States and England* (Chicago: Quadrangle Books, 1969), 34ff.
19. Antoinette Brown Blackwell, "On Marriage and Work," in *Root of Bitterness: Documents of the Social History of American Women*, ed. Nancy Cott (New York: E. P. Dutton & Co., 1972), 353–54.
20. See Buenker et al., *Progressivism*; Crunden, *Ministers of Reform*.
21. Lucy Williams was Harriet Haynes's sister; she suffered from arthritis and usually spent her summers in the James home.
22. HWH to HNJ, 20 January 1887, CJCP.
23. HWH to HNJ, 29 December 1891, CJCP.
24. Ibid.
25. Marian Cannon Schlesinger, Henry's granddaughter, compares him to Dickens's lovable spendthrift Wilkins Micawber from *David Copperfield* in her Cambridge memoir *Snatched from Oblivion*.
26. Arthur Schlesinger Jr. used the adjective "self-contained" to characterize the Cannon family of the 1930s and 1940s (*A Life*, 184).
27. CJC to FHJ, 31 January 1927, CJCP.
28. Barbara Welter, "The Cult of True Womanhood, 1820–1860," *American Quarterly* 18 (1966): 165.
29. O'Neill, *The Woman Movement*, 44.
30. Ibid.; see also Helen L. Horowitz, *Alma Mater: Design and Experience in the Women's Colleges from Their Nineteenth-Century Beginnings to the 1930s* (Boston: Beacon Press, 1986); Mabel Newcomer, *A Century of Higher Education for American Women* (New York: Harper and Row, 1959).
31. See Richardson, *Love and Eugenics*, 30, 40–41; Pickens, *Eugenics*.
32. See Cott, *Root of Bitterness*, 20.
33. See Richardson, *Love and Eugenics*, 46–57.
34. See Heideking and Mauch, *Geschichte*, 167–69; Lewis Gould, *America in the Progressive Era, 1890–1914* (New York: Longman, 2001); Martin J. Sklar, *The Corporate Reconstruction of American Capitalism, 1890–1916: The Market, the Law, and Politics* (Cambridge: Cambridge University Press, 1988).
35. CJ to FHJ, 9 March 1893, CJCP.
36. Russell, "New Boston Road," 55.
37. CJ to the James family, 9 January 1893, CJCP.
38. CJ to FHJ, 19 February 1893, CJCP.
39. See Ann Ardis, *New Women, New Novels: Feminism and Early Modernism* (New Brunswick: Rutgers University Press, 1990).

2. "Four Years of Unorthodox Study"

1. CJC, "Radcliffe 1855 [*sic*]–1899," SL, Radcliffe Reminiscences, Papers (1968–1973), SC 94, Box 1, Folder 8.
2. Schlesinger, *Snatched*, 37.
3. Cited in "The New Founders Award and the Alumnae Recognition Award," *RQ* (August 1965): 3.
4. CJC, "Radcliffe 1855–1899."

5. See Banner, *Women in Modern America,* 5.

6. Dora E. Howells, *A Century to Celebrate: Radcliffe College, 1879–1979* (Cambridge: Radcliffe College, 1978), 13; Horowitz, *Alma Mater.*

7. Most prominently Walter B. Cannon, Cornelia's future husband.

8. That year admission exams for Radcliffe were held "in Minneapolis, Cleveland, Portland, Albany, Exeter, Concord, Groton, and Washington, as well as in Cambridge and New York." Mary Coes, "Radcliffe College," *Harvard Graduates Magazine* 4 (1895–96): 94.

9. Cited in Schlesinger, *Snatched,* 36.

10. Howells, *A Century,* 43.

11. See David L. Lewis, *W. E. B. Du Bois: Biography of a Race, 1868–1919* (New York: Henry Holt, 1993), 155.

12. CJ to FHJ, undated but September 1895, CJCP.

13. CJ to FHJ, 30 September 1897, CJCP.

14. Cited in Mary Coes, "Radcliffe College: Academic and Social," *Harvard Graduates Magazine* 7, no. 28 (1899): 563; see also Elizabeth R. Briggs, "Early Days on Appian Way and Fay House," *RQ* (May 1937): 11–14.

15. CJC, "Radcliffe 1855–1899."

16. Schlesinger, *Snatched,* 88.

17. CJC to FHJ, 27 April 1923, CJCP.

18. See Newcomer, *A Century of Higher Education.*

19. Cited in Howells, *A Century,* viii.

20. "President Eliot's Commencement Address," *Harvard Graduates Magazine* 7, no. 25 (1898): 83.

21. Louise B. Crothers, *A Family Chronicle* (Cambridge, Mass.: privately printed, 1966), 154.

22. "President Eliot's Commencement Address," 83; see also Charles W. Eliot, "The Higher Education for Women," in *Charles W. Eliot: The Man and His Beliefs,* ed. William A. Nielson (New York: Harper and Brothers, 1926); Mary Moser, "The Eliot Years," *RQ* (June 1976): 44–46.

23. CJC, "Science at Radcliffe," 24–25, unpublished manuscript, CJCP.

24. This episode was recounted by Billy James, son of William James, and reported to me by Linda Cannon Burgess in a letter of 16 September 1992.

25. Gertrude Stein, *The Autobiography of Alice B. Toklas,* in *Selected Writings of Gertrude Stein,* ed. Carl Van Vechten (New York: Random House, 1962), 74–75.

26. David M. Kennedy, *Birth Control in America: The Career of Margaret Sanger* (New Haven: Yale University Press, 1970), 114; Barry Mehler, "The History of the American Eugenics Society, 1921–1940" (Ph.D. diss., University of Illinois, Urbana-Champaign, 1988), 329–30; Ordover, *American Eugenics,* 11, 141.

27. CJ to FHJ, 17 January 1896, CJCP.

28. CJ to Margaret James, 2 June 1897, CJCP.

29. CJ to Helen James, 11 May 1899, CJCP.

30. CJ to FHJ, 28 January 1898, CJCP.

31. For a detailed discussion of the role of class at Harvard, see Doris K. Goodwin, *The Fitzgeralds and the Kennedys* (New York: St. Martin's Press, 1987), chap. 13.

32. CJ to Frances James, 29 September 1895, CJCP.

33. See Radcliffe '99, Class Day Book, 25, Radcliffe College Archives, Cambridge, Mass.

34. See Carrie M. Harper, "The Place of Dramatics in College Life," *RQ* (December 1916): 13–14; Mary S. Stimpson, "Radcliffe Women in Literature and Drama," *New England Magazine* (January 1908): 223–37.
35. Cited in William G. B. Carson, *Dear Josephine: The Theatrical Career of Josephine Hull* (Norman: University of Oklahoma Press, 1963), 10.
36. CJ to FHJ, 15 April 1897, CJCP.
37. CJ to FHJ, 19 May 1897, CJCP.
38. FHJ to Margaret James, n.d., CJCP.
39. CJ to FHJ, 22 October 1897, CJCP.
40. Goodwin, *The Fitzgeralds and the Kennedys,* 252.
41. After her marriage to Walter B. Cannon, the Crotherses became intimate friends.
42. Banner, *Women in Modern America,* 22.
43. CJ to FHJ, 2 February 1896, CJCP.
44. In 1922 she repaid the loan through a $750 donation to the Radcliffe Endowment Fund, money earned through her publications in the *Atlantic Monthly;* see CJC to FHJ, 18 April 1922, CJCP.
45. CJ to FHJ, 5 April 1897, CJCP.
46. Stein, *Autobiography,* 73.
47. Schlesinger, *Snatched,* 157–59; Helen Cannon Bond in conversation with author.
48. Stein, *Autobiography,* 74.
49. Harriet Scott Chessman, "Gertrude Stein," in *Modern American Women Writers,* ed. Elaine Showalter, Lea Baechler, and W. Walton Litz (New York: Macmillan, 1991), 339.
50. See Marianne DeKoven, *Rich and Strange: Gender, History, Modernism* (Princeton: Princeton University Press, 1991); Heinz Ickstadt and Hubert Zapf, "Die amerikanische Moderne," in *Amerikanische Literaturgeschichte,* ed. Zapf (Stuttgart: Metzler, 2004), 222–27.
51. See Allegra Stewart, "The Quality of Gertrude Stein's Creativity," *American Literature* 28 (1957): 491–93.
52. Gertrude Stein, *Wars I Have Seen* (London: Brilliance Books, 1984), 44; Maria I. Diedrich, "'A Book in Translation about Eggs and Butter': Gertrude Stein's World War II," in *Women and War: The Changing Status of American Women from the 1930s to the 1940s,* ed. Diedrich and Dorothea Fischer-Hornung (New York: Berg, 1990), 87–106.
53. Stein, *Autobiography,* 72; see also Marianne DeKoven, *A Different Language: Gertrude Stein's Experimental Writing* (Madison: University of Wisconsin Press, 1983).
54. Chessman, "Gertrude Stein," 338.
55. Stein, *Autobiography,* 79.
56. English, *Unnatural Selections,* 93–117. See also Jaime Hovey, "Sapphic Primitivism in Gertrude Stein's *Q.E.D.,*" *Modern Fiction Studies* 42, no. 3 (1996): 547–68; Laura Doyle, "The Flat, the Round, and Gertrude Stein: Race and the Shape of Modern(ist) History," *Modernism/Modernity* 7, no. 2 (2000): 249–71.
57. CJ to FHJ, 1 January 1898, CJCP.
58. CJ to Helen James, 28 May 1897, CJCP.
59. CJC, "Reaction of a Radical," 715.
60. "Birthday Tribute to CJC," CJC to FHJ, 17 November 1922, CJCP.

61. Mary Coes, "Radcliffe College: Academic and Social," *Harvard Graduates Magazine* 8, no. 29 (September 1899): 63.
62. Cited ibid., 68.
63. CJ to WBC, 17 September 1899, WBCP, S VIII B 146 F 2058.
64. CJ to WBC, 15 May 1900, WBCP, S VIII B 146 F 2062.
65. Charles W. Eliot to Cornelia James, 30 October 1899, CJCP.

3. "WALTER CANNON IS MY COMFORT"

1. CJ to FHJ, 15 August 1897, CJCP.
2. CJ to FHJ, 8 August 1897, CJCP.
3. CJ to FHJ, 26 January 1898, CJCP.
4. CJ to Helen James, 12 December 1895, CJCP.
5. Cott, introduction to *Root of Bitterness,* 11; see also Welter, "Cult of True Womanhood," 151ff.
6. Cott, introduction, 19.
7. CJC's children informed me that their parents continued this tradition: in their relationship to their children they avoided the subject of sexuality in every possible way. Avoidance and evasion were the means of teaching. In that they were thoroughly Victorian—"Puritan," as their daughter Helen Bond called it.
8. This episode was related to me by John Fairbank during an interview in Franklin, New Hampshire, in August 1991 a few months before his death. He suggested that CJC was always afraid of similar relationships developing in her own family, and he also claimed that the romantic involvement between Matts and his stepdaughter Christina in Cannon's novel *Red Rust* is related to this experience.
9. CJ to FHJ, 22 April 1899, CJCP.
10. CJ to FHJ, 26 April 1899, CJCP.
11. CJ to FHJ, 30 April 1899, CJCP.
12. CJ to Helen James, 21 May 1899, CJCP.
13. See CJ to FHJ, 25 June 1899, CJCP.
14. See CJ to Henry C. James, 20 October 1895, CJCP.
15. For biographical background, see WBC, *The Way of an Investigator: A Scientist's Experiences in Medical Research* (1945; reprint, New York: Norton, 1984), chap. 1; Schlesinger, *Snatched,* 42ff.; Saul A. Benison, Clifford Barger, and Elin L. Wolfe, *Walter B. Cannon: The Life and Times of a Young Scientist* (Cambridge: Harvard University Press, 1987), chaps. 1 and 2 (hereafter Benison, Barger, and Wolfe, *WBC*).
16. May Newson to CJ, 5 February 1893, WBCP, S VIII B 145 B 2039.
17. CJ to Helen James, 12 December 1895, CJCP.
18. CJ to FHJ, 27 March 1897, CJCP.
19. CJ to FHJ, 16 December 1898, CJCP.
20. CJ to FHJ, 25 November 1898, CJCP.
21. CJ to FHJ, 16 December 1897, CJCP.
22. See WBC, *The Way,* 16.
23. John Fairbank made these remarks in an interview with me shortly before his death.
24. CJ to FHJ, 11 April 1897, CJCP.

25. CJ to FHJ, undated but May 1898, CJCP.
26. See Benison, Barger, and Wolfe, *WBC*, 72.
27. See Schlesinger, *Snatched*, 40.
28. WBC to CJ, undated but between 29 April and 4 May 1900, WBCP, S VIII B 146 F 2059.
29. Quoted in Cott, *Root of Bitterness*, 295.
30. WBC to CJ, 4 May 1900, WBCP, S VIII B 146 F 2059.
31. Linda Cannon Burgess, interview by author, fall 1994.
32. G. J. Barker-Benfield, *The Horrors of Half-Known Life: Male Attitudes toward Women and Sexuality in Nineteenth-Century America* (New York: Harper & Row, 1976), 72; see also Mark H. Haller, *Eugenics: Hereditarian Attitudes in American Thought* (New Brunswick: Rutgers University Press, 1963), 63ff.; Daniel Kevles, *In the Name of Eugenics: Genetics and the Uses of Human Heredity* (New York: Knopf, 1985); Kenneth M. Ludmerer, *Genetics and American Society* (Baltimore: Johns Hopkins University Press, 1968), 7ff., 45ff.; Richardson, *Love and Eugenics*, 49.
33. Quoted in Barker-Benfield, *The Horrors*, 72.
34. Ibid.
35. Richardson, *Love and Eugenics*, 49–50.
36. WBC Diaries, entry of 25 June 1901, WBCP, S IX B 167 F-.
37. See WBC, "Diary of Wedding Journey, 1901, Remembered in 1903," WBCP.
38. Schlesinger, *Snatched*, 46.
39. See WBC to Colbert H. Cannon, 21 July 1901, CJCP; WBC S VIII B/63 F 23/2; WBC, *The Way*, chap. 2.
40. See Peggy Pascoe, "Miscegenation Law, Court Cases, and Ideologies of 'Race' in Twentieth-Century America," in *Interracialism: Black-White Intermarriage in American History, Literature, and Law*, ed. Werner Sollors (New York: Oxford University Press, 2000), 193 n. 53.
41. Haller, *Eugenics*, 5.
42. Pascoe, "Miscegenation Law," 193.
43. Kennedy, *Birth Control in America*, 114–15.
44. WBC, *The Way*, 19.
45. Benison, Barger, and Wolfe, *WBC*, 134.
46. Schlesinger, *Snatched*, 68.
47. Glenna Matthews, *The Rise of Public Woman: Woman's Power and Woman's Place in the United States, 1630–1970* (New York: Oxford University Press, 1992).
48. O'Neill, *The Woman Movement*, 47.
49. See Lori D. Ginzberg, *Women and the Work of Benevolence: Morality Politics and Class in the Nineteenth-Century United States* (New Haven: Yale University Press, 1990); Matthews, *The Rise of Public Woman*.
50. See Marvin Lazerson, *Origins of the Urban School: Public Education in Massachusetts, 1870–1915* (Cambridge: Harvard University Press, 1971), 6–7.
51. See Andrew Bunie and Alan Rogers, *Boston: City on a Hill* (Boston: Winsor Publications, 1984), 88–95; J. Anthony Lukas, *Common Ground: A Turbulent Decade in the Lives of Three American Families* (New York: Knopf, 1985), 60; Thomas H. O'Connor, *Bible, Brahmins, and Bosses: A Short History of Boston*, 2nd ed. (Boston: Boston Public Library, 1984), 119–52.

52. Paul Boyer, *Urban Masses and Moral Order in America, 1820–1920* (Cambridge: Harvard University Press, 1978), 190.

53. On this concept of consanguine whiteness, see Matthew F. Jacobson, *Whiteness of a Different Color: European Immigrants and the Alchemy of Race* (Cambridge: Harvard University Press, 1998).

54. See Deutsch, *Women and the City,* chaps. 1 and 7.

55. Crunden, *Ministers of Reform,* 39.

56. William James, *Pragmatism and Four Essays from the Meaning of Truth,* ed. Ralph Barton Perry (Cleveland: Meridian Books, 1955), 167.

57. Greenberg, "Twentieth-Century Liberalism," 59; See Paul Boyer, "The Chameleon with Nine Lives: American Religion in the Twentieth Century," in Sitkoff, *Perspectives on Modern America,* 249–55; see John E. Smith, *Purpose Thought: The Meaning of Pragmatism* (Chicago: University of Chicago Press, 1978).

58. Cited in Cott, *Root of Bitterness,* 293.

59. Theodore Roosevelt cited in Pickens, *Eugenics,* 79.

60. Helen James Sommers to CJC, 2 June 1902, CJCP.

61. See F. Tilden Brown and Alfred T. Osgood, "X-Rays and Sterility," *American Journal of Surgery* 18 (1907): 179–82.

62. Benison, Barger, and Wolfe, *WBC,* 89.

63. Helen James to CJC, undated but October 1901, CJCP.

64. See WBC Diaries, entry of 22 March 1906, WBCP S IX B/67 F-.

65. Benison, Barger, and Wolfe, *WBC,* 149.

66. See WBC Diaries, entry of 27 March 1907, WBCP.

67. FHJ to CJC, 29 October 1901, CJCP.

68. CJC to Bradford Cannon, 31 October 1938, CJCP.

69. For a detailed account of the event, see WBC, *The Way,* chap. 17; Benison, Barger, and Wolfe, *WBC,* 149–50.

70. CJC to FHJ, undated letter of January 1907, CJCP.

71. Ibid.

72. See WBC, *The Way,* 188–94.

73. See Louise W. Knight, *Citizen: Jane Addams and the Struggle for Democracy* (Chicago: University of Chicago Press, 2006).

74. See Ida M. Cannon, *On the Social Frontier of Medicine: Pioneering in Medical Social Service* (Cambridge: Harvard University Press, 1952); Harriet Bartlett, "Ida M. Cannon: Pioneer of Medical Social Work," *Social Service Review* 49 (1975): 208–29; Anette Bickmeyer, "'The Best Way to Explain It Is to Do It': Ida Cannon and the Professionalization of Medical Social Work during the Progressive Era and the 1920s" (Ph.D. diss., University of Hannover, 1999); Ida M. Cannon, *Medical Social Work in Hospitals: A Contribution to Progressive Medicine* (New York: Survey Associates, 1913).

75. See Benison, Barger, and Wolfe, *WBC,* 213–15.

76. In the thirties she lost her position at Filene's and opened a store for children in Harvard Square, another successful business venture.

77. "Reports of Cannon Psychiatric Clinic" (December 1932), unpaginated, CJCP.

78. Ida Cannon to CJC, undated but September 1912, WBCP, S VIII B 163 F 2313; see Schlesinger, *Snatched,* 63.

79. Ida Cannon to CJC, undated but September 1912, WBCP S VIII B 163 F 2313.

80. FHJ to CJC, 15 September 1907, CJCP; see also Dr. Cannon's diary entries between April and December 1907, WBCP S IX B/67 F-.

81. On 23 November 1907 Helen James Sommers wrote to her sister: "Dear Cornelia, we do love you and we do think of you and long for the time to be over and you to be happy with the little daughter. Frances expresses a wicked wish that you may be surprised by a son!" CJCP.

82. WBC to the James family, 2 December 1907, CJCP.

83. Schlesinger, *A Life,* 184.

84. Dickstein, "Pragmatism Then and Now," 2.

85. CJC to FHJ, 10 May 1927, CJCP.

86. See Schlesinger, *Snatched,* 60.

87. See Lawrence A. Cremin, "The Progressive Movement in American Education: A Perspective," *Harvard Educational Review* 27, no. 4 (1957): 251–70.

88. Crunden, *Ministers of Reform,* 61.

89. CJC, "Public Schools," *RQ* (May 1917): 73.

90. See Lazerson, *Origins of the Urban School,* 6–7.

91. Ibid., xii.

92. Cited in Lawrence A. Cremin, *The Transformation of the School: Progressivism in American Education, 1876–1957* (New York: Knopf, 1961), 69.

93. John E. Smith, *The Spirit of American Philosophy* (New York: Oxford University Press, 1963), 117.

94. John Dewey, "Education as Politics," in *Middle Works of John Dewey,* vol. 13, ed. Jo Ann Boydston (Carbondale: Southern Illinois University Press, 1978), 334.

95. Lazerson, *Origins of the Urban School,* 194 n.

96. CJC, "The Responsibility of University Women in Public Education," *Journal of the American Association of University Women* (October 1924): unpaginated.

97. CJC, "Public Schools," 74.

98. Cott, *Root of Bitterness,* 27.

99. CJC, "The Responsibility."

100. Schlesinger, *Snatched,* 23–25.

101. See O'Connor, *Bible, Brahmins, and Bosses,* 167–69; Stephen Thernstrom, *The Other Bostonians: Poverty and Progress in the American Metropolis, 1880–1970* (Cambridge: Harvard University Press, 1973), 176–219.

102. Schlesinger, *Snatched,* 23–25.

103. Frankenberg, "The Mirage of an Unmarked Whiteness," 80.

104. See Adelaide Cromwell, *The Other Brahmins: Boston's Black Upper Class, 1750–1950* (Fayetteville: University of Arkansas Press, 1994); John Daniels, *In Freedom's Birthplace: A Study of Negro Boston* (Boston: Houghton Mifflin, 1914), 468–69; James O. Horton and Lois E. Horton, *Black Bostonians: Family Life and Community Struggle in the Antebellum North* (New York: Homes and Meiner, 1979); O'Connor, *Bible, Brahmins and Bosses,* 74; Elizabeth H. Pleck, *Black Migration and Poverty: Boston, 1865–1900* (New York: Academic Press, 1979); Mark Perry, *Lift Up Thy Voice: The Grimké Family's Journey from Slaveholders to Civil Rights Leaders* (New York: Putnam, 2001), 255ff.; Violet Showers Johnson, *The Other Black Bostonians: West Indians in Boston, 1900–1950* (Bloomington: Indiana University Press, 2006), 36–38.

105. Schlesinger, *A Life,* 182.
106. See CJC to FHJ, 6 August 1923, CJCP.

4. "THE WOMAN WHO STAYS BEHIND"

1. Goodwin, *The Fitzgeralds and the Kennedys,* 311.
2. President Wilson cited in Zinn, *A People's History,* 361.
3. See Heideking and Mauch, *Geschichte,* 219–20.
4. WBC Diary, February 1915, 370, WBCP, S IX B 167 F-.
5. CJC to FHJ, 26 February 1915, CJCP.
6. Heideking and Mauch, *Geschichte,* 220–21.
7. WBC, *The Way,* 130; see also Benison, Barger, and Wolfe, *WBC,* 383ff; Elin L. Wolfe, Clifford Barger, and Saul A. Benison, *Walter B. Cannon: Science and Society* (Cambridge: Harvard University Press, 2000), chaps. 1–3 (hereafter Wolfe, Barger, and Benison, *Science and Society*).
8. CJC, "Our International Baby," *WC,* 21 May 1925, unpaginated.
9. CJC to FHJ, 14 January 1915, CJCP.
10. See Benison, Barger, and Wolfe, *WBC,* 386ff.
11. For concepts of republican motherhood, see Lora Romero, *Home Fronts: Domesticity and Its Critics in the Antebellum United States* (Durham: Duke University Press, 1997), 14.
12. CJC to FHJ, 3 December 1916, CJCP.
13. WBC reports on his war experience and work in his autobiography, *The Way of an Investigator,* chap. 12; for an excellent analysis of WBC's work on shock, see Saul A. Benison, Clifford Barger, and Elin L. Wolfe, "Walter B. Cannon and the Mystery of Shock: A Study of Anglo-American Cooperation in World War I," *Medical History* 35 (1991): 217–49; Wolfe, Barger, and Benison, *Science and Society,* chaps. 1–3.
14. CJC to FHJ, 2 April 1917, CJCP.
15. See William Jordan, "'The Damnable Dilemma': African-American Accommodation and Protest during World War I," *Journal of American History* 81, no. 4 (1995): 1562–83.
16. Zinn, *A People's History,* 364.
17. See CJC to FHJ, 29 March 1917, CJCP.
18. See CJC to FHJ, 30 April 1917, CJCP.
19. See George M. Fredrickson, *The Black Image in the White Mind: The Debate on Afro-American Character and Destiny, 1817–1914* (New York: Harper & Row, 1971).
20. See Diedrich and Fischer-Hornung, introduction to *Women and War,* 7ff.
21. CJC, "The Women Who Stay Behind," 1917, CJCP.
22. See Amy Bentley, *Eating for Victory: Food Rationing and the Politics of Domesticity* (Urbana: University of Illinois Press, 1998), chap. 1.
23. CJC, "The Day," CJCP.
24. Randolph S. Bourne, *War and the Intellectuals: Essays, 1915–1919* (New York: Harper & Row, 1964), 10.
25. WBC to CJC, 17 July 1918, WBCP, S XI B 183 F-.
26. WBC to CJC, 16 July 1918, WBCP, S XI B 183 F-.
27. WBC to CJC, 20 July 1918, WBCP, S XI B 183 F-.

28. CJC to WBC, 5 September 1917, WBCP, S XI B 184 F-.
29. CJC, "A Middle-Aged Adventure" (August 1917), 10, 1, unpublished manuscript, CJCP. Cited in the text as "AMA."
30. O'Neill, *The Woman Movement,* 80.
31. Schlesinger, *A Life,* 183.
32. WBC to CJC, 5 January 1918, WBCP, S XI B 183 F-.
33. See David M. Kennedy, "World War I," in *The Reader's Companion to American History,* ed. Eric Foner and John A. Garraty (Boston: Houghton Mifflin, 1991), 1172.
34. See William O'Neill, *Everyone Was Brave: The Rise and Fall of Feminism in America* (Chicago: Quadrangle Books, 1969), 189ff.
35. See Richardson, *Love and Eugenics,* 46–57. See also Martin S. Pernick, *The Black Stork: Eugenics and the Death of "Defective" Babies in American Medicine and Motion Pictures since 1915* (New York: Oxford University Press, 1996), chaps. 2–3.
36. Mark Thomas Connelly, "Prostitutes, Venereal Disease, and American Medicine," in *Women and Health in America: Historical Readings,* ed. Judith W. Leavitt (Madison: University of Wisconsin Press, 1984), 196.
37. Ibid., 200, 215 n. 45.
38. WBC to CJC, 5 January 1918, WBCP, S XI B 184 F-.
39. WBC to CJC, 21 April 1918, WBCP, S XI B 184 F-.
40. After the war Dr. Cannon became a member of the Committee for Research in Problems of Sex; he worked on this committee for more than twenty years. See WBC, *The Way,* 150–51; Wolfe, Barger, and Benison, *Science and Society,* 136ff.
41. Margaret Sanger, *An Autobiography* (New York: Norton, 1938), 256.
42. For a detailed report on these activities, see CJC, "From a Hostess House, 1917–1918," unpublished manuscript, CJCP.
43. CJC to FJC, 5 December 1917, CJCP.
44. See Diedrich and Fischer-Hornung, introduction, 7ff.; Ruth Milkman, *Gender at Work: The Dynamics of Job Segregation by Sex during World War II* (Urbana: University of Illinois Press, 1987).
45. WBC, *The Way,* 132.
46. CJC, "From a Hostess House."
47. WBC to CJC, 23 June 1917, WBCP, S XI B 183 F-.
48. WBC to CJC, 14 November 1917, WBCP, S XI B 183 F-.
49. WBC to CJC, 16 July 1918, WBCP, S XI B 183 F-.
50. WBC to CJC, 20 November 1918, WBCP, S XI B 184 F-.
51. See George H. Douglas, *Women of the Twenties* (Dallas: Saybrook Publishers, 1986), 14–15.
52. CJC to WBC, 13 November 1918, WBCP, S XI B 184 F-.
53. WBC, *The Way,* 142.
54. CJC to WBC, 13 November 1918, WBCP, S XI B 184 F-.

5. "Can Our Civilization Maintain Itself?"

1. CJC, "From a Hostess House," 9.
2. See CJC to FHJ, 30 September 1918, CJCP.
3. CJC to FHJ, 22 January 1919, CJCP.

4. CJC to FHJ, 6 February 1919, CJCP.

5. CJC, "The Lost Fruits of Victory," unpublished manuscript, CJCP/MCS.

6. Zinn, *A People's History*, 375.

7. Ordover, *American Eugenics*, 22; Spickard, *Almost All Aliens*, 276–81.

8. Étienne Balibar, "Racism and Crisis," in *Race, Nation, Class: Ambiguous Identities*, ed. Balibar and Immanuel Wallerstein (New York: Verso, 1991), 219.

9. Michelle Wright, *Becoming Black: Creating Identity in the African Diaspora* (Durham: Duke University Press, 2004), 8.

10. W. E. B. Du Bois, "Returning Soldiers," *The Crisis* 18 (May 1919): 14.

11. Claude McKay, "If We Must Die," in *The Norton Anthology of African American Literature*, ed. Henry Louis Gates Jr. and Nellie Y. McKay (New York: Norton, 1997), 984.

12. Madison Grant cited in Ordover, *American Eugenics*, xvii.

13. CJC, "The Reaction of a Radical," 714.

14. See Greenberg, "Twentieth-Century Liberalism," 61.

15. Cited in Zinn, *A People's History*, 374.

16. Schlesinger, *A Life*, 184.

17. CJC, "The Dissociated School," *AM* (November 1923): 610.

18. CJC to FHJ, 1 July 1921, CJCP.

19. See John Dewey, *The Public and Its Problems* (New York: Henry Holt, 1927), 147–48; Robert Westbrook, *John Dewey and American Democracy* (Ithaca: Cornell University Press, 1991), xv.

20. See CJC, "The Dissociated School"; CJC, "The Great September Event," *WC*, 22 September 1923; CJC, "Parents and the School," *Child-Welfare Magazine* (February 1924): 252–53.

21. See CJC, "Philanthropic Doubts," *AM* (September 1921): 289–300.

22. CJC, "Can Our Civilization Maintain Itself?" *AM* (November 1920): 636.

23. CJC, "Are Women Worth Their Salt?" *WC*, 6 May 1922.

24. CJC, "The Bonus and Idealism" *WC*, 23 September 1922.

25. CJC, "Our International Baby," *WC*, 21 March 1925.

26. CJC, "You and I and Public Health," *Hygeia* (February 1924).

27. CJC, "The Test of the Genteel," *Harper's Monthly Magazine* (June 1926): 69–74.

28. CJC, "Prohibition and the Younger Generation," *NAR* (September–November 1925): 37.

29. CJC, *The History of the Women's Educational and Industrial Union: A Civic Laboratory* (Boston: Thomas Todd, 1927).

30. CJC to FHJ, 16 July 1925, CJCP.

31. CJC, "The Crabbing of Youth by Age," *AM* (June 1923): 795.

32. Heideking and Mauch, *Geschichte*, 237–38.

33. See Spickard, *Almost All Aliens*, 257–81; George E. Mowry, *The Era of Theodore Roosevelt and the Birth of Modern America, 1900–1912* (New York: Harper & Row, 1958), 103ff.; John Higham, *Strangers in the Land: Patterns of American Nativism, 1860–1925* (New Brunswick: Rutgers University Press, 1992).

34. See Michael Grossberg, "Guarding the Altar: Physiological Restrictions and the Rise of State Intervention in Matrimony," *American Journal of Legal History* 26 (July 1982): 221–24.

35. See Ordover, *American Eugenics*, 51–53; Kennedy, *Birth Control*, 114–16; English, *Unnatural Selections*, chap. 5.

36. See Wolfe, Barger, and Benison, *Science and Society,* 140ff.; Stephen Jay Gould, *The Mismeasure of Man* (New York: Norton, 1981), 192–233; Spickard, *Almost All Aliens,* 271–72; Raymond E. Fancher, *The Intelligence Men: Makers of the IQ Controversy* (New York: Norton, 1985); Allan Chase, *The Legacy of Malthus: The Costs of the New Scientific Racism* (New York: Knopf, 1977), chap. 11; Howard F. Taylor, *The IQ Game: A Methodological Inquiry into the Heredity–Environment Controversy* (New Brunswick: Rutgers University Press, 1980).

37. Ordover, *American Eugenics,* 25.

38. Mae M. Ngai characterizes the Immigration Act of 1924 as follows: "At one level, the new immigration law differentiated Europeans according to nationality and ranked them in a hierarchy of desirability. At another level, the law constructed a white American race, in which persons of European descent shared a common whiteness that made them distinct from those deemed to be not white. Euro-Americans acquired both ethnicities—that is, nationality-based identities that were presumed to be transformable—*and* a racial identity based on whiteness that was presumed to be unchangeable. . . . But, while Euro-Americans' ethnic and racial identities became uncoupled, non-European immigrants—among them Japanese, Chinese, Mexicans, and Filipinos—acquired ethnic and racial identities that were one and the same. The racialization of the latter groups' national origins rendered them unalterably foreign and unassimilable to the nation." Mae M. Ngai, "Architecture of Race in American Immigration Law: A Reexamination of the Immigration Act of 1924," *Journal of American History* 86 (June 1999): 69–70; see also Robert Divine, *American Immigration Policy, 1924–1952* (New Haven: Yale University Press, 1957); Ian Haney Lopez, *White by Law: The Legal Construction of Race* (New York: New York University Press, 1996); Michael Novate, *The Rise of the Unmeltable Ethnics* (New York: Macmillan, 1973); Spickard, *Almost All Aliens,* 257–61.

39. See Mowry, *The Era of Theodore Roosevelt,* 103ff.; Higham, *Strangers in the Land.*

40. See Oscar Handlin, *Boston's Immigrants: A Study in Acculturation* (Cambridge: Harvard University Press, 1959); Handlin, *The Uprooted* (Boston: Little, Brown, 1951); Thernstrom, *The Other Bostonians.*

41. Peggy Pascoe, "Democracy, Citizenship, and Race: The West in the Twentieth Century" in Sitkoff, *Perspectives on Modern America,* 233–34.

42. Robert Yerkes cited in Ordover, *American Eugenics,* 26.

43. All data are from CJC, "American Misgivings," *AM* (February 1922): 145–57 (cited in the text as AmM).

44. Cited in Gary Gerstle, "Immigration and Ethnicity in the American Century," in Sitkoff, *Perspectives on Modern America,* 281; see James J. Connolly, *The Triumph of Ethnic Progressivism: Urban Political Culture in Boston, 1900–1925* (Cambridge: Harvard University Press, 1998); John Haller, *Outcasts from Evolution: Scientific Attitudes of Racial Inferiority, 1859–1900* (Urbana: University of Illinois Press, 1971).

45. Cited in Ngai, "The Architecture of Race," 68.

46. See WBC, *The Way,* chap. 11.

47. A few years later she had found a solution: voluntary or coercive sterilization. See chapters 9 through 10.

48. See Robert B. Westbrook, "Pragmatism and Democracy: Reconstructing the Logic of John Dewey's Faith," in Dickstein, *The Revival of Pragmatism*, 135–37. For the relationship between expertise and control in progressivism, see Arthur Link and Richard L. McCormick, *Progressivism* (Arlington Heights, Ill.: Harlan Davidson, 1983), 8–9.

49. In a letter of 6 June 1921 to her mother she reported on a dinner conversation with public health officials from Ellis Island who expressed concern at the large number of "Balkan Jews" entering the country. For Cannon these were "pure Orientals and as difficult to assimilate as the Japanese and a worse element." She claimed that American Jews were funding this—often—illegal immigration, charging that this "reflects great discredit on the Jews already here" (CJCP). See Nathan Glazer, *American Judaism* (1957; reprint, Chicago: University of Chicago Press, 1972), chaps. 5 and 6; Milton M. Gordon, *Assimilation in American Life: The Role of Race, Religion, and National Origins* (New York: Oxford University Press, 1964), chaps. 4–6; David M. Kennedy, *Freedom from Fear: The American People in Depression and War, 1929–1945* (New York: Oxford University Press, 1999), 410ff; Frederic C. Jaher, *A Scapegoat in the Wilderness: The Origins and Rise of Anti-Semitism in America* (Cambridge: Harvard University Press, 1994).

50. For a more detailed analysis of Cannon's attitude toward "the Asiatic," see chapter 10.

51. Cited in English, *Unnatural Selections*, 17.

52. CJC to FHJ, 16 January 1923, CJCP. Tom Perry was a neighbor and friend.

53. Kwame Anthony Appiah, "The Uncompleted Argument: Du Bois and the Illusion of Race," in Gates, *"Race," Writing, and Difference*, 35–36.

54. CJC, "Philanthropic Doubts," 293.

55. "What do you think of that?" she triumphed after having received a letter from the *American Monthly* eliciting yet another article, "not only having things accepted by the Atlantic, but being run after for some more pearls." CJC to FHJ, 30 March 1921, CJCP.

56. Wolfe, Barger, and Benison, *Science and Society*, 142, 212ff.

57. "Birthday Tribute," 17 November 1922, CJCP.

58. CJC to FHJ, 1 January 1924, CJCP.

59. Cited in Pickens, *Eugenics*, 121.

60. G. Linda Gordon, *Woman's Body, Woman's Right: A Social History of Birth Control in America* (New York: Grossman, 1976), 136.

61. Ellen Chesler, *Woman of Valor: Margaret Sanger and the Birth Control Movement in America* (New York: Simon & Schuster, 1992), 141.

62. BCLM Constitution, adopted 6 November 1916, SL, B-20 B.

63. James Reed, *From Private Vice to Public Virtue: The Birth Control Movement and American Society* (1978; reprint, Princeton: Princeton University Press, 1983), 144.

64. Ibid.

65. John K. Fairbank, *Chinabound: A Fifty-Year Memoir* (New York: Harper and Row, 1982), 26.

66. After the war Dr. Cannon became a member of the Committee for Research in Problems of Sex; he worked on this committee for more than twenty years. See WBC, *The Way*, 150–51; Wolfe, Barger, and Benison, *Science and Society*, 136ff.

67. CJC, "Birth Control in the United States, 1900–1965: For the Family Chronicles" (1965), unpaginated, CJCP.
68. CJC, "Birth Control in the United States," CJCP.
69. Gordon, *Woman's Body,* 284.
70. Sanger, *Autobiography,* 301.
71. Reed, *Private Vice,* 108; Gordon, *Woman's Body,* 284ff.
72. Sanger, *Autobiography,* 304.
73. CJC to FHJ, 14 November 1921, CJCP.
74. CJC, "Freedom of Speech," WC (November 1921).
75. Cited in Schlesinger, *Snatched,* 104.
76. Fairbank, *Chinabound,* 26.
77. CJC to FHJ, 14 November 1921, CJCP; Schlesinger, *Snatched,* 103–4.
78. Cited in Schlesinger, *Snatched,* 104.
79. See Childs, *Modernism and Eugenics,* 8; Kevles, *In the Name of Eugenics,* 64–66.
80. Gordon, *Woman's Body,* 299–300.
81. Sanger, *New Race,* 101.
82. Sanger, *Autobiography,* 134ff; Arthur Calder-Marshall, *Havelock Ellis: A Biography* (London: Rupert Hart-Davis, 1959), 196ff.
83. Reed, *Private Vice,* 58.
84. Pickens, *Eugenics,* 28.
85. Gordon, *Woman's Body,* 283.
86. Ordover, *American Eugenics,* 129.
87. CJC to FHJ, 24 March 1924, CJCP.
88. Gordon, *Woman's Body,* 268.
89. Marian Cannon Schlesinger, interview by author, March 2002.

6. "STONE-AGE INDIVIDUALS"

1. It resurfaced when Walter Cannon's biographers raided the place for his documents; it is now in CJCP. Cornelia Cannon always called *Red Rust* her first novel.
2. See Paul Fussell, *The Great War and Modern Memory* (New York: Oxford University Press, 1975).
3. See John W. Aldridge, *After the Lost Generation: A Critical Study of the Writers of Two Wars* (New York: Arbor House, 1985); Peter G. Jones, *War and the Novelist: Appraising the American War Novel* (New York: Columbia University Press, 1976); Diedrich and Fischer-Hornung, introduction, 11–19.
4. Ordover, *American Eugenics,* 7.
5. See Diedrich and Fischer-Hornung, introduction, 1–20.
6. See O'Connor, *Boston Irish;* John F. Maguire, *The Irish in America* (New York: Arno, 1969); Lawrence McCaffery, *The Irish Diaspora in America* (Bloomington: Indiana University Press, 1976); William Shannon, *The American Irish* (New York: Macmillan, 1966); Noel Ignatiev, *How the Irish Became White* (New York: Routledge, 1995); L. Perry Curtis Jr., *Apes and Angels: The Irishman in Victorian Caricature* (Washington, D.C.: Smithsonian Institution Press, 1996); Richard Stivers, *Hair of the Dog: Irish Drinking and Its American Stereotype,* rev. ed. (New York: Continuum, 2000); Dale T. Knoble, *Paddy and the Republic: Ethnicity and Nationality in Antebellum America* (Middletown, Conn.: Wesleyan University Press, 1986); Timothy J. Meagher, ed., *From Paddy to Studs: Irish*

American Communities in the Turn of the Century Era, 1880–1920 (Westport, Conn.: Greenwood Press, 1986).

7. The Carnahans landed in Boston Harbor in August 1718; they later changed the family name to Cannon. See WBC, *The Way*, 12–13.

8. Henry Cabot Lodge cited in Goodwin, *The Fitzgeralds and the Kennedys*, 368.

9. CJC to FHJ, 22 September 1919, CJCP.

10. Carrie Chapman Catt, "Danger to Our Government," in *Up from the Pedestal: Selected Writings in the History of American Feminism*, ed. Aileen S. Kraditor (Chicago: Quadrangle Books, 1968), 261.

11. See Pernick, *The Black Stork*, 75–78, 106–7; Susan Currell, *The March of Spare Time* (Philadelphia: University of Pennsylvania Press, 2005), 70–73.

12. Bunie and Rogers, *Boston*, chap. 5; O'Connor, *Boston Irish*, xv–xvi.

13. See Ordover, *American Eugenics*, 10–11.

14. Cannon's opposition to denominational schools was articulated in her article "The Dissociated School," which *AM* published in November 1928, and in dozens of letters to local newspapers.

15. In a family letter of 4 October 1920 she quoted a Miss Driscoll, a member of the Cambridge school committee, as saying, "We Catholics have control of the public schools now, and we must keep it!"

16. See Joseph F. Dinneen, *Ward Eight* (New York: Harper and Row, 1936).

17. CJC to FHJ, 14 November 1921, CJCP.

18. See James B. Cullen, *The Irish in Boston* (Boston: J. B. Cullen, 1889); O'Connor, *Boston Irish*; Goodwin, *The Fitzgeralds and the Kennedys*, chaps. 1–4.

19. See Gerstle, "Immigration and Ethnicity," 276.

20. See Blight, *Race and Reunion*, 112–22.

21. See Heideking and Mauch, *Geschichte*, 176–77.

22. Crunden, *Ministers of Reform*, 197.

23. This policy of withdrawal, of leaving the unregenerate to their fate, is also characteristic of Cannon's response to political events in Ireland. "Doesn't Ireland make you sick!" she exclaimed in a letter to Minnesota on 28 August 1920. "Why doesn't England get out and let the Kilkenny cats destroy each other?" Again the responsibility for violence is sought exclusively among the Irish.

24. See CJC to FHJ, 15 February 1923, CJCP.

25. Ordover, *American Eugenics*, 26.

7. "I've Got a Little Fame Myself"

1. CJC, "The Writing of *Pueblo Boy*," *RQ* (February 1958): 4.

2. Schlesinger, *Snatched*, 121.

3. Ibid., 123.

4. Ibid., 124.

5. CJC, "The Writing of *Pueblo Boy*," 4.

6. Marion B. Cook to CJC, 17 July 1943, CJCP.

7. CJC to FHJ, 21 July 1926, CJCP.

8. See CJC to FHJ, 15 August 1926, CJCP.

9. CJC, *The Pueblo Boy: A Story of Coronado's Search for the Seven Cities of Cibola* (Boston: Riverside Press/Houghton Mifflin, 1926).

10. CJC to FHJ, 24 October 1926, CJCP.

11. See Perry Miller's fascination with an American historiography that he perceived as a "massive narrative of the movement of European culture into the vacant wilderness of America." Perry Miller, *Errand into the Wilderness* (Cambridge: Harvard University Press, 1964), vii; Henry N. Smith, *Virgin Land: The American West as Symbol and Myth* (Cambridge: Harvard University Press, 1978).

12. See Robert F. Berkhofer Jr., *The White Man's Burden: Images of the American Indian from Columbus to the Present* (New York: Knopf, 1978); Ray A. Billington, *Land of Savagery, Land of Promise: The European Image of the American Frontier* (Norman: University of Oklahoma Press, 1981).

13. Mary L. Pratt, "Scratches on the Face of the Country; or, What Mr. Barrow Saw in the Land of the Bushman," in Gates, *"Race," Writing, and Difference*, 139; see also Pratt, *Imperial Eyes: Travel Writing and Transculturation* (London: Routledge, 1992).

14. See Edward W. Said, *Orientalism: Western Conceptions of the Orient* (New York: Columbia University Press, 1978), 7ff.

15. Benjamin Franklin, "Observations Concerning the Increase of Mankind, Peopling of Countries, etc.," in *Benjamin Franklin: Representative Selections*, ed. F. L. Mott and C. E. Jorgenson (New York: American Book Company, 1936), 223.

16. For the concept of assimilation in colonial discourse, see David Spurr, *The Rhetoric of Empire: Colonial Discourse in Journalism, Travel Writing, and Imperial Administration* (Durham: Duke University Press, 1993), 22.

17. Cited in Homi Bhabha, "Signs Taken for Wonders: Questions of Ambivalence and Authority under a Tree Outside Delhi, May 1817," in Gates, *"Race," Writing, and Difference*, 181; see Bhabha, "Of Mimicry and Man: The Ambiguity of Colonial Discourse," *October* 28 (Spring 1984): 132.

18. Pratt, "Scratches on the Face," 139.

19. For an analysis of this process of bifurcation, see JanMohamed, "Manichean Allegory," 98ff.

20. CJC, *Red Rust* (Boston: Little, Brown, 1928). Quotations in the text are from the Pocket Book edition (New York, 1960).

21. Schlesinger, *Snatched*, 128.

22. Cited ibid., 125.

23. Ibid., 126.

24. CJC, "The Genesis of *Red Rust*" (1928), 4, unpublished manuscript, CJCP.

25. CJC to FHJ, 16 August 1926, CJCP.

26. Marian Cannon to CJC, undated but January 1927, CJCP. The name of the character Matts was probably derived from Hans Mattson, a Swedish American land agent for the Lake Superior & Mississippi Railroad, who played an important role in attracting Swedish immigrants to Minnesota. See Lars Ljungmark, "'Come to the New North West': Immigration Promotion among the Swedes in America and in the Old Country, 1869–1876," in *Perspectives on Swedish Immigration: Proceedings of the International Conference on the Swedish Heritage in the Upper Midwest*, ed. Nils Hasselmo (Chicago: Swedish Pioneer Historical Society, 1978), 110–11.

27. See Deborah Carlin, "Willa Cather," in Showalter, Baechler, and Litz, *Modern American Women Writers*, 36–38; S. P. Harvey, *Redefining the American Dream: The Novels of Willa Cather* (Rutherford, N.J.: Fairleigh Dickinson University Press, 1995).

28. Allan Nevins, review of *Red Rust, Saturday Review of Literature* 4 (February 1928): 630.
29. M. E. Chase, review of *Red Rust, Atlantic Bookshelf* (April 1928): 48.
30. Cited in Ordover, *American Eugenics*, 32–33.
31. Ibid., 222 n. 11.
32. See CJC to FHJ, 31 January 1927, CJCP.
33. Sten Carlsson, *Swedes in North America, 1638–1988: Technical, Cultural, and Political Achievements* (Stockholm: Steiffert, 1988), 109–10.
34. CJC, "The Genesis," 5.
35. See CJC to FHJ, 8 June 1926, CJCP.
36. See Sten Carlsson, "Why Did They Leave?" in Hasselmo, *Perspectives,* 25–27; see also Vilhelm Moberg, *The Unknown Swedes: A Book about Swedes and America, Past and Present* (Carbondale: Southern Illinois University Press, 1988), 8–9; Carlsson, *Swedes in North America,* 33–35.
37. See Ljungmark, "Come to the New North West," 109ff.
38. See John G. Rice, "Marriage Behavior and the Persistence of Swedish Communities in Rural Minnesota," in Hasselmo, *Perspectives,* 136; Sten Carlsson uses the term "stock effect" to characterize this pattern of culturally contained settling, meaning "that many immigrants went to the households and places where they could be with relatives and former neighbors" (*Swedes in North America,* 49).
39. In 1921 the Swedish American Carl Jonar Love Almquist complained, "To our farmers no other books seem to reach except the hymn book, the catechysm, and sometimes the Bible." Cited in Göran Stockenström, "Sociological Aspects of Swedish-American Literature," in Hasselmo, *Perspectives,* 263.
40. Carlin, "Willa Cather," 41.
41. Moberg writes, "In these Swedish settlements the absence of what we call secular culture is immediately obvious to a foreigner; church life is practically the only form of cultural intercourse between people." Moberg, *The Unknown Swedes,* 82.
42. CJC to FHJ, 15 January 1921, CJCP.
43. See Dorothy B. Skardal, *The Divided Heart: Scandinavian Immigrant Experience through Literary Sources* (Lincoln: University of Nebraska Press, 1974); Stockenström, "Sociological Aspects," 265ff.
44. Ngai, "Architecture of Race," 70.
45. CJC, "The Genesis," 1.
46. See Paul de Kruif, *The Sweeping Wind: A Memoir* (New York: Harcourt, Brace and World 1962); Charles E. Rosenberg, "*Martin Arrowsmith:* The Scientist as Hero," *American Quarterly* 15, no. 3 (1963): 448ff; Marcel C. La Follette, *Making Science Our Own: Public Images of Science, 1910–1955* (Chicago: University of Chicago Press, 1990).
47. CJC, "The Genesis," 4.
48. See Beverly Stoeltje, "A Helpmate for Man Indeed: The Image of Frontier Woman," *Journal of American Folklore* 88 (January–March 1975): 347.
49. See Annette Kolodny, *The Lay of the Land: Metaphor as Experience and History in American Letters* (Chapel Hill: University of North Carolina Press, 1975), chap. 1.
50. According to Sten Carlsson, 56 percent of Swedish American women working outside the home in 1900 were employed as domestic servants or waitresses. See Carlsson, *Swedes in North America,* 83.

51. Melody Graulich, "Violence against Women: Power Dynamics in the Literature of the Western Family" in *The Women's West,* ed. Susan Armitage and Elizabeth Jameson (Norman: University of Oklahoma Press, 1987), 113; see G. Linda Gordon, *Heroes of Their Own Lives: The Politics and History of Family Violence* (New York: Viking, 1988).
52. CJC to FHJ, 31 January 1927, CJCP.
53. On alcoholism in the Swedish American community, see Skardal, *The Divided Heart,* 224ff.
54. Ralph Barton Perry, "Walter's Fame," 25 October 1931, CJCP.
55. CJC to Minnesota family, 24 June 1928, CJCP.
56. Schlesinger, *Snatched,* 129; see Wolfe, Barger, and Benison. *Science and Society,* 252ff.
57. Schlesinger, *Snatched,* 133.
58. Ibid., 158.
59. Ibid., 167.
60. See Wolfe, Barger, and Benison, *Science and Society,* 259ff.
61. See Kennedy, *Freedom from Fear,* 9, 381ff.

8. "The Melting Pot in Action!"

1. Charles Trout, *Boston: The Great Depression and the New Deal* (New York: Oxford University Press, 1977).
2. See John Kenneth Galbraith, *The Great Crash: 1929* (Boston: Houghton Mifflin, 1972).
3. Heideking and Mauch, *Geschichte,* 385–90.
4. Franklin D. Roosevelt cited in Currell, *The March of Spare Time,* 5. See also Susan Currell, ed., *Popular Eugenics: National Efficiency and American Mass Culture in the 1930s* (Athens: Ohio University Press, 2006), 4–6.
5. Cited in Zinn, *A People's History,* 387.
6. Cited in Ordover, *American Eugenics,* 148. See Currell, *The March of Spare Time,* 11.
7. Earnest Hooton cited in Currell, *The March of Spare Time,* 166.
8. Mencken cited ibid., 165.
9. See *Recent Social Trends in the United States: Report of the President's Research Committee on Social Trends,* 2 vols. (New York: McGraw-Hill, 1933); Currell, *The March of Spare Time,* 158–82; Currell, *Popular Eugenics;* Pernick, *The Black Stork;* Childs, *Modernism and Eugenics,* 10–12; Karen A. Keely, "Poverty, Sterilization, and Eugenics in Erskine Caldwell's *Tobacco Road," Journal of American Studies* 36, no. 1 (2002): 23–42.
10. Cited in Currell, *The March of Spare Time,* 166.
11. See Kennedy, *Freedom from Fear,* 242–43.
12. See Currell, *The March of Spare Time,* 168.
13. See Wolfe, Barger, and Benison, *Science and Society,* 290–91.
14. See CJC to Wilma and John K. Fairbank, 23 June 1932, CJCP.
15. See CJC to Family, 11 April 1939, CJCP.
16. CJC to Family, 16 June 1933, CJCP.
17. CJC to FHJ, 26 November 1925, CJCP.
18. See CJC to Bradford Cannon, undated but fall 1933, CJCP; Joseph C. Aub

et al., "Mycosis Fungoides Followed for Fourteen Years: The Case of Dr. W. B. Cannon," *AMA Archives of Pathology* 60 (November 1955), 535–47; Wolfe, Barger, and Benison, *Science and Society,* 293ff.

19. CJC mentioned her intention of writing another novel only one month after signing the contract for *Red Rust*: "I am bursting with ideas, the only difficulty is choosing." CJC to FHJ, 7 March 1927, CJCP.

20. Bradford Cannon to CJC, letter undated except "Monday" (must be 1930), WBCP, S VIII B 163 F 2315.

21. CJC, "What Ideals," 808.

22. On a more personal level this representation of overrefinement and loss of vitality among New England dynasties enabled Cannon to express her resentment against those Cambridge "ladies" who continued to snub the unconventional Mrs. Cannon as an outsider, not only because they marginalized newcomers from the Midwest to the Harvard elite, but also because she offended their notions of propriety and good taste. Imagine a Harvard professor's wife who proudly displayed her litter of healthy, unruly children as a midwesterner's contribution to the rehabilitation of a sterile and sapless New England, Marian Cannon Schlesinger proposes in *Snatched from Oblivion.*

23. See CJC, SC, 330.

24. Cited in Pickens, *Eugenics,* 79; see Thomas G. Dyer, *Theodore Roosevelt and the Idea of Race* (Baton Rouge: Louisiana State University Press, 1992).

25. See Edward Pinkowski, "The Great Influx of Polish Immigrants and the Industries They Entered," in *Poles in America: Bicentennial Essays,* ed. Frank Mocha (Stevens Point, Wis.: Worzalla Publishing, 1978), 305.

26. CJC to FHJ, 29 August 1922, CJCP.

27. See Pinkowski, "The Great Influx," 320.

28. See Thaddeus M. Piotrowski, *Manchester's Polonia, 1888–1974* (Manchester, N.H.: Piotrowski, 1974), 2ff.

29. Daniel C. Brewer, *The Conquest of New England by the Immigrants* (New York: Knickerbocker, 1926), 252, 256.

30. *Fifty Years of Boston, 1880–1930: A Memorial Volume* (Boston: Tercentenary Committee, 1930), 65ff.

31. CJC to FHJ, 29 August 1922, CJCP.

32. Cited in Pinkowski, "The Great Influx," 310.

33. Ewa Morawska claims, "Memories of possible Old Country's scarcities and spectacular effects of the New Country's affluence reinforce each other, thus stimulating efforts toward material advancement." Ewa T. Morawska, *Maintenance of Ethnicity: Case Study of the Polish American Community in Greater Boston* (San Francisco: R & E Research Associates, 1977), 80.

34. Ibid., 15.

35. CJC to FHJ, 20 August 1923, CJCP.

36. Michael Kammen, "The Problem of American Exceptionalism: A Reconsideration," *American Quarterly* 45, no. 1 (March 1993): 29; Gordon, *Assimilation in American Life,* chap. 1.

37. See Michael Novate, *The Rise of the Unmeltable Ethnics* (New York: Macmillan, 1973); Rudolf J. Vecoli, "Ethnicity: A Neglected Dimension in American History," in *The State of American History,* ed. Herbert J. Bass (Chicago: Quadrangle Books, 1970), 70–89.

38. Thomas Carlyle, "Chartism," in *Thomas Carlyle: Selected Writings,* ed. Alan Shelston (Harmondsworth: Penguin, 1971), 189.

39. For strategic reasons she chose to ignore the importance of parochial schools within the Polish American community. See Ellen Marie Kuzniki, "The Polish American Parochial Schools," in Mocha, *Poles in America,* 435–60.

40. For an analysis of Polish-American intermarriage, see Mieczyslaw W. Friedel, *This Polish Blood in America's Veins: Sketches from the Life of Polish Immigrants and Their Descendants in America* (New York: Vantage, 1978).

41. Mills, *The Racial Contract,* 81.

9. "STARVED KITTENS"

1. Cited in Ordover, *American Eugenics,* 148.

2. The investment for work programs alone amounted to $11 billion by 1939. Heideking and Mauch, *Geschichte,* 261–63.

3. Gordon, *Woman's Body,* 304.

4. CJC to Family, 27 December 1934, CJCP.

5. Schlesinger, *A Life,* 183.

6. Currell, *The March of Spare Time,* 158. See also Currell, *Popular Eugenics,* 1–4.

7. Gordon, *Woman's Body,* 268.

8. Cited ibid., 269.

9. Eugene L. Belisle, "Birth Control in Massachusetts," *New Republic,* 8 December 1941, 760.

10. "Statement by the President of the BCLM," Sophia Smith Collection, Smith College, PPLM, Box 31, Folder: Publicity.

11. CJC, "Birth Control in the United States," 3, CJCP.

12. Like the manuscript of *The Clan Betrays,* the 280-page manuscript of *Denial* was discovered by WBC's biographer Elin Wolfe during a research trip to Franklin. I am deeply grateful to her for sharing this information with me. The manuscript is in the CJCP.

13. Sanger, *Autobiography,* 86–92; see Chesler, *Woman of Valor,* 63.

14. See Alfred Kazin, *Starting Out in the Thirties* (London: Secker and Warburg, 1966); Marcus Klein, *Foreigners: The Making of American Literature, 1900–1940* (Chicago: University of Chicago Press, 1981).

15. See Keely, "Poverty, Sterilization, and Eugenics," 23–42.

16. See Cuddy and Roche, *Evolution and Eugenics,* 17–32.

17. Gordon, *Woman's Body,* 295.

18. See Currell, *The March of Spare Time,* 166.

19. See Paul, "Eugenics and the Left."

20. Emma Goldman, *Living My Life* (Garden City, N.Y.: Garden City Publishers, 1934), 185; Reed, *Private Vice,* 47.

21. As Elizabeth Jameson has shown, there was a folk knowledge that was shared among women and passed from one generation to the next. The study of private women's writing—diaries, letters—shows how essential it is to differentiate between notions of what women should talk about and "the reality of what women did discuss." The genteel language women used was often a mask they wore to maintain their public respectability; it was "corseted" for public display.

Elizabeth Jameson, "Women as Workers, Women as Civilizers: True Womanhood in the American West," in Armitage and Jameson, *The Women's West*, 153.

22. On abortion, see Patricia G. Miller, *The Worst of Times: Illegal Abortion Survivors, Practitioners, Coroners, Cops, and Children of Women Who Died Talk about Its Horrors* (New York: HarperCollins, 1993); Marvin Olasky, *Abortion Rites: A Social History of Abortion in America* (Wheaton, Ill.: Crossway Books, 1992).

23. Carlyle, "Chartism," 189.

24. Cited in Gould, *The Mismeasure of Man*, 223.

25. Goldman, *Living My Life*, 556.

26. See Paul, "Eugenics and the Left," 568–69.

27. See Nicole Hahn Rafter, ed., *White Trash: The Eugenic Family Studies, 1877–1919* (Boston: Northeastern University Press, 1988).

28. See Keely, "Poverty, Sterilization, and Eugenics"; Currell, *The March of Spare Time*, 163–64; Susan C. Holmes, "Re-examining the Political Left: Erskine Caldwell and the Doctrine of Eugenics," in Cuddy and Roche, *Evolution and Eugenics*, 240–57.

29. See Cuddy and Roche, *Evolution and Eugenics*, 13.

30. Cited in Thomas Shapiro, *Population Control Politics: Women, Sterilization, and Reproductive Choice* (Philadelphia: Temple University Press, 1985), 40.

31. Ordover, *American Eugenics*, 39–42.

32. Ibid., 134.

33. CJC to Wilma and John Fairbank, 11 January 1933, CJCP.

34. Ordover, *American Eugenics*, 128.

35. See Kennedy, *Freedom from Fear*, 242, 271ff.

36. A woman physician wrote to the president of the American Birth Control League in 1935: "The most sensitive nerve center in which to hit the public is their pocketbook. Sick poor mothers and the high mothers' death rate leave them cold." Cited in Gordon, *Woman's Body*, 304.

37. Letter from Blanche Ames Ames to Dear Fellow Members, 10 January 1935, Sophia Smith Collection, Smith College, PPLM, Box 31, Folder: Publicity.

38. Blanche Ames Ames to CJC, 6 January 1935, ibid.

39. "Cornelia James Cannon Leaving Birth Control Assn.," *Boston Herald*, 18 January 1935, CJCP/MCS.

40. See Lee Rainwater, *And the Poor Get Children: Sex, Contraception, and Family Planning in the Working Class* (Chicago: Quadrangle Books, 1960); Wendy Kline, *Building a Better Race: Gender, Sexuality, and Eugenics from the Turn of the Century to the Baby Boom* (Berkeley: University of California Press, 2001).

10. "IN THE FACE OF WHAT WE SEE"

1. See CJC to Family, 16 September 1934, CJCP.

2. Dr. Cannon had organized financial support for Pavlov in the early twenties, and when Pavlov traveled to the United States in 1923 and again in 1929, he spent several days with the Cannons in Cambridge and Franklin. See WBC, *The Way*, 184–87; Benison, Barger, and Wolfe, *Science and Society*, 331–32; Schlesinger, *Snatched*, 218–21.

3. See CJC to Family, 31 January 1935, CJCP. For a detailed account of this tour from WBC's angle, see Wolfe, Barger, and Benison, *Science and Society*, chap. 17.

4. See CJC to Mary Howland, 25 April 1935, CJCP.

5. CJC quoted in "Birth Control in China," *North China Daily News*, 29 May 1935, CJCP.

6. CJC to Family, 22 May 1935, CJCP.

7. CJC to Family, 26 April 1935, CJCP.

8. CJC to Family, 5 May 1935, CJCP.

9. CJC to Family, 26 April 1935, CJCP.

10. CJC to Family, 18 April 1935, CJCP.

11. CJC to Family, 22 May 1935, CJCP.

12. Schlesinger, *Snatched*, 205–6.

13. CJC to Family, 5 May 1935, CJCP.

14. CJC to Family, 27 May 1935, CJCP.

15. For the concept of "distancing," see Tzvetan Todorov, "'Race,' Writing, and Culture," in Gates, *"Race," Writing, and Difference*, 372ff.

16. CJC to Family, 5 May 1935, CJCP.

17. CJC to Mary Howland, 7 June 1935, CJCP.

18. CJC to Family, 9 June 1935, CJCP.

19. CJC to Family, 10 June 1935, CJCP.

20. CJC to Family, 24 June 1935, CJCP.

21. For the concept of boundary management, see Nira Yuval-Davis and Floya Anthias, *Racialized Boundaries: Race, Nation, Gender, Color, and Class and the Anti-racist Struggle* (New York: Routledge, 1992), 5ff.

22. Schlesinger, *Snatched*, 213.

23. CJC to Family, 10 July 1935, CJCP.

24. Ibid.

25. CJC to Family, 11 July 1935, CJCP.

26. CJC to Family, 31 July 1935, CJCP. See also Paul, "Eugenics and the Left," 569–71.

27. CJC, "Why So Panicky about Communism?" (November 1937), 3, unpublished manuscript, CJCP.

28. WBC's address at the Fifteenth International Physiology Congress, WBCP.

29. CJC to Family, 16 July 1935, CJCP.

30. CJC to Family, 27 July 1935, CJCP.

31. CJC to Family, 17 July 1935, CJCP.

32. CJC, "An Open Letter to Stalin," 30 August 1935, 2, 5, CJCP. She sent this letter to the editor of the *Saturday Evening Post*; it did not appear in print.

33. CJC to Family, 25 July 1935, CJCP.

34. CJC to Family, 13 July 1935, CJCP.

35. CJC to Family, 17 August 1935, CJCP.

36. CJC to Family, 14 July 1935, CJCP.

37. CJC to Family, 17 August 1935, CJCP.

38. CJC to Family, 27 August 1935, CJCP.

39. Cited in Ordover, *American Eugenics*, 22.

40. See Jacobson, *Whiteness of a Different Color*.

41. CJC to Family, 14 September 1935, CJCP.

42. See Premier Juan Negrin's letter to WBC in CJC to Family, 19 May 1938, CJCP; WBC, *The Way*, 159–62.

43. See CJC to Family, 30 January and 10 May 1939, CJCP.

44. See Wolfe, Barger, and Benison, *Science and Society*, chaps. 18 and 24.

45. WBC, *The Way,* 162.
46. Schlesinger, *A Life,* 183.
47. CJC, "Why So Panicky?" 4.
48. Gates, "Writing 'Race,'" 5.
49. Cited in Anne McClintock and Rob Nixon, "No Names Apart: The Separation of World and History in Derrida's 'Le Dernier Mot du Racisme,'" in Gates, *"Race," Writing, and Difference,* 353.
50. CJC to Family, 19 April 1933, CJCP.
51. See Wolfe, Barger, and Benison, *Science and Society,* chap. 18.
52. See Fredrick C. Jaher, *A Scapegoat in the Wilderness: The Origins and Rise of Anti-Semitism in America* (Cambridge: Harvard University Press, 1994), chap. 1; Deborah E. Lipstadt, *Beyond Belief: The American Press and the Coming of the Holocaust, 1933–1945* (New York: Free, 1986); David Wyman, *The Abandonment of the Jews: America and the Holocaust, 1941–1945* (New York: Pantheon, 1984).
53. CJC, "Can the Jews Save Themselves?" unpublished manuscript, CJCP.
54. See CJC to Family, 23 April 1939, CJCP.
55. See Aub et al., "Mycosis Fungoides," 2–5; "Interview of Dr. Joseph Aub," by Paul Benison, 19 August 1957, 360, WBCP.
56. See WBC, *The Way,* 20, 221; Wolfe, Barger, and Benison, *Science and Society,* chap. 23.
57. See WBC, *The Way,* 211.
58. Together they wrote *Autonomic Neuro-Effector Systems;* see WBC, *The Way,* 105.
59. CJC to Family, 17 May 1944, CJCP.
60. See Bernard B. Perry to V. Stevens, 17 July 1944, CJCP.
61. They later adopted two girls. See CJC, "Our Family Data" (undated), CJCP.
62. See "New Boston Colony Small but Busy," *Franklin Transcript,* 8 July 1943, CJCP.
63. Aub et al., "Mycosis Fungoides," 11.
64. Schlesinger, *Snatched,* 239.
65. CJC to Family, 20 October 1946, CJCP.
66. CJC, *Feasting with the Bear: The USSR and a Medical Congress* (undated), CJCP.
67. See Catherine Milton, "Is the Travel Yen Inherited? Meet the Cannon Family," *Boston Sunday Globe,* 7 April 1968.
68. Quoted in Schlesinger, *Snatched,* 242.
69. Linda Cannon Burgess to author in conversation.
70. See Kline, *Building a Better Race.*
71. Schlesinger, *A Life,* 184.
72. CJC to Family, 3 June 1933, CJCP.
73. Linda Cannon Burgess to author in conversation.
74. *Boston Herald,* 12 December 1969, CJCP.
75. CJC to FHJ, 30 May 1919, CJCP.

INDEX